KU-737-479

Tinker, Tiller, Technical Change

Technologies from the people

Edited by MATTHEW GAMSER,
HELEN APPLETON and NICOLA CARTER

INTERMEDIATE TECHNOLOGY PUBLICATIONS   1990

Acknowledgements

First and foremost, thanks should go to all the case study authors and their organizations who have given this work both its objectives and its conclusions. Being alongside them as they planned and implemented the 'Tinker, Tiller' project has been a valuable experience.

We are grateful to Geraldine Skinner for translating the Latin American case studies for this book.

Thanks must go also to the organizations that have funded this work, the Overseas Development Administration, the Ford Foundation, the Hilden Trust, the Dr L.H.A. Pilkington Trust, and Shell International. Without their generosity, none of this work would have been possible. We are especially grateful that these institutions accepted the project's flexible approach which enabled methods to adapt to fit the knowledge and experience of the authors. The results are much richer because of the understanding nature of our funders.

Finally, special thanks to our colleagues Priyanthi Fernando, Ebbie Dengu, Andrew Maskrey, Adam Platt and Jill Georgiou of ITDG's Policy and Country Representation Unit who have helped many times during this project, often saving the day.

Intermediate Technology Publications
103-105 Southampton Row, London WC1B 4HH, UK.

Published in North America by
The Bootstrap Press, an imprint of
the Intermediate Technology Development Group
of North America,
777 United Nations Plaza,
New York, NY 10017

© Intermediate Technology Publications 1990

British Library Cataloguing in Publication Data

Tinker, tiller, technical change.
1. Technological innovation
I. Gamser, Matthew S.   II. Appleton, Helen   III. Carter,
Nicola
600

ISBN 1 85339 061 5 (UK)
ISBN 0 942850 31 9 (USA)

Typeset by Inforum Typesetting, Portsmouth
and printed in Great Britain by BPCC Wheatons Ltd, Exeter

Social Science Library
Oxford University Library Services
Manor Road
Oxford OX1 3UQ

WITHDRAWN

University of Oxford
71191
2 0 DEC 1990

T
173
.8
.TIN

TINKER, TILLER, TECHNICAL CHANGE

300545597

Social Science Library
Oxford University Library Services
Manor Road
Oxford OX1 3UQ

UNIVERSITY OF OXFORD
INTERNATIONAL DEVELOPMENT
CENTRE LIBRARY

DATE CATALOGUED 20.12.90

CLASS-MARK Q 5 A

WITHDRAWN

Contents

v

Preface

The process of development assistance has to tackle the problems of ignorance, backwardness, helplessness, and resistance to change — not amongst the rural poor but amongst development agencies themselves.

Although few members of the development community would wish to apply such characteristics to themselves, these are still implicit in the behaviour of many institutions. This is especially true when work focuses on the areas of technology adaptation and innovation. Few development workers can honestly say that they are not guilty in some measure.

The ignorance of development agencies is ignorance of unfamiliar technological approaches and ignorance of the richness of traditional resources of knowledge. This richness is now being recognized widely, for example in the area of ethnobotany, where indigenous knowledge of genetic stocks of plants and their practical applications far outstrips that of the professional biologist and agriculturalist. The *Tinker, Tiller, Technical Change* case studies demonstrate that equivalent levels of knowledge exist in other areas of indigenous technology.

The backwardness of development agencies is in not taking account of the extent of local knowledge, and in not recognizing that communities living in close balance with their environment have had to develop survival strategies that depend on an ability to innovate and change. One of the papers illustrates a remarkable degree of experimentation and innovation among fishing communities in southern India. In the face of declining fish stocks, local fishermen experimented with and developed artificial reefs, lines, bait and other items of fishing gear.

The helplessness of development agencies is enshrined in programmes which do not build on local knowledge, skills and enterprise, but which seek to impose agencies' systems and create yet more institutions to prop up external assistance structures. Schumacher said 'help the poor to help themselves'. He did not tell us to assume that the poor are helpless, and to impose aid as a charitable exercise. One of the *Tinker, Tiller, Technical Change* case studies illustrates how an artisanal fishing industry in Nicaragua was stultified by a totally misconceived and overwhelming programme of support. The case study refreshingly and honestly analyses the failure of the project. This is something far too rare amongst development agencies anxious not to prejudice chances of funding in the future.

The resistance to change of development agencies is perpetuated by monolithic organizations and complex procedures which keep agencies distant from people in fields and villages. These barriers do not allow agencies to appreciate the real needs of local populations.

As an agency, Intermediate Technology (ITDG) believes that development assistance must be guided by the participants themselves, and must start from and build on a clear knowledge of the resources, capabilities and knowledge of local communities. The case study work for the *Tinker, Tiller, Technical Change* project was planned and executed by workers within the countries represented. The seminar that presented this work to an international audience was also designed by these workers.

Participation in programmes of work with local partners helps ITDG to develop a fuller understanding of the development process: not just an understanding of the technologies themselves and their economic environments, but also the processes by which technologies can be adopted, adapted and spread. ITDG also seeks to communicate that experience — to inform, influence and persuade all those who in some way participate in the development process. An important aspect of this role is the provision of channels which may help the exchange of experience, and help other people and agencies to articulate their views and experiences. The *Tinker Tiller, Technical Change* project is but one example of how this may be achieved.

Frank Almond
Chief Executive, ITDG

Introduction

MATTHEW GAMSER, HELEN APPLETON and NICOLA CARTER

Poor people in poorer countries are not ignorant, backward, or helpless regarding technological change. These people are no more mystified by machines and products from industrialized countries than are many people from these richer countries. Villagers' knowledge of local flora, fauna, and environmental management can be more extensive than trained scientists'. Artisan solutions for effective use of available raw materials are often far superior to solutions proposed by trained engineers.

So why do so many attempts to introduce 'Western' technology to developing countries end in failure? The answer is not because poor people in those countries resist change, or because they are not prepared to work with new machines and ideas. Considering the limited time during which Western technology has been present in many of these countries, the speed with which the poor have adapted to its presence is quite remarkable. In some cases, adaptation has allowed for the use of new materials and products. In some cases adaptation has allowed traditional production to survive in a competitive environment where Western technology is present. In some cases local innovation is not enough to sustain traditional livelihoods. But in all cases the poor are experimenting constantly, innovating in a struggle to survive.

Peoples' technology in a global perspective

Cases documented in this book show that the development process in most countries has marginalized poor people, their local knowledge, and their innovations. Technological development in most countries is dominated by imports of products and machinery from outside which can hinder peoples' innovation. Formally-trained scientists and engineers are put 'up-front' while artisans and other 'informal' innovators are at the back. Such policies lead to poor people losing control over local resources and decision-making that affects their lives.

MATTHEW GAMSER is the policy economist within the Intermediate Technology Development Group's Policy and Country Representation Unit (ITDG/PCRU).
HELEN APPLETON is the social scientist, ITDG/PCRU.
NICOLA CARTER is the co-ordinator, ITDG/PCRU.

Paradoxically, this situation can encourage the development of peoples' technology. Government actions may hinder local innovators and innovations but the worsening plight of the marginalized groups can provide a greater motivation to innovate. Unlike research scientists who innovate to satisfy their professional aspirations, peoples' technology innovators work to survive. Increased poverty can encourage the growth of peoples' technologies.

Peoples' technologies grow in different ways from technologies 'transferred' from outside. The latter are often parachuted into a country in a fixed package. Hardware and skill needs are set before arrival and may bear little relation to local skills and experiences. Labour and management requirements are established in countries of origin and are based on those countries' socio-economic priorities and cultural norms. Natural resource requirements, too, are based on economic and ecological concerns at points of origin.

Peoples' technologies, on the other hand, develop and diffuse slowly and steadily through a trial-and-error process. They rely on close communication between users and producers to identify changes required for improvement. Because of this close consultation, the technologies develop in a way that retains and builds upon local skills and closely reflects the priorities of local people. Such technologies show greater consideration of gender roles. Use is less likely to require men or women to do things that are physically, socially, or culturally difficult or unacceptable. Because people don't like to pollute their own neighbourhoods, peoples' technologies tend to be more ecologically sound.

Although poverty often stimulates development of peoples' technologies, spreading these technologies can be difficult. Local innovation is not recognized by the formal scientific and industrial community. This denies peoples' technologies access to technical information and to the financial and communications channels open to the formal sector. The growth of peoples' technology occurs in a horizontal pattern, across groups of poor people. Prevailing social, political, and institutional structures are barriers against this sort of poor-to-poor interaction and so the full potential of these technologies is seldom realized. Where peoples' technologies have become widespread, a re-organization and adaptation of these structures has taken place. This is often made necessary by an economic, political, or environmental crisis.

The 'ignored' technological revolution

From the perspective of large and expensive 'technology-transfer' projects, the history of technology in developing countries is a tale full of problems and short on progress. However, from the perspective of poor people and the technologies they employ in daily life, recent history shows many dramatic innovations. Africa is often singled out as the region most resistant to technological change, but it is in Africa that some of the most rapid and remarkable changes have occurred at the grass roots level.

Tanzanian people were not permitted to grow coffee until the 1920s (Europeans originally controlled everything). Now, Tanzanian smallholders account for most coffee production and for most processing of arabica and robusta beans. The small-scale processing equipment is virtually all made locally. Far from being intimidated by foreign crops and technology, Tanzanian farmers absorbed outside influences at an impressive speed. By comparison, Scandinavian nations, now regarded as advanced industrial states, took far longer to assimilate the tools and products of the English industrial revolution!

Nigeria's people faced a food crisis in the early 1980s. Economic recession forced an end to expensive cereals imports, upon which many people depended. But famine never arrived. Today the population relies on locally grown, locally processed cassava. For some of Nigeria, this is simply going back to a traditional food with a new marketing and processing system. Other Nigerians are learning to accept cassava as a new staple.

How did such change occur in the largest country in Africa? It was not simply a result of government laboratory products being introduced through gifts of development aid. Change came mostly through the work of small artisans, traders and farmers. Ordinary men and women increased cassava production, developed processing machinery and organized processing enterprises to increase the consumption of *gari, fufu* and other cassava food products in Nigeria.

The 1980s brought a similar crisis to Sierra Leone's salt supplies. These were made up largely of rock salt imports from Senegal. When foreign exchange grew scarce, imports dropped. A development agency tried and failed to introduce solar salt manufacturing. Local salt producers, extracting salt from filtering brine-rich silts, saved the day. These producers improved their techniques and expanded their output. Today they provide 35 per cent of national supplies and their production and market share continue to grow.

Asia is seen by many as less of a technological problem area than Africa but some of the poorest countries and regions of Asia are often derided. Yet cases from some of the poorest parts of Asia demonstrate impressive innovations that have transformed life at grass roots level.

Nepal is one of the world's poorest and most technologically backward countries. In the 1950s it had virtually no local engineering capacity. Today it has at least eight private companies designing and installing hundreds of micro-hydro schemes. These provide mechanical and electrical power for crop processing and other rural needs. Small firms are literally lighting up the countryside and are transforming rural women's lives by reducing the time and drudgery of crop processing tasks. The firms are nurturing local engineering skills that support other initiatives, such as large-scale electrification projects and the growth of new manufacturing industries. Nepali companies now export turbines and other micro-hydro system components to other Asian countries, and to Spain.

In Bangladesh, blacksmiths have attracted little public attention but they account for 5 per cent of the country's gross output, 9 per cent of its value added, and 11 per cent of total manufacturing GDP. About 10,000 blacksmithing enterprises are a major source of non-farm employment in a nation with an estimated 65 million landless poor. Blacksmiths also help in import substitution, producing spare parts for power tillers and tractors. Without the blacksmiths, these parts would have to be imported — at twice the cost!

Official recognition and local innovation

Technologies arising from research laboratories have a support system to nurture their development. Government and aid agency funding supports introduction to new countries and markets. Academic and aid agency literature describes the potential of 'official' technology and promotes its use. Peoples' technologies generally have no such help. Poor people are not recognized as sources of new technology, so their initiatives are rarely examined, much less promoted. Yet the few cases where such recognition has taken place show what great potential there is for collaboration between scientists, policy makers, and local innovators.

Development of the local micro-hydro industry in Nepal accelerated rapidly after the National Electricity Authority repealed a ban on private electricity generation for small mills — and even more rapidly after the Agricultural Development Bank offered capital subsidies for upgrading mills. Local fabricators and foreign hydro experts have co-operated in experiments on new component designs and production techniques to reduce costs further. This has made the benefits of micro-hydro innovations affordable to poorer mill owners and communities.

In Gujarat, India, staff from an engineering research institution encouraged local artisans to persevere with attempts to produce multi-purpose, animal-drawn farm implements. Staff helped to persuade the government to include this type of tool in its farm equipment subsidy scheme. The multi-purpose tool bar has become one of the most popular new implements in the state. It has saved farmers time and has increased yields by enabling greater control over fertilizer application. New manufacturers have set up in rural areas to produce the implement. Agricultural labourers, increasingly displaced by tractors and other large-scale machinery, retain their jobs on farms using the tool bar.

Most official recognition of peoples' technology seems to have occurred in Asia, but there are examples from other regions. Since 1981 the

Tanzanian Academy of Sciences has run the TASTA (Tanzania Awards for Scientific and Technological Achievement) programme to recognize and reward local innovation. One producer of the widely used coffee pulper received this award, which has assisted his further refinement and promotion of the technology.

However, recognition can be a double-edged sword. Artisans require a certain degree of freedom and recognition can deprive them of vital room to manoeuvre. The provision of equipment, infrastructure and credit for artisanal fishermen on the Pacific coast of Nicaragua has driven off the few artisans that originally plied their trade in the Aserradores area. After $1.5m of 'help', only three of the 25 original members of the fishing community remain.

The environment and peoples' technologies

There is great concern about the impact of new technologies upon the environment. Poor people feel this impact most acutely, for they are the ones in closest contact with threatened natural resources. What is little appreciated is that poor people are often at the forefront of technological change to protect and restore local environments.

In the 1950s, artisanal fishermen from Kerala, the poorest state in India, first protested against the introduction of mechanized trawling in the Arabian sea. Their claim that fish stocks would be decimated was dismissed by fisheries scientists, but the people have been proved correct. With their superior understanding of the local ecosystem, the fishermen are leading the way in developing technologies such as artificial reefs and species-specific baits to restore the shallow water marine habitat and populations. The state government now supports the fishermen's research under its Five-Year Plan, and funds a collaborative research project on artificial reefs by its Marine Fisheries Research Institute and the fishermen's union.

The local community in the Ica valley of Peru saw its lands and livelihood threatened by government land grants to rich outsiders. Expropriation was limited only by the difficulty in irrigating the arid lands effectively. Borewells delivered required water, but the crops fared poorly. Local farmers knew this was because of nutrient deficiencies in surface water-based irrigation. When the government promised to build a canal from the Choclococha river to provide newcomers with irrigation water, the community did not react by just lamenting the lot of the poor. Instead, the community carried out its own 18km extension of an existing canal that dated back to Inca times so that irrigation might be under its control. In the end, poor farmers lost out to larger landowning interests — but not as a result of a lack of technological knowledge or creativity. Indeed, the local peoples' 'civil engineering' provided the base upon which agricultural productivity expanded greatly in the region.

People living in the most difficult environments often show the greatest skill and innovation in dealing with environmental problems. In the poor, arid Coquimbo region of Chile, the greatest skill and initiative in water supply and irrigation is found in the community of Los Rulos, where water resources are scarce even by regional standards. Farmers can detect underground water sources through surface inspection. They build specially designed hillside excavations (*piques*) to obtain subsurface water and elaborate systems of dams and canals for water delivery.

In the squatter settlements of Santo Domingo in the Dominican Republic and in Huancayo in Peru, people build houses in some of the most densely populated and difficult environments imaginable. Their homes are not pretty, but they are affordable and they enable families to survive. A wide variety of materials are used in construction, in hillside stabilization, and in the provision of basic services such as water, roads and power.

Energy innovation: power from the people

One of the most widely researched and reported areas of energy technology in development is that of stoves for the poor. Scientific institutions and aid agencies have invested much time and effort in this cause, but few of their stoves are reaching rural households. This could be cause for despair, but the case studies of peoples' energy technology provide a different, brighter perspective.

In Zimbabwe, a cooking system consisting of a metal grate provided by metalworking artisans, and a hearth and windscreen constructed by women users in their kitchens, can be found in the vast majority of rural homes. This system has evolved over time as cooking practices and cooking pots have changed. The system owes virtually nothing to formal research and development and has been unreported in stove literature — but it is the innovation upon which rural Zimbabwean food preparation depends. The grate system provides a versatile and energy-efficient way to use firewood to cook local dishes.

The seeds of a similarly dramatic innovation could be present in Kenya. Deforestation and rising fuelwood prices have led artisans and households in the Meru area to develop stoves that can use agricultural residues in place of wood. Up to 30 per cent of households in the local villages are now using the new stoves.

Fuelwood scarcity is fostering local innovations of a different form in the Coquimbo area of Chile. At the beginning of this century, all houses cooked on open fires. Bread was baked by preheating stones with wood or dung. As wood became scarcer, ceramic stoves and ovens were developed. These evolved in size and in construction materials to make them suitable for all types of cooking and baking. As kerosene and liquefied petroleum gas fuels have become available, stoves using these have been introduced in many homes.

Local innovators in Villanueva in the Venezuelan Andes have adapted stove designs from Brazil and Ghana. The resulting stoves and ovens are suited to village cooking needs, such as the preparation of local pancakes (*arepas*). One important element of these innovators' success has been the ability to evolve and adjust new models to meet changing household needs. Initially villagers sought new stoves primarily to reduce cooking time. But after using the new stoves for a while, people began to ask as well for changes to reduce smoke emitted during cooking. Local builders were able to recognize and respond to these changing tastes and priorities.

Bolivian farmers from the harsh *altiplano* region, where frosts, dust storms and droughts are common, have demonstrated great ingenuity in using solar energy to protect their crops. Drawing upon designs imported by various aid organizations, the farmers have produced greenhouses and cold frames affordable to poor people. Scrap tin and *adobe* (rammed earth blocks) replaced imported metal for doors, window frames and roofs. Local fibres served as ties and screens in place of wire mesh. Greenhouses were made smaller and built partly below ground to increase insulation and reduce construction materials required. Temporary covers were developed for cold frames, reducing costs and allowing farmers to expose crops during good weather. This shows that the farmers, far from resisting change, critically assess all options put before them. Non-adoption of particular hardware is not rejection of change, but rejection of what is impractical or inappropriate.

The Tinker, Tiller, Technical Change project

The case studies in this book are the work of a group of 17 investigators from 14 countries in Asia, Africa, and Latin America. These authors — scientists, social scientists and engineers — represent a variety of organizations, working in a wide range of social, cultural and economic situations. The differences between them are great but they have found a common ground in 'peoples' technology'. All feel that too little attention has been paid to the role of farmers, artisans, and other 'non-scientists' in the development of new technologies, particularly those most useful for poor people.

The 'Tinker, Tiller' investigators each selected a technology from his or her country and carried out detailed field studies of its evolution, its social and economic importance and its limitations. Investigators examined the background to see how the skills associated with technological change have developed and spread.

At the same time, investigators met colleagues in their region to learn how factors supporting and hindering locally developed stoves compared with those affecting building materials, and those affecting food processing machinery. Investigators noted how local innovators fared in Bangladesh compared to Nepal, in Kenya versus Zimbabwe, and in Chile versus the

Dominican Republic. These discussions identified common issues to consider during their field studies.

Having carried out their field work, the group met altogether to see how peoples' technology in Asia differed from that in Africa, and in Latin America. The group shared their work with representatives of donor agencies, non-government agencies and research institutions at a seminar at the London Business School in June 1989. The material in this book is the product of both field work and group discussion.

How to support peoples' technology

The cases presented in this book demonstrate the need to put peoples' technology and the local innovation behind it on the same footing as 'formal' research and development. Recognition of the value of peoples' technology is the necessary first step towards strengthening this technology and organizations behind it. From recognition comes an important re-examination of development relationships. Reforms should bring local innovators into greater prominence and should combine local experience and scientific knowledge in the development of new technologies. Examples of these reforms include:

1 government financial and policy support for water-mill innovation by artisan manufacturers in Nepal;
2 Kerala state government inclusion of fishworker-originated experiments on artificial reef construction in the state's new five-year science and technology development programme;
3 the Zimbabwe government decision to provide permanent land for metalworking artisans involved in the manufacture of cooking grates and other essential products;
4 Nigerian polytechnics' inclusion of lectures and training sessions involving practising artisans in their courses, to add a new dimension to their students' technological education.

Such reforms can help to stop reinforcing the structures that are marginalizing peoples' technology and its innovators. Reforms must strengthen whatever peoples' organizations exist. Over time, there must be more institutional bridges between these popular organizations and formal science, technology, and aid bodies. This will combine the useful knowledge and experience developed by all.

At the same time, support for peoples' technology has to respect the informality under which it thrives. What is needed are policies that facilitate but do not 'bureaucratize', policies that ease access to credit, information, and markets but that do not over-regulate. These case studies suggest a variety of ways in which these reforms can arise. Perhaps they can provide the initial impetus for a global revitalization of peoples' technology.

The world knows of Leonardo da Vinci, Marie Curie, and Thomas Edison and the impact they have made on human life. Few have heard of Nigeria's Ologbon Ori or Nepal's Akkal Man Nakarmi, but they and others like them are playing a similar role for their people. Gathering information about such local innovators helps an understanding of their skills, their potential, and the obstacles they face. Learning what they are doing, what they can do, and what they want to do is a first step for any outsiders wanting to help.

A note on currencies

The following conversion rates, dating from June 1989 (the time of the completion of the field research for the case studies), will give the reader a general idea of the values.

	£ sterling	*US$*
Bangladesh	49.8 laka	31.5
Bolivia	4.1 bolivianos	2.6
Chile	405 pesos	256
Dominican Republic	10.2 D. pesos	6.5
India	25.6 rupees	16.2
Kenya	33 shillings	20.9
Nepal	38.2 rupees	24.2
Nicaragua	11725 cordobas	7414
Nigeria	11.8 nairas	7.5
Peru	5034 intis	3183
Sierra Leone	99.8 leches	63.1
Tanzania	219 shillings	139
Venezuela	61.5 bolivars	38.9
Zimbabwe	3.3 dollars	2.1

PART I

Africa

AFRICA — Regional overview

J.G.M. MASSAQUOI

Background

Six case studies were prepared from Africa. One study covered the evolution of cassava processing technology in Nigeria. Another study, also from Nigeria, discussed the diffusion of one specific hardware in the cassava processing technology, namely the cassava grater. A third case study which was conducted in Sierra Leone examined the traditional method of salt production from salt-bearing silts. This study examined the evolution and diffusion of both the processing activities and the hardware involved. A fourth case study looked into the history of the development of the Tanzania coffee pulper which evolved from a simple stone crusher to a motorized machine. The last two studies dealt with energy and the ability of people to adapt to the decline in fuelwood supply. In one case, the traditional Kenya fuelwood stove was adapted by the people in order to use agricultural residues in areas where there was scarcity of fuelwood. In another case study, the evolution of the Zimbabwean cooking grid was examined. This cooking system developed not only from the point of view of saving fuelwood but also to take account of other needs, such as a highly rigid pot clamp to withstand heavy mixing. Space heating needs were helped as well.

All six studies addressed very important issues that affect the socio-economic development of the countries in which they were carried out. Cassava, especially in its processed form *gari*, is a very important foodstuff in Nigeria. In Sierra Leone, salt processing in the informal sector is important because there is no organized salt production. In Tanzania, coffee is a main export crop which brings large amounts of valuable foreign exchange every year. Finally, set in the deforested areas of southern and eastern Africa, there is a study of the innovative capability of rural people to use efficiently whatever energy is available. The six studies show that rural innovators are making contributions in vital areas of the socio-economic development of their countries.

DR J.G.M. MASSAQUOI (Sierra Leone) is Dean of the Faculty of Engineering at Fourah Bay College, University of Sierra Leone, Freetown. He has nearly 15 years' research and teaching experience in Energy, Appropriate Technology and Technology Policy and has published over 25 papers.

Common themes

Although all the studies were very diverse both in terms of the topics covered and the regions in which they were carried out, it was still possible to identify common themes. A total of four such themes were identified: the evolution process and stimuli of the innovation; the beneficiaries of the technology; the viability/diffusion of the technology; and the knowledge/ skills acquisition.

In all the case studies, innovation was stimulated by needs identified within the community by the people themselves. This may arise as a result of a government policy, changes in the natural environment or any other factors affecting demand for the product of the technology. The Nigerian case studies clearly illustrate how a government decision to ban the import of foodstuffs led to a big demand for the cassava product *gari* and the consequent evolution and diffusion of the cassava grater. In Sierra Leone, scarcity of foreign exchange to import salt, coupled with unfavourable climatic conditions for the operation of solar salt fields, helped to increase the demand for salt produced from salt-bearing silts. In Tanzania, it was the need to improve income from a major cash crop that stimulated the innovation in the coffee pulper. In Kenya and Zimbabwe it was changes in the environment and effects on energy supply that encouraged innovation in cooking stoves.

In all cases, the various activities of the technologies considered were traditionally carried out by women. However, it was observed in each case that, as the technology evolved, the role of women changed. They ceased to be operators and became merely users of the technology. This was observed in all cases but was more vivid where mechanization was introduced e.g. the examples of the cassava grater and coffee pulper. In both cases the women traditionally operated the hand grater and pulper. However, when the technology developed to the level of mechanization, the men carried out the operations.

It was also observed in all cases that the contribution of the peoples' technology to the supply of products in the market was very significant, ranging from 30 to 60 per cent of the total supply.

The case studies also showed that the traditional technologies under investigation were economically viable. There were even instances where the traditional coped satisfactorily with challenges from imported technologies. The traditional technologies were also diffused widely which is reasonable in view of the fact that people developed these technologies in response to perceived needs within the community.

With regard to skills/knowledge acquisition, it was reported in all cases that there is no formal system for this. The transfer of skills/knowledge was always through a system of apprenticeship, learning-by-doing.

4

Common constraints

Three common areas of constraints were identified. These were technical, financial, and the lack of official recognition. With regard to technical constraints, researchers felt that the peoples' technologies under investigation had now evolved to the highest possible level taking into account facilities and information available to the innovators. There was a definite need to link up with the formal R & D sector to tap the knowledge available there. The innovative capability will still be with the people but inputs into the innovative process should be enlarged to include information from the R & D sector.

Financial constraint was mainly in the lack of either working or fixed capital. There were little or no credit facilities available to acquire the technologies. Most users relied on their personal savings to finance the acquisition of the technology.

Finally, lack of recognition was identified as a major problem. Since the existence of these innovations was not noticed in official circles, it was not possible for the improved technologies to benefit from any government policy. In some cases, governments actually took policy decisions that inadvertently stifled the innovations of rural people.

Recommendations

The general recommendations for all the projects were in line with overcoming the constraints highlighted above. However, there was one case (Sierra Leone) where it was recommended that innovators of a particular technology organize themselves to impose some quality control. It was felt by the researchers that quality control was necessary to build up consumer confidence.

The coffee pulper in northern Tanzania

SIMON R. NKONOKI

Introduction

Coffee in Tanzania's economy

Coffee is Tanzania's number one cash crop for generating foreign exchange. Other cash crops are, in decreasing order of importance to the country's economy, cotton, tobacco, cloves, sisal, cashew nuts, tea and pyrethrum. Taken together, these eight cash crops earn the country about 80 per cent of its foreign exchange. Of that 80 per cent, coffee alone accounts for about 40 per cent of the country's annual foreign exchange earnings. This may be up to 50 per cent when harvests are good and world prices are high.

Coffee is grown in five of the 25 provinces of the country — in Kilimanjaro and Arusha in the north, Kagera in the north-west and in Mbeya and Ruvuma provinces of the south-west. The processing of coffee is a very important activity for Tanzania's economy, not only because of the crop's contribution to the nation's treasury but also because the activity engages and absorbs a lot of otherwise idle or excess labour in rural areas.

An historical overview

Coffee was first grown before the 1890s in the Kagera Region of the former Tanganyika. Robusta-type coffee was grown there for two main reasons. Coffee chewing has been a cherished tradition amongst the Haya people ever since the pre-colonial period. Even today, courtesy in a Haya family is to serve roast coffee beans to the visitor for chewing. (Robusta is ideal for chewing because of its mild, sweet taste.) Also, coffee has been symbolic among the Haya for use in rituals. For example, coffee has been used in ceremonies for cementing friendships and robusta is best for this as well.

Robusta coffee is also preferred because it is resistant to diseases, reproduces better than arabica coffee and flourishes well in the soils of that part of Tanzania. Hard bourborn (arabica) coffee was introduced in the area

PROFESSOR S.R. NKONOKI (Tanzania) is Professor of Science and Technology in the Institute of Development Studies at the University of Dar es Salaam. Research interests in rural energy technologies including biogas technology and dissemination of improved woodfuel cookstoves.

in the early 1930s but today about 70 per cent of coffee grown in Kagera is robusta. The 1934 Report of the Department of Agriculture noted that 'fourty pounds of bourborn coffee seed has been obtained from Moshi and six nurseries have been started two years earlier at Ntungano in Biharamulo'. Ihangiro and Western Kiango, Bukoba District, now Muleba District, and Wenyarwanda are reported to have started growing arabica coffee in 1934. The leading province for arabica coffee production in Tanzania is Kilimanjaro, a province which lies largely on the southern slopes of Mount Kilimanjaro, while Kagera leads in robusta coffee production.

Coffee growing in the Kilimanjaro and Arusha provinces began in the early 1890s for settlers and in the early 1920s for African peasants. Coffee growing was introduced by German Missionaries at Kilema Catholic Mission Station in 1906. 'The planting of the first coffee tree at Kilema Mission over 60 years ago was the beginning of a period of sustained development in Kilimanjaro. This brought the Chagga people a prosperity in agriculture which surpassed that of most other peoples of Tanzania'. (Brewin, 1965)

Initially, only Europeans were permitted to grow coffee in Tanganyika, now mainland Tanzania. Africans began to grow coffee in 1921 on a significant scale, following the repeal of the 1890s rule that coffee was to be grown by settlers only. It was out of the Chagga Chief Kilamia Marealle's instigation and campaign that African peasants could and ought to grow coffee that the British colonial rulers finally bowed to such demands.

Arabica coffee production in the south-western part of Tanzania, Ruvuma province, began in 1926 when the local chief of Mbinga, Chief Chrysostomus Makita, introduced coffee from Moshi, Kilimanjaro province. Chief Makita had visited Kilimanjaro and northern Tanzania on several occasions. He made close observations and acquired basic skills in tending coffee plants. Chief Makita sent several groups of his people on study tours to Kilimanjaro to learn about coffee husbandry and the processing of ripe coffee. Thus, the coffee which was introduced and continues to be grown in Mbinga district to date is mild arabica. Likewise, the technology for processing ripe arabica coffee in Mbinga district, from the time it is harvested up to the stage when it is marketed as dry coffee beans, is almost exactly as it is for the processing of coffee in Kilimanjaro and Arusha provinces.

Nowadays, in Kilimanjaro and Arusha provinces of north-eastern Tanzania, arabica coffee is the number-one cash crop which is grown by virtually every small-holder. There are also large-scale coffee estates which belonged to settlers before the promulgation of the Arusha Declaration in 1967. In Kagera province, a comparable situation exists regarding robusta coffee growing. In Arusha and Kilimanjaro provinces, large-scale, settler-owned coffee estates were nationalized in 1967. These were then owned and managed by the appropriate Co-operative Union: Kilimanjaro Native Co-operative Union (KNCU) in the case of Kilimanjaro, Vuasu Co-operative Union (VCU) for Pare District and Arusha Co-operative Union

(ARCU) for the coffee estates in Arusha province. Up to 1976, coffee pulping was done either at a central coffee factory or at family homesteads. After the dissolution of Co-operative Unions in 1976, coffee processing, especially coffee pulping, became more and more the activity of each small-holder's family. A locally developed and produced coffee pulper was used.

The small-holder coffee farmer
Small-holder farmers in Tanzania are those whose farms range from one to three hectares or about two to six acres. Such small-holder farmers constitute about 85 per cent of all farmers in the country. Large-scale farms and estates utilize about 13 per cent of the cultivated land which totals 4,465,000 ha. Small farmers cultivate 3,880,000 ha and 585,000 ha are large-scale farms and estates. Up to 1980, large-scale farms and estates produced slightly below 50 per cent of export crops while they employed about 5 per cent of the agricultural labour force. Before 1980, small farmers produced 50–55 per cent of the cash crops plus nearly all food crops. Currently, the contribution of cash crops by small-holders has risen to about 70 per cent. Small-holder farmers use mainly hand-tool technologies, including the traditional hand-hoes and manual crop-processing technologies. Both technologies involve intensive use of muscular energy. Apart from inefficient hand-hoe technology, the other reasons for lower productivity of the small farmers, compared to the large-scale farmers or estate owners, are:

1 inadequate technical know-how;
2 inadequate organization for effective production programmes;
3 limited capital outlay;
4 inadequate professional advice and too many farmers per extension worker (1,500 farmers per field technician).

Coffee production trend
The average annual production of coffee in Tanzania from 1966 to 1985 was between 45,000 and 55,000 metric tons. A major bottleneck in the coffee industry has been non-availability and/or inadequate agro-chemicals to combat coffee berry disease. The slump of coffee prices on the world market up to the early 1980s was also responsible for the fall in coffee production in Tanzania. During the early 1980s, with the deepening of the economic crisis, soaring inflation and a slump of coffee prices on the world market, some Chagga small-holder coffee growers turned to growing other crops such as vegetables and fruits. This raised concern in government circles because of the negative impact on coffee's vital contribution to foreign exchange earnings. With better prices domestically and internationally, the situation has reverted to normal.

Nevertheless, poor technology in the overall small-holder farming system in Tanzania is largely responsible for low productivity. This now stands at only 300kg per hectare as against a possible average yield of 500kg per hectare if modern crop husbandry is used.

Objectives of the study

1 to study the origins/evolution of the coffee pulping technology;
2 to establish the extent of product diffusion;
3 to identify present bottlenecks and policy issues related to mass production improvement and wider dissemination of the technology;
4 to formulate specific policy recommendations.

Research methodology

The primary method used in this research was to interview peasant/small-holder coffee farmers in their villages in Kilimanjaro, Arusha and Ruvuma provinces. The researcher concentrated mainly on Kilimanjaro province for details of the technology that was being studied. A total of 40 peasant farmers growing coffee were interviewed in their village communities — 25 in Kilimanjaro, 8 in Arusha and 7 in Ruvuma province.

A further 6 small-holder peasant farmers from Mbeya province and 7 from Kagera province were interviewed. This was not on their farms, but either in their province's or district's headquarters or in Dar es Salaam. With regard to artisans who make coffee pulpers and/or train others to make coffee pulpers, 7 were interviewed in the Kilimanjaro/Arusha provinces, 4 in the Kagera region and only 2 in the Ruvuma province. Thus, the total number of farmer-interviewees was 53.

Apart from interviews, researchers obtained secondary information from documentary evidence, such as the *Journal of the Tanzania Society, Tanzania Notes and Records*, records on early Christian missions in mainland Tanzania and reports of the Ministry of Agriculture.

Significance of the study

The coffee pulping technology which is used by small-holder peasant farmers is diffused very widely in the arabica coffee growing provinces of Arusha, Kilimanjaro, Mbeya and Ruvuma in Tanzania.

Similar technology has been developed by local artisans, almost independent of foreign influence, in the Kagera province in north-western Tanzania, where the coffee grown is mainly the robusta type.

The evolution of indigenous coffee pulping technology

Fermentation and manual removal of pulp
Coffee pulping had been done by hand long before German colonial rule

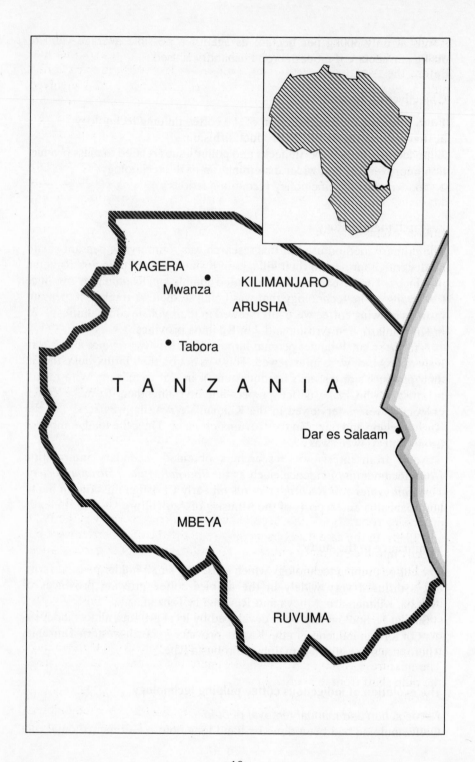

KAGERA

Mwanza •   KILIMANJARO

ARUSHA

• Tabora

T A N Z A N I A

Dar es Salaam •

MBEYA

RUVUMA

started in Tanganyika in the 1890s. This was especially so in the north-western province of Kagera which lies to the west of Lake Victoria. Before the twentieth century, and even up to the 1920s, arabica coffee pulping was done by a cumbersome and tedious process. This involved soaking the arabica coffee berries in water for a period of three days or more, followed by the manual removal of the pulp from the ripe berries. In that way, coffee beans were separated from the pulp. This method of pulping was not only extremely tiring but also time consuming. To process and obtain a volume of 20 litres of clean/pulped coffee beans would occupy at least one adult working hard for at least two days, each working day being eight hours. Such was the earliest traditional coffee pulping technique for arabica coffee. This type of coffee was grown initially almost exclusively in the north-eastern provinces of Arusha and Kilimanjaro.

In the case of robusta coffee, traditional coffee pulping consisted of spreading the ripe coffee berries on a mat in an open space outside the homestead immediately after harvest. Drying used rays from the sun and usually took three to four days. After that, a flat crusher-stone of about 30cm length by 15cm width and about 5cm thickness was used to grind the dried coffee berries against another, stationary stone of a much wider surface area. The big stone was sometimes ten to fifteen times larger than the crusher-stone.

Using this stone-crusher method, pulp was separated from the coffee beans. Manual winnowing using natural wind followed. However, often the crushing had to be re-done two or three times for about half of the dried coffee berries until the coffee beans were all separated from the pulp.

The pestle and mortar pulping process
The pestle and mortar method of pulping was later used widely as an improvement of the stone and stone-crusher method. This method for processing robusta and arabica coffee was dominant especially in the 1920s and 1930s. In the case of robusta coffee, sun-dried coffee berries were put directly into the mortar in quantities of about 6kg weight at a time. About one litre of water was added to each lot before pounding started.

Through repeated manual pounding using the pestle, the berries were hulled, leaving the coffee beans either intact or split into the two cotyledons. Pounding took about half-an-hour for each lot of 5–8kg. After every half-hour or so, the mixture of the pulp and the beans was removed from the mortar and put in a wide basin-shaped papyrus-made container. The mixture was subjected to winnowing, using natural wind to separate the pulp chaff from the coffee beans.

Coffee berries which had not been completely separated from all pulp were put back into the mortar for further pounding for about ten to fifteen minutes. This was followed again by winnowing. A fresh lot of coffee

11

berries was taken only after a previous lot had been pounded thoroughly and the separation of coffee pulp from coffee beans had been completed. As with the pestle and mortar, this method was extremely strenuous as it demanded a lot of physical labour.

Unlike robusta coffee, arabica coffee was usually soaked for two to three days before pounding using the pestle and mortar. The soaking made the pulp almost 'rotten' and hence helped the separation of the pulp from the coffee beans.

The indigenous coffee pulper

Arabica coffee berries are picked when they are ripe, that is, when the colour of the berries is red. These berries are then put in a pulping machine for processing. Some water, about one litre, is added to the berries to 'lubricate' and cool the machine. The bowl in which the ripe coffee berries are put varies in size depending on the size of the machine. Some bowls can take one tinful of coffee berries (about 20 litres volume) or two or three tinfuls at a time. Two metal channels lead the berries to the pulping chamber when the roller is rotated by using the handle. The berries are crushed as they come between the pulper and the bottom of the bowl. Coffee beans come out the front while the pulp-cum-husks drop out of the pulping chamber through an opening at the rear of the pulper.

Depending on how efficient the machine is — and particularly the actual pulping system — the husks are not supposed to be mixed with seed as they come out. If mixing occurs then both the husks and beans are spread separately for sorting. If some whole berries come out by the front with the seeds, they are sorted out and re-pulped. The coffee seeds are collected into a receiver-basin just in front of the machine. The coffee beans drop to a container on the ground.

The metal parts of the coffee pulping machines are made out of scrap — old paraffin or edible-oil tins. These parts include the handle for rotating the roller, the two tube-like channels which lead to the pulping chamber and the cover over the wooden roller. The machine stand and bowl for holding berries before they drop into the pulping chamber are made out of wood.

The popularity of locally-developed arabica coffee pulpers

As noted earlier, the first portable, family-size arabica coffee-pulping machine was made locally by African artisans in the mid-1920s. African artisans, mainly blacksmiths and carpenters, were encouraged and given some short training in the use of simple workshop tools by German missionaries. The missionaries had keen interest in promoting the participation of Africans in coffee growing. Local craftsmen were trained to make these machines using locally available materials. Each machine was made out of wood with a few metal parts. The pulping roller was made out of wood and covered with lanced sheet metal.

12

It was not until the mid-1930s that imported coffee pulpers were brought into Tanganyika. Such imported coffee pulpers were usually sold to rich coffee growers, initially through the Kilimanjaro Native Coffee Growers Association. Later, from the late 1930s to 1976, pulpers were sold through the Kilimanjaro Native Co-operative Union. Those who bought the imported machines were mostly rich farmers. When the co-operative unions were dissolved, there was a critical shortage of imported coffee machines and appropriate spare parts. This situation forced the majority of coffee growers, including rich farmers, to go for the locally produced coffee pulpers.

Central coffee pulperies were built by the co-operative unions, throughout Kilimanjaro, Pare and Arusha. However, nearly all coffee growers preferred to do the pulping at home before sending the coffee beans to market at the nearest Co-operative Society's store. The price obtained for pulped coffee was nearly ten times the price of unprocessed, raw coffee berries. The locally made coffee pulper is so popular that of the over one million people who live in Kilimanjaro province, approximately 210,000 homesteads, there are about 120,000 locally produced and operating coffee pulpers. Some are small while others are relatively large.

Small pulpers sold at 18,000 and 20,000TShs at early 1989 free-market prices, while the larger pulper sold at 35,000TShs. A small pulper can pulp up to 20 litres (one debe) of coffee by volume at a time while the larger pulper can take up to two debes at a time.

The fabrication and use of such indigenous coffee pulpers was started initially by local blacksmiths and carpenters but has now spread almost all over Chaggaland. This is an amazingly high rate of diffusion and social acceptability. This type of arabica coffee pulper has spread to all coffee growing provinces in Tanzania except for Kagera province where a similar but slightly different pulping machine has emerged. This other machine is extremely popular among the robusta coffee growers.

Nearly half of the smaller coffee pulping machines are made locally. These machines process approximately 60 per cent of all the arabica coffee which is produced by the average Kilimanjaro small-holder and up to 40 per cent of all coffee that is produced in Arusha, Ruvuma, Kagera and Mbeya provinces. This means that imported machines process only 40–55 per cent of all the small-holder produced coffee.

Locally-made coffee pulpers do create some problems from time to time. The operation of these machines is an extremely tedious job. Normally the machine is made out of wood with a few metal parts. The metal parts used are usually of lower quality and of little strength and this accelerates the wearing-out of parts. Another problem is that the pulping roller is made out of wood. The wooden roller absorbs water during the pulping operations. This in turn causes swelling and increases the roller's size. During

13

the off-season, the roller loses water and shrinks, thus reducing its length and its diameter. This intermittent change in the size of the pulping roller affects pulping efficiency. Sometimes coffee berries can be crushed whereas sometimes the berries pass through the pulping stage without actually being pulped. After some time, the machines become less efficient due to variations in the size of the wooden roller.

After observing such problems on a systematic basis, it was found necessary to make modifications to these local coffee pulpers. In the coffee growing provinces of Ruvuma, Mbeya and Arusha, coffee pulping is done mainly by the same Kilimanjaro-developed pulper alongside a comparable number of imported manually-operated small machines.

The modified arabica coffee pulper

The locally made machine has been modified and improved by replacing the wooden roller with a concrete roller. The modifications have been made by and through the joint efforts of the Arusha based Centre for Agricultural Mechanization and Rural Technology (CAMARTEC) and a long standing rural-based artisan Mr Wilson Msami from Mlangarini Village in Hai District, Kilimanjaro. The concrete roller does not vary in size because it does not swell or shrink due to moisture. The rest of the parts, other than the roller's handle, are made of wood and the roller is covered by lanced sheet metal. The collecting tray which conveys the coffee beans to a container is made of sheet metal.

There are two main versions: the conventional hand-operated version which is very popular amongst ordinary coffee growers and a bigger machine with a large capacity. This bigger machine is also hand-operated but it can be motorized.

This whole idea of improving the performance or efficiency of the local coffee pulper came from Mr Msami, a local craftsman who has been making coffee pulping machines for nearly 20 years. He was invited to CAMARTEC Workshop at Tengeru, Arusha, and collaborated with CAMARTEC specialists, engineers and technicians on production of the modified version. Another main modification made on the local coffee pulper is that the metal parts used are stronger than those used in the local version, so that the parts last longer. The benefit of these modifications is that the pulping efficiency has been increased since the pulping roller does not vary in size. Also, the pulper lasts longer since it is made of hard wood and stronger metal parts.

The modified coffee pulper is composed of three types of material — metal, wood and concrete. The main components of the machine are:

1 the roller: This is cast out of concrete and reinforced by rings of wires of about 3.5mm diameter which are placed near the ends of the roller. During casting, provision for holes is made on the surface of the roller to

14

Table 1 Requirements for fabrication of small hand-operated machine

S/R	Material specification	Qty
1	MS round bar: Ø19mm × 71mm	1pc
2	MS round bar: Ø38mm × 30mm	2pcs
3	MS sheet: 0.8mm × 229mm × 305mm	1pc
4	MS sheet: 0.8mm × 309mm × 503mm	1pc
5	bolts and nuts: M12 × 127mm	2pcs
6	nails (1", 2½", 3", 4")	1kg
7	cement:	5kg
8	sand:	5kg
9	timber: *(Mringaringa)* – 2" × 12" × 7' – 1" × 12" × 2' – 4" × 7" × 2' – 2" × 2½" × 3' – 2" × 4" × 1'	

accommodate small pieces of wood about 25mm diameter and 35mm long on to which the lanced sheet metal is nailed. The roller is 20.3cm in diameter and 30cm long.

2 the hopper: The box-like hopper is made of wood and holds the coffee berries before dropping them into the pulping chamber.

3 the pulping chamber: The pulping chamber is made of hard wood (*mringaringa*). The chamber is lined on the inside with sheet metal. The pulping chamber is the space between the roller and front of the machine.

4 the cranking handle: The cranking handle is made of a mild steel round bar 19mm diameter and 762mm long. It is fixed to the roller when concrete is being cast. The round bar is drilled and metal rods are placed in the holes to prevent the cranking handle from rotating in the roller.

5 the collecter tray: This is made of sheet metal sized ⅟₃₂″ × 9″ × 14″ (0.8mm × 229mm × 3,356mm). The tray is used for collecting and conveying coffee beans from the pulping chamber to the container.

Material requirements: For the conventional machine there are two sizes, a small hand-operated machine and a large hand-operated version.

Five prototypes of the CAMARTEC-improved arabica coffee pulper have been made so far. The Mang'ula Mechanical Tools Company Ltd has also made some prototypes of an improved Kilimanjaro arabica coffee pulper. However, these improved coffee pulpers have not yet been diffused on any appreciable scale in any of the coffee growing provinces.

Indigenous robusta coffee pulper
In Bukoba, Kagera province, where most of the coffee grown is robusta, the popular indigenous coffee pulper consists of a wooden roller into which metal strips/bands are nailed lengthwise at regular intervals.

Table 2 Requirements for fabrication large hand-operated machine

S/R	Material specification	Qty or ct
1	MS round bar: Q19mm × 762mm	1pc
2	MS round bar: Q38mm × 30mm	2pcs
3	MS sheet: 0.8mm × 229mm × 356mm	1pc
4	MS sheet: 0.8mm × 305mm × 704mm	1pc
5	bolts and nuts: M12 × 127mm	2pcs
6	nails (1", 2½", 3", 4")	1kg
7	cement:	6¼kg
8	sand:	7½kg
9	timber: *(Mringaringa)*	
	– 2" × 12" × 7'	
	– 1" × 12" × 2'	
	– 4" × 7" × 2'	
	– 2" × 2½" × 3'	
	– 2" × 4" × 1'	

This roller is encased in a concentric wooden tube of a slightly larger diameter. In making the outer cylinder, metal bands/strips are nailed on the inside of the cylinder length-wise, when the cylinder is still open into two halves. Between the inner wall of this outer tube-like cylinder and outer wall of the roller, there is a thin hollow cylindrical shell of air which just facilitates the free entry of berries in the space. This space is the machine's pulping chamber.

When the roller is rotated, the space facilitates crushing or shaving of the pulp from the ripe, dried robusta coffee berries. The space between the two cylinder walls is just big enough to allow the berries to drop. The rotating roller has shavers in the form of metal strips which crush the berries and remove the pulp. The roller is usually made from wood derived from a tree called *omushambya* in the Hay language. During the pulping process, a little water is added to the berries to ease the removal of the pulp while at the same time cooling the metal and wooden parts. Coffee pulping using this machine started in Kagera province in the 1930s, following commercialization of coffee in that province. Use of the machine was encouraged by the price differential in the market between pulped and unpulped coffee. Coffee pulping at home was and still is preferred not only because pulped coffee fetches a much higher price on the market but also because coffee processing productively occupies excess family labour.

The only two major improvements which the local robusta coffee pulper has undergone are the identification of tree-species which has long-lasting wood for use as rollers and the use of longer-lasting metal strips. Otherwise, the locally-produced robusta coffee pulper has remained much the same in design over the last 55 years.

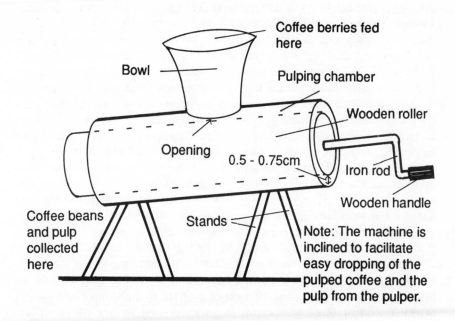

Coffee berries fed here

Bowl

Pulping chamber

Wooden roller

Opening

0.5 - 0.75cm

Iron rod

Wooden handle

Coffee beans and pulp collected here

Stands

Note: The machine is inclined to facilitate easy dropping of the pulped coffee and the pulp from the pulper.

The Kagera robusta coffee pulper

Acquisition of knowledge and skills

There are no formal training courses for artisans who intend making indigenous arabica or robusta coffee pulpers. Anyone who wants to know how to make the coffee pulper usually 'attaches' himself to an artisan who has extensive experience. The learner goes to live at the master artisan's home. The apprentice usually takes some grains, beans and/or bananas as his contribution for food. This is done weekly.

Step-by-step, the person being initiated into the art acquires the skills of making various parts of the pulper. He learns practically how to use the tools and is under the close eye and regular monitoring of the master artisan. After knowing how to make the various parts of the coffee pulper, the apprentice is then taught how to assemble the whole machine.

Usually such apprenticeship takes from two to three months depending on the pace at which the apprentice picks up the skill and dexterity required. Apprentices are, on average, aged between 25 and 30 years.

Apprentices usually are not charged any monetary fees but such apprentices are made to work for the master artisan on tasks such as harvesting or pulping coffee on days when there is no activity involving actual making of parts or assembling a coffee pulper.

As the apprentice begins to 'mature' in the industrial art of making coffee pulpers, and begins to make whole machines, the unwritten yet well-understood and respected contract between the master artisan and the apprentice takes hold. This is that all the money from the sale of pulpers made by the apprentice is the property of the master artisan. After all, it is the master artisan who also provides the materials for making the pulpers. If the master artisan so wishes, he can give the apprentice a few shillings for buying cigarettes or *mbege*, the local banana brew in Kilimanjaro.

In a typical week, three working days may be devoted to teaching the apprentice, and the other days are for agricultural activities. The apprentice is often allowed two days off so that he can go to his home to help with agricultural work or sort out any other issues. Very rarely would a master artisan accept more than one or two apprentices at a time.

At the end of an apprenticeship, the new graduate is expected to make a voluntary donation to the teacher, such as one or two goats or a calf as a token appreciation for the knowledge and skills he has acquired. Some apprentices master the skill of making pulpers so well that their master artisans request them to stay on as partners in a joint venture. Alternatively, the newly 'graduated/initiated' artisans may become employees of the master artisan.

Bottlenecks

On the whole, neither the arabica coffee pulper nor the robusta coffee pulper has serious bottlenecks with regard to dissemination. All materials used, including scrap metal and wood, are available locally and skills for fabricating such machines are available within village communities throughout the coffee growing areas, especially in Kilimanjaro and Kagera provinces. The coffee pulpers are extremely popular. Even those few families who cannot afford to buy and own such pulpers borrow one from neighbours in the village so that they can process their coffee berries before taking them to the co-operative market. Coffee growers who harvest a bumper crop of coffee berries, or people incapacitated because of old age or some other cause, usually hire young men to pulp their berries.

However, both types of coffee pulper are inefficient and their operation, though less vigorous and less tiring than straight manual pulping, is cumbersome. There are possibilities for improving pulper performance through some modifications.

A small arabica pulper cost 15,000TShs and a large one cost 30,000 to 35,000TShs in 1989 prices. The costs are rising so fast that it is imperative to arrange for subsidy or credit to small-holder farmers.

18

Finally, there are no larger-scale pulper manufacturing units or enterprises in Tanzania. Mass production of improved pulpers could reduce spending on expensive, imported coffee pulpers. Such mass production could in the long run reduce the pace at which pulper prices are rising. All production of pulpers is by hundreds of scattered, rural-based artisans whose skills are not updated. Artisans could improve through short practical workshops or through a bringing together of artisans for an exchange of experiences and expertise. Current quality of production varies greatly.

On a regional level, there has never been in Africa a single opportunity for artisans engaged in the production of indigenous crop processing technologies to meet and exchange views on their experiences, work environments and problems of production and/or marketing.

Major findings

Coffee occupies a central role in the overall economy of Tanzania, especially among small-scale producers and in terms of being the number-one export cash crop.

Coffee pulping is done both by modern, large-scale technology at centralized, co-operatively owned factories and by locally made pulping machines. The bulk of coffee processing, about 60 per cent, is done at homesteads using the locally-made machines.

Locally made pulping machines have been widely diffused in Tanzania and are extremely popular, mainly due to economic necessity and demand. Coffee pulping technology has evolved from manual to semi-mechanized pulping equipment but it is still labour-intensive and inefficient. There is the technical possibility of improving machine performance.

Nearly all artisans who produce the locally made coffee pulping machines have learnt the trade through informal apprenticeship at the homes of master-artisans. They in turn learned their skills through similar apprenticeship.

The cost of producing coffee pulping machines is becoming too high for the ordinary artisan to afford to buy the materials required. Production of such machines may be in danger of declining, if the government will not intervene to assist such artisans.

The cost of acquiring/purchasing locally made coffee pulping machines is escalating very fast. Many ordinary, poor small-scale holders/producers will not be able to afford such coffee pulping devices if no subsidy and/or credit schemes are introduced.

The skills of artisans are not up-graded on a formal, regular basis in order to improve the quality of their productive efforts. Their working tools are both poor and inadequate.

Recommendations

In view of the economic importance of coffee to the country's foreign currency earnings, it is recommended that the government should encourage and assist local artisans to set up efficient production lines for improved local coffee pulpers, on a co-operative basis, if possible. These could reduce heavy expenditure on imported pulpers and at the same time improve the efficiency of locally produced pulpers. Such a step would not hurt the business of isolated, single artisan-manufacturers in villages as the demand for such machines is quite high. The government should formulate a subsidy or credit scheme to assist small-holder coffee growers to acquire efficient, locally made coffee pulpers.

Rural-based artisans who fabricate local coffee pulpers, whether individually or in co-operative groups, should be assisted by the Government, NGOs and financial institutions to improve their skills. Seminars and assistance for acquiring better but simple tools would help. This would recognize the crucial contribution of these artisans to the coffee processing industry in Tanzania.

The international community, including international banks, NGOs, the UN system and donor agencies, should assist indigenous technologists in up-grading their skills. Short-term international training and provision of small credit facilities to improve the quality and range of working tools are needed.

Residue stoves in Kenya

MOHAMMED MWAMADZINGO

Introduction

Rural people are not ignorant or helpless when it comes to matters pertaining to new sources of energy. They can use their knowledge of the local environment to modify, change and improve the existing production system for their own benefit. This is an issue normally ignored by researchers, scientists and donor agencies.

Local artisans in Kenya have been able to modify existing stove design to have an effective combustion that takes advantage of abundant agricultural and forestry residues. Since the inception of the traditional residue stove around 1976, it has undergone minor changes and modifications aimed at improving the burning potential. These modifications were carried out in close co-operation between artisans and users, with almost no influence by or support from external agencies.

There are certain factors which hinder the wider dissemination of the stoves. These include lack of explicit policies to help accumulation of the local technological capacity, and the lack of financial, institutional and structural support. Thus, the study proves that what local people lack is not the technology, but rather the ability to enhance and put the technology into best practice.

As a way of minimizing the impact of the energy crisis, many donor agencies in conjunction with Third World governments and non-government organizations instituted various efforts. These included either increasing the supply of fuelwood by afforestation programmes or decreasing demand by the introduction of fuel-intensive stoves, the so-called 'improved' cooking stoves.

The promotion of improved stoves in developing countries started in the late 1940s. However, it was the 1970s before they had a substantial impact. Various reasons have been put forward to explain the 'failure' of the early improved stoves programmes. Some of these reasons include the neglect of the role and perception of the user, unprecedented efficiency and convenience of traditional cooking methods, high stove costs, the divergence

MR M. MWAMADZINGO (Kenya) is a research assistant with the African Centre for Technology Studies (ACTS). ACTS is a non-profit organization based in Nairobi. His main interests include biotechnology and the accumulation of indigenous technological capabilities in developing countries.

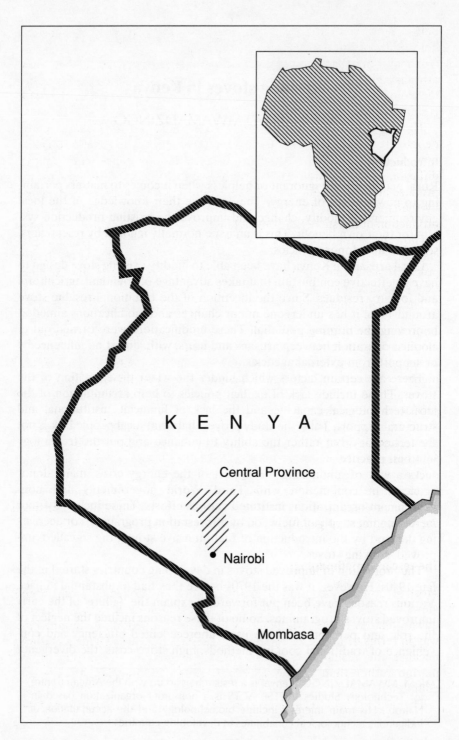

between the laboratory tests and the field performance, the impact on deforestation, and the stove design and testing.

A major drawback of many stove programmes is that they assume rural artisans and users do not have a part to play in the search for better technologies, new sources of energy, and new conservation measures. This is shown by the lack of research in this area.

The main objective of this study is to show the importance of the people's technology in general economic development, in terms of why and how residue stoves evolved in Kenya, and the importance and extent of diffusion of the technology. The study also looks at why it is attractive to produce and use residue stoves in the country. Other matters investigated by the study include the process involved in acquiring knowledge about production of the stoves and development of skills. This involves determining how these 'traditional' processes relate to scientific methods and understandings. The study ends by identifying major obstacles and the future potential and achievements of the technology. The aim is to suggest practical ways of helping people to help themselves.

The specific objectives of the study can be summarized as follows:

1 to trace the origin of the residue stove in Kenya, and to spell out various modifications undertaken during the evolution process;
2 to establish the extent of stove diffusion in the country, in terms of the number of producers, consumers, marketing and distribution agents;
3 to analyse the economic and social viability of the technology on the producers and users;
4 to examine the training, knowledge and skill development process in the accumulation of indigenous technological capability;
5 to identify the main bottlenecks and policy issues relating to the production and usage of the technology;
6 to suggest policy recommendations to the government, non-government institutions, scientists, and donor agencies on how to enhance the development of people's technology.

The research methodology

Most information contained in this report was collected from interviews with the users and producers of the technology, using a structured questionnaire. However, the interviews were carried out in an informal way in terms of group discussions i.e. 'panel interviews'. This was done because the researcher was interested mainly in maximizing information rather than maximizing the number of questionnaires to be completed.

The research is based mainly on information collected in Nairobi and the Central province of Kenya. The locations considered include Kikuyu,

Thogoto, Ruiru, Mukurweini, and Limuru in Central Province, and Kawangware, Shauri-Moyo, Kibera, and Dagoretti in Nairobi.

After the above areas were identified, only a few of the most informative
artisans and users were interviewed, in a group wherever possible. The
most informative interviewees were selected based on their knowledge and
experience about the residue stoves. Other information was collected also
from the Ministry of Energy, the Kenya Energy and Environment Organizations Associations (KENGO), the Apro Energy Enterprises, and the
Appropriate Technology Centre of Kenyatta University.

The energy situation in Kenya

There are only three main energy sources in Kenya — woodfuel,
petroleum and hydro-electricity — despite various efforts undertaken to
identify new sources. Wood and forestry products account for more than 98
per cent of the country's total energy supply. It has been forecast that wood
products will continue to supply more than half of energy requirements
well into the twenty-first century.

The main uses of woodfuel in Kenya are to be found in the household
sector, but industry is also a significant consumer. It is estimated that as
much as 26 per cent of the total national consumption of fuelwood and 12
per cent of charcoal are for industrial purposes.

There is much concern about increasing woodfuel consumption in
Kenya. The total use of fuelwood in the rural areas is said to be increasing
at the rate of 3.6 per cent per annum, while that of charcoal is growing at 7
per cent per annum. Projecting these trends reveals a highly alarming
situation, with widespread depletion of forests by the turn of the century. It
is because of this realization that the Kenyan Ministry of Energy is developing a comprehensive woodfuel policy. This includes agro-forestry,
peri-urban and industrial plantations, as well as the promotion of improved
methods of charcoal making and the dissemination of the more efficient
wood and charcoal stoves.

Table 1 Energy supply in Kenya

	Giga joules	% of total energy
Fuel wood	209.7	63
Petroleum and coal	82.2	25
Charcoal	25.3	8
Crop residue	9	3
Hydro-electricity	5.8	2
TOTAL	332	100

Source: O'Keefe et al, 1984

24

An omission in the Ministry of Energy's woodfuel policy is the lack of recognition of the importance of agricultural and forestry residues in meeting Kenya's energy demand. This is the basis of the evolution of the residue stoves examined in this study.

The experience of improved-cooking stoves in Kenya

Before the emergence of the improved stoves programmes in the early 1980s, all charcoal stoves available in the country were the traditional metal stove (TMS). This was first introduced at the coastal town of Mombasa by the Indian railway workers in the late 1890s. This early stove received immediate and rapid dissemination to other areas of the country because it was considered to be superior to traditional open fires and because it used a new fuel—'charcoal'.

The traditional metal stove is made entirely of recycled metal. It has a cylindrical shape with a door for air combustion and ash removal. There are three triangular-shaped flaps for supporting the cooking pans. It is estimated that over 560,000 traditional stoves are used for heating and cooking in Kenya. The stove is not insulated and can be used as well for space heating in cold areas of the country.

Since 1981 there has been a major campaign by the Kenya Government, donor agencies and the non-governmental organizations (NGOs) to introduce fuel-efficient stoves. At present, three types of stove can be identified:

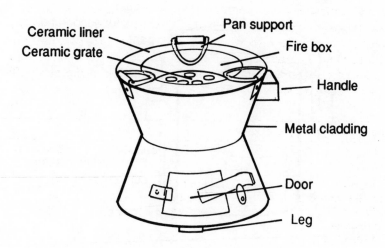

The Kenyan traditional metal stove

1   the charcoal stoves, aimed at the urban population;
2   the woodstoves, mainly found in the rural areas;
3   the institutional or community stoves, aimed for use by large institutions.

The main significant charcoal stove is the Kenya ceramic *Jiko* (KCJ) which is a lined stove adapted from the TMS and the Thai Bucket to suit Kenyan cooking practices. The development of the KCJ involved many institutions such as the KENGO, the Appropriate Technology Centre of Kenyatta University, the Intermediate Technology Development Group (ITDG), the United States Agency for International Development (USAID), the Kenya Government, the International Development Research Centre (IDRC), and many other NGOs.

The KCJ project is now considered to be one of the most successful in Africa. By mid-1986 more than 250,000 stoves had been produced and sold to urban dwellers, and the demand consistently exceeds the supply. The stoves now account for more than 50 per cent of traditional stoves in Nairobi and over 10 per cent of the national stove market. As a result of large market sales, the price of the stoves has come down from 250KShs when they were introduced to less than 80KShs, depending on the size.

In contrast with the urban programme, only 10,000 woodstoves for rural areas have been introduced. This is largely because, unlike urban dwellers, rural users rarely have to pay for their fuel. Thus, there is little direct

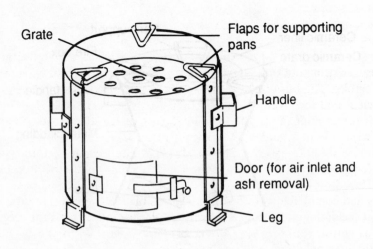

The Kenyan ceramic jiko

economic incentive to improve the efficiency with which fuel is burnt. The cost of the woodstoves is also high which inhibits widespread use to the rural communities. (One woodstove costs 150KShs.)

The residue stoves

It is not easy to identify exactly the origin of the traditional residue stove. It was suggested by artisans interviewed that the stove first emerged around the Meru area in 1976. At that time the diffusion of the stove was too limited to warrant much knowledge of its existence.

The reasons that led to the emergence of the residue stove in the country include:

1 increased biomass waste from the sawmills, rice mills, carpentry shops, and the sisal factories;
2 the 'woodfuel crisis' in terms of increased cost of charcoal and firewood;
3 the capability and the need on the part of local artisans to modify existing stove designs.

Kenya produces large quantities of agricultural waste associated with food and industrial production. Often these wastes create problems of disposal. It has been estimated that rice mills alone throw away over 40,000 tons of rice husks every year while coffee and sisal factories all over the country may throw away an even higher tonnage of waste. The volume of rice husks disposed of by the Mwea Rice Mills alone is said to be sufficient to cook meals for 30,000 families for a whole year. It is also estimated that Kenya produces more than 100,000 tons of sawdust in its sawmills and carpentry shops.

Much potential energy locked up in this waste biomass was lost as the technology for efficient combustion was unavailable. In some cases, agricultural waste like rice husks and sawdust was burnt directly for commercial use, creating not only a nuisance but also a health hazard by emitting toxic smoke. The burning of these wastes in conventional stoves was very inefficient and inconvenient, giving only 5 to 9 per cent of useful energy output for cooking. With the introduction of the residue stoves, the biomass waste has now gained an economic price.

Rural households and peri-urban dwellers often cannot afford to pay cash for cooking fuel but have access to free wood and agricultural residues. Sawdust, rice husks, and coffee husks are commonly used as supplements and complements to firewood and charcoal. These residues need a special technology to burn effectively. There are other types of residue, such as cotton stalks, maize cobs and maize stalks, which can be burnt directly in an open fire or in some woodstoves.

Most of the improved stoves developed in Kenya are associated with donor programmes. However, the stoves under review differ from these initiatives in one aspect — the stoves are not linked with any donors and are from rural artisans who design, produce and market their own products. The stoves are made by the same artisans who make the traditional stoves.

The residue stoves are a modification of the traditional metal stove, with specific adaptations and designs to burn loose biomass. There are three types of residue stoves in Kenya — the traditional, the modified clay-liner household stove and the institutional stove.

The main feature of the traditional residue stove is that it is made of recycled metal, as in the traditional metal stove. It can be distinguished from the TMS by the absence of a grate, the presence of the top lid with a hole at the centre used for channelling heat radiation during cooking time and a smaller door for allowing in air.

The inner cylindrical wall body acts as the central combustion chamber, where both the residue and the firewood is held. The outer door has a door frame and some stoves have a door to control air intake. The size of the stove varies according to the customer's specifications.

Various changes and modifications can be identified since traditional residue stoves first came into being. These changes can be classified as incremental (minor) and radical (major). Incremental changes include:

1 removal of legs: As mentioned earlier, the design of residue stoves originated from the traditional metal stove. Originally, the residue stove

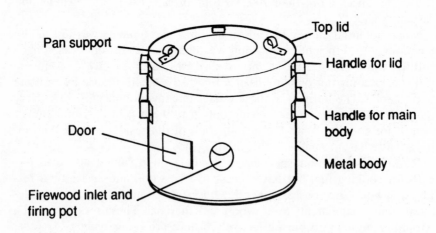

The traditional residue stove

28

had legs. However, due to the heavier weight caused by the residue plus the weight of the food cooked, the legs were found to be weak. To respond to this problem, artisans decided to make the stoves without legs. It was considered that removing legs would not affect the performance of the stove.

2 strengthening the pan supports: Because of the weight of the cooking pots and the need for vigorous stirring of the staple food *ugali*, there was a need to strengthen the pan supports (flaps). This has been done by the use of heavier metal gauge as flaps.

3 reduction of the inside diameter of the top lid: This was done to increase the time and extent of combustion of the residue.

Dissemination of the technology

Residue stoves have been disseminated widely, mainly in the residue-excess area of Central Province and Nairobi. A very preliminary survey by the researchers found that up to 30 per cent of households in the locations selected were using the stove. The main areas which are known to use the residue stoves are Ruiru, Kikuyu, Karai, Thogoto, and Limuru (Kiambu district), Athi River (Machakos district), Njoro (Nakuru district), Mukurweini (Nyeri district), Karatina (Murang'a district) and Kibera, Dagoretti, Shauri Moyo, and Kawangware (Nairobi).

The following were identified as the main contributing factors:

1 availability of residue: In all these areas sawdust, coffee husks and rice husks were always available from the sawmills, rice mills, carpentry shops, and coffee mills.

2 low price of the stoves: The price of the residue stoves is around 40KShs. This is much lower than the price of the Kenya ceramic Jiko (80 KShs) but is the same price as the traditional metal stove.

3 low price of fuel: The residue is normally obtained free of charge or at very low prices, mainly to cover transport costs and a small profit margin. The survey found that the price of the residue varied from place to place. For instance, a 70kg bag of sawdust cost 3KShs in Ruiru, but cost up to 30KShs in the Kikuyu division.

Viability and economics of the technology

Although there has been no official efficiency testing of the stove, users find it more convenient than the open fire. The stove is said to be efficient in terms of combustion of the biomass and produces a clear flame with little smoke. To show the efficiency of the residue stove two types of test were carried out:

29

1 Burning (combustion) efficiency: 40kg of sawdust can be used to cook for a family of eight for a period of two weeks, but a 40kg load of firewood used in the open fire lasts for only four days. If we assume that the open-fire stove is 10 per cent efficient, the residue stove was found to be 17.1 per cent more efficient in terms of burning capacity (see Table 2). This means that the stove saves 71 per cent of the equivalent fuel used in the traditional open-fire stove.

Table 2 Combustion efficiency of the residue and open-fire stoves

	Residue stove	Open-fire stove
specific daily combustion	40kg/14 days = 2.86	40kg/4 days 10
percentage saving = $\dfrac{10 - 2.86}{10}$ = 71.4%		
combustion efficiency	17.1%	10%

Source: *Field Survey, 1989*

Preliminary efficiency tests carried out by some students of the Appropriate Technology Centre at Kenyatta University reveal that the residue stove saves around 29–30 per cent of the fuel used by the traditional metal charcoal stove.

2 Cost efficiency: The residue stove is economical to users in that it saves fuel, as Table 3 shows.

Table 3 Cost benefits of the residue stoves and the traditional charcoal stove

	Residue stove	Charcoal stove
price per 70kg bag (KShs)	30	120
duration (for a family of eight)	4 weeks	4 days
average cost per month (KShs)	30	900
saving ratio	1 :	30

Source: *Field Survey, 1989*

It is estimated that approximately 5 per cent of artisans involved in the production of stoves in the areas surveyed are involved in the production of the residue stoves. This implies that residue stove-making is becoming more important as a generator of rural and peri-urban employment.

More people will be employed as the importance of the stove is realized by more users. Currently most of the stoves are sold directly from the artisans' workshops but a new distribution system is evolving. This involves

30

distribution through middlemen, particularly those people involved in the selling of the residue as fuel. The following illustrates the distribution network:

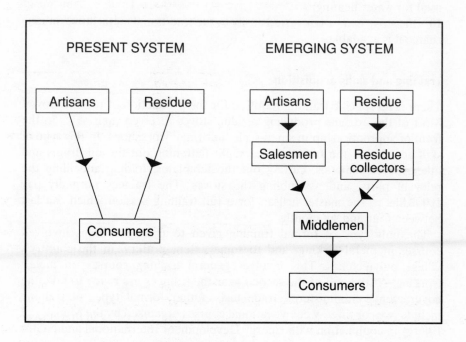

The distribution network of the residue stove

Other benefits of residue stoves include:

3 the sale of materials that would otherwise be wasted;
4 less pressure on wood resources through the reduction of consumption of firewood and charcoal, in line with the need to preserve the environment;
5 a contribution to the accumulation and building of indigenous technological capability;
6 a reduction of problems of waste disposal and risks of fire from the mills;
7 health and safety considerations: the stove emits less smoke and is safe to the users and children because residue acts as an insulator with minimal heat loss;
8 the stove is easy to use, does not change traditional cooking habits and uses the same type and size of pot currently available to users, and it gives a

stronger user-artisan relationship or collaboration with the aim of improving the efficiency of the stoves;

9 the stove has a long-burning capacity compared to traditional stoves; it is normally used to cook meals for the whole family and residual heat is used for water heating;

10 the stove can be converted easily to the traditional metal stove, in case charcoal is available.

Training and skills acquisition

There is no specific training required for the production of residue stoves. Most of the artisans producing residue stoves received their skills in the form of apprenticeship in small-scale 'informal' workshops. In this type of skill acquisition the trainees are taught flattening out the oil drums and other recycled metals, cutting out the templates, folding and filing the relevant parts, and assembling the stoves. The trainees normally pay 1000KShs to the master-artisan for a full training session which can last between four and six months.

The only type of formal training given to trainee artisans involved courses in metalworking, and to some extent pottery, in the country's village polytechnics. This involves general training courses on metalworking. At the end of the second year the trainees are ready to take the government's administered trade tests. Other formal types of training include two- or three-week vocational courses organized by the Ministry of Energy in conjunction with Energy Development International and NGOs (such as KENGO).

The major problems faced during the training period include the lack of teaching materials such as reference books and tools. There is also a shortage of instructors in the village polytechnics. For example, in one of the training centres visited there was only one instructor who was supposed to be teaching both the first and second years in the same classroom.

Obstacles to increased dissemination and production

Despite successful dissemination of the residue stoves in the country there are a number of factors that inhibit wider diffusion.

1 reduced market potential: There are a large number of people, even in areas with excess sawdust and rice husks, who do not have any information on the stoves. The interviews found some residents who were amazed by the idea that there existed locally-made stoves which could use what they considered to be waste.

2 weaknesses of the stove design: It should be noted that although the stove is widely disseminated, there are a few disadvantages. These include o smoke emission, particularly in the initial burning stage;

o the residues do not burn completely and

o it is not possible to add more fuel (the residue) while the stove is burning.

3   poor man's technology: Some of the users declined to use the stove for fear of being seen as too poor to afford charcoal or firewood.

4   financial constraints: Major problems faced on the part of artisans include lack of working capital and unavailability of infrastructural support. The artisans claimed that they have the capacity to produce and sell more stoves if they had enough money to buy raw materials and equipment. They claimed that at the moment the demand for the residue stoves far exceeds the supply. Some artisans ask users to bring their own materials, mainly the recycled metal, so that they can charge only their labour costs. This reduces the burden on the part of the artisans and also the price of the final product.

Recommendations for increased dissemination

1   Research and development: In order to increase the use of residue stoves in the relevant areas there is a need to carry out more research and development aimed at improving the burning efficiency of existing stove designs. This has to be followed by appropriate field tests to find the viability of the stoves to the users.

2   Marketing support: Residue stoves can be used by more Kenyans in the residue-excess areas if advertising on fuel and cost efficiency is emphasized. There is a need for strategic marketing surveys to determine which areas have excess agricultural residues and to find the types of fuels used by local people.

3   Infrastructural support: To increase the production of the stove there is a need to provide more infrastructural support such as more credit (either in kind or in cash), electricity, water and roads.

The grate cooking system in Zimbabwe

MTHULI NCUBE

Introduction

This study is centred on the metal grate, a cooking device which is currently in use in rural Zimbabwe. The popular structure of the cooking metal grate consists of a rectangular frame with four legs. To enable pots and other cooking containers to sit on it, pieces of metal rods are welded inside the rectangular frame. The grate is then put over a fire. Most of the grates have three rings of different sizes welded inside the frame to hold round-bottomed pots. It is a technology produced by the informal sector, and its durability, portability and modern appearance contribute to its popularity. The size, height and quality of the grates invariably varies and so does performance as a cooking device.

Consumers and producers

Consumers are located in rural areas while producers are in the peripheral informal sector within urban areas. Chihota, a rural area south of Harare, the capital of Zimbabwe, was chosen as a target research area. Chihota has a problem of wood shortage due to deforestation. This is an important issue for fuel conservation. The aim was to determine the response of rural people to this cooking technology, given their wood problem.

A total of 50 households were interviewed. People answered questionnaires about characteristics of the metal grate, its links with health, their willingness to pay and household characteristics. The income range of the households was between Z$200 and Z$7,500 a year, with a mean of Z$1,758 a year. Chihota is a high income area by rural standards. Most households receive income from monthly remittances, sale of crops, sale of garden vegetables, local part-time wages, occasional remittances, local full-time wages and other sources.

Producers of the metal grate are located in the informal sector in urban areas. This is where the market is concentrated, as most wage earners of

MR M. NCUBE (Zimbabwe) is a lecturer in the Economics Department at the University of Zimbabwe. He has worked as a consultant for SADCC Mining Unit, World Bank, ILO, NAM, ITDG and other organizations, as well as lecturing at the University of Zimbabwe and sitting on the Zimbabwe Stock Exchange Board.

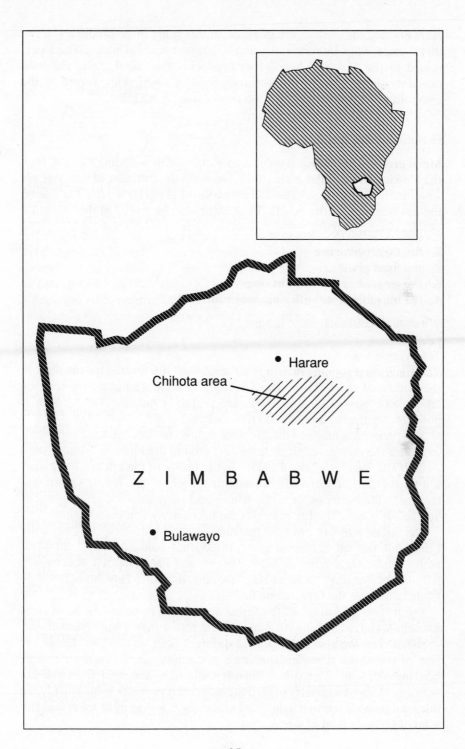

Chihota area

● Harare

Z I M B A B W E

● Bulawayo

35

rural households work in urban areas. In this study three producers of the metal grate were interviewed using a questionnaire. The questions pertained to the cost and benefits of producing the metal grate, the time producers have been in the business, acquisition of skills, future of the technology and bottlenecks for the production of the grate.

Evolution of the metal grate

Metal grate technology is part of a cooking system including the pot, fuel, the cooking site and the grate itself. The main determinant of the system's structure is the pot. To discuss the evolution of the grate we need to discuss the development of the hearth. Four stages can be traced in the evolution of the cooking hearth:

1 **the three-stone fire**
2 **the fixed grate**
3 **the movable grate without rings**
4 **the movable grate with rings and with 'grill'.**

We shall discuss each stage in turn.

Three-stone fire

The traditional cooking hearth is a three-stone fire located on the floor in the middle of the kitchen. The kitchen is a separate hut where cooking takes place but sometimes meals are prepared outside. The kitchen is preferred by the women who do the cooking.

A depression is made in the fireplace to hold the hot charcoal and ashes, to reduce the dangers of them spreading around the kitchen. Wood is used as fuel. The location of the fireplace in the centre of the kitchen hut makes it a focal point for social life in traditional society. The family sits around the fire in the evenings, or in the winter and rainy season discussing social and family issues. The fire provides the necessary warmth and light.

The three-stone fire can hold traditional round-bottomed clay pots quite firmly but the flat-bottomed iron pots do not balance well. Traditional maize food, *sadza*, requires heavy stirring and flat-bottomed pots usually fall out of the fire, thus making cooking difficult. Few households in Chihota still use the three-stone fire.

The biggest advantage of the three-stone fire is its economy. Most rural households have an ability-to-pay problem rather than a willingness-to-pay problem. The fire also holds pots of different sizes, as one can change the size of the stone triangle. The fire's portability allows users to change cooking locations. The stones absorb some heat and light from the fire hence only about a quarter of respondents feel it provides heat. Most feel it does not provide enough light. Fuel efficiency is low as most users feel this kind of fire uses a lot of wood.

Because of the openness of the fire, the carbon in the smoke sticks on the grass thatch. From the survey, 16 per cent of households feel this type of fire protects thatch from termites and reduces permeability to rain water. About 36 per cent of households feel the fire produces too much smoke, which is a health hazard. The open fire has its dangers. Of those interviewed, 60 per cent highlighted the danger of burning people while 24 per cent expressed the danger of burning the kitchen.

Because of the fire's structure, 58 per cent of households feel it cannot sit several pots at a time. This slows down the cooking process. Generally, users did not feel this kind of fire cooks a particular pot slowly. Because of wind and eddy currents, the fire makes the kitchen dirty (say 44 per cent) as ashes are blown about.

What has rendered the three-stone fire obsolete is the development of the pot. Traditionally, round-bottomed clay pots were used. But as industrialization took effect in the urban areas, flat-bottomed iron pots were introduced. These are available for purchase in the cities, including rural shops in service centres. The flat-bottomed pot cannot balance well on the three-stone fire. The pot is part of the cooking system, and therefore the three-stone fire had to be transformed to fit with the changing cooking system.

Even the round-bottomed pot has problems in balancing as users cook traditional food. *Sadza* requires heavy stirring and the stones move apart, making cooking difficult. A much firmer cooking device had to be introduced, which was the fixed grate. Of course some households use both the three-stone fire *and* the fixed grate. Thus we have an overlapping evolutionary process, leading to the phasing out of the stone fire, and the emergence of the fixed grate.

Fixed grate
The fixed grate has four corner-mounds of clay into which connecting metal bars are embedded. The connecting bars can hold both flat-bottomed and round-bottomed pots.

Unlike the three-stove fire which could be used outside, the fixed grate is fixed in the centre of the kitchen and is immobile. The fixed grate is also a people's technology as each household makes its own. The clay for the four mounds is available locally and the metal bars are from scrap metal. The technology is household-based and it is for the use of the family only. In other words, it has *use* value but no *exchange* value.

In Chihota, people value the fixed grate for its ability to hold up to three pots, both round and flat-bottomed. Households learn the design from neighbours and relations. People see the grate in use and they duplicate it. It is a technology that is simple to copy and that simplicity facilitates diffusion.

The obsolescence of the fixed grate is due to negative characteristics that outweigh positive ones. Firstly, the fixed grate is immovable, which does

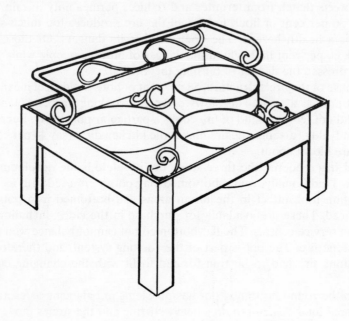

Movable metal grate with rings

not allow households to use it outside the kitchen hut. When it is too hot in the kitchen, the need arises to cook outside. For this, the fixed grate is a disadvantage. Secondly, clay mounds and metal bars have different expansion co-efficients which causes the clay to crack, breaking up the whole structure. This makes cooking difficult and there is a need to replace the clay mounds. Thirdly, the differential expansion rates of the bars under heat causes them to bend inwards to different degrees. As a result, the pots cannot sit firmly. The bars have to be removed and straightened requiring complete reconstruction each time the bars are straightened. These disadvantages are the source of obsolescence of the technology and a motivation for the development of the movable metal grate without rings.

Movable metal grate without rings
This grate comprises a metal frame welded together, without rings. Metal bars are welded inside the frame. The grate was designed by the informal

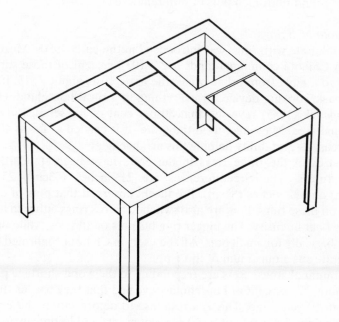

Movable grate without rings

sector in the urban sector, out of scrap metal. Having been introduced about 30 years ago, it came about nine years after the flat-bottomed pot.

The production of the movable grate shifted from the rural household to the informal sector in the urban areas of cities. It became more dependent on the metal sector of the manufacturing industrial sector. The informal sector is responsible for the changes. This is not difficult because most of the informal sector producers belong to both the rural peasant class and urban working class. This sector is aware of the needs of the rural sector, because of its dual character.

The firm structure and movability of the metal grate are its advantages. But its design was not conceived in line with the other component of the cooking system, the pot. Round-bottomed pots were not eliminated with the introduction of the fixed grate. But the movable grate can hold only flat-bottomed pots firmly. There was need for corrective engineering to accommodate the round-bottomed pot.

39

This saw the birth of the next stage in the design of the grate, which included rings of different diameters welded inside the metal frame. These cater for round-bottomed pots of different sizes.

Metal grate with rings
The metal grate with rings was introduced in the early 1980s. Most households in Chihota communal lands use it (93 per cent of those surveyed). Purchased mainly from urban areas, the grate costs about Z$15. It is used as the basic cooking device for everything in a rural household. Hancock and Hancock (1985) revealed that 80 per cent of households in another communal area, Masvingo, used the grate. It is carried as far as 400km to rural areas, its portability helping this arrangement.

The sizes of the three rings in the grate have been standardized by manufacturers. The circumferences are 21 inches (53cm), 25 inches (63.5cm) and 32 inches (81cm). Producers observed that pots of different sizes fit on these rings. Pots are also switched across rings either to lessen or increase heat intensity. The bigger ring fits pots of all sizes, while the other two are basically for small pots. All the users in Chihota confirmed that the metal grate sits a maximum of three pots.

In communal areas, users are responding to the wood-shortage problem. In Chihota, 72 per cent of households revealed that they use less firewood now than 10 years ago. This is a response to deforestation and expensive wood, costing an average of Z$20 per scotch cart and lasting an average of two to three months. In general, it is the women and children who fetch firewood and they generally feel the sources becoming more distant.

With the new cooking grate, users have responded by drying wood, using a windbreak, lowering the grate, using crop residue and cow dung and putting out the fire after use. Of direct relevance to the metal grate, the windbreak is the most popular method of fuel conservation. The windbreak is constructed either at the doorway side or opposite the doorway side; 32 per cent were on the doorway side and 30 per cent opposite the doorway side.

The windbreak stops the wind coming in through the doorway from blowing fire away from the pots. The material of the grate is usually bricks and mud, bricks and concrete or mud. Most windbreaks are made from bricks and mud (59.4 per cent) while the rest are made from bricks and concrete (22 per cent) and mud/other materials (18.6 per cent).

About 87 per cent of windbreaks are straight while the rest, 13 per cent, are comma shaped. The height of the windbreaks varies from 14cm to 28cm, but the average height is 21cm.

The fuel conservation measure of lowering the grate is done in several ways: by cutting off the legs of the grate, digging it into the ground, raising the ground, raising the fireplace ground and using extension below the grate.

In the Chihota communal area, most grates (70 per cent) are dug into the ground while the rest are not lowered at all. The distance between the pot and the ground varies from 12cm to 26cm with an average of 17cm.

The fire is still centrally located for equitable distribution of heat and light, and for social gathering in the kitchen hut. At the centre of the fireplace, a hole measuring about 5cm in depth is dug. The depressed fireplace traps ashes and stops them being blown about the hut. The small hole also traps hot charcoal which is protected by ashes. This makes re-lighting easier.

The advantages of the movable metal grate have popularized it — especially its portability, durability and its capacity to hold pots firmly. However, the grate has not solved the fundamental disadvantages of an open hearth cooking system. Such disadvantages pertain to health hazards of burns and smoke.

How have the changes been made? Changes in the metal grate came about through a communication system between producers and consumers. The producers belong to a dual class with peasant and urban-worker characteristic. They know what the people want. Most of all, the pot sizes dictated the size of the three rings welded in the grate. The producers respond to the desires of the consumers. The designers respond to people's tastes — and they change people's tastes as well.

Viability and economics of the technology

The production of the metal grate is by small-scale producers on oligopolistic markets. The average size of each production unit is three workers. In an eight-hour working day, 15–20 grates can be produced. Production is basically in the informal sector and located in high density sites of Mbare, in Harare, for market reasons.

This small-scale production has characteristics which distinguish it from the formal sector. Firstly, the means of production are owned by workers and therefore the benefits accrue to them. This is so because the required level of investment is small and techniques are easy to operate.

Secondly, the metal grate is not produced on its own. All producers make other commodities, such as door frames, window frames and scotch carts. In terms of profitability, window frames and door frames are most profitable. Product diversification exists, with producers aiming at widening markets and hedging against the risk of non-profitable commodities.

Thirdly, the production process does not have barriers to entry for entrepreneurs — in contrast to the formal sector. Prior skill in making the grate is not a prerequisite. Often general welding and metalwork knowledge is the requirement, hence the product diversification. Skill requirements are not acquired from the formal education system, but from on-the-job training in the formal sector. All producers were either high school or primary school dropouts or a product of formal sector retrenchment.

Fourthly, monopoly in the form of control of vital inputs or skilled labour does not exist. Metal bars come from the metal industries, and every producer has access to this market.

Lastly, while prices in the formal sector are dictated by government regulations and competition, metal grate prices are set mainly through a cartel (implicit collusion) of producers. In the survey done both at Mbare and Chihota, the average price of the metal grate was Z$15.

Basically, producers informally agree on the price to charge. But approached by a potential buyer, a seller may quickly abandon the cartel price and bargain with the buyer. In this case, the price is not fixed but depends on the bargaining strength of the two parties.

In general, such characteristics define the informal sector in sharp contrast to the formal sector. An exception on the ownership structure is one producer in Mbare whom we shall refer to as Mr X. Mr X is an informal sector entrepreneur who employs four workers and is the most prolific producer. We shall refer to him later.

Inputs for the production of the metal grate come from the Zimbabwe Iron and Steel Company (ZISCO). Some inputs are scrap metal from engineering companies. Mr X and other producers have contracts with ZISCO for the supply of flat, angled and round metal bars. The scrap metal from engineering companies is also a product of ZISCO.

This is the strongest linkage between the formal sector and the informal metal grate sector. This backward linkage is the lifeline of the metal grate without which it cannot exist. Such a parasitic character is typical of informal sector production.

The market for the metal grate is located in rural areas even though the product is sold in the urban informal sector. How then does the grate find its way to the rural sector? The grate is sold in the vicinity of the rural bus terminus, at Mbare. This is one of the busiest parts of Harare City, with people moving about all the time. In this market, other commodities are sold including furniture products, car parts and other metalwork.

Members of rural households who work in Harare purchase the metal grate and the rural buses are the mode of transporting grates to the rural areas. The Mbare market therefore acts as an intermediary market between the producers and the final users in rural areas.

Costs of production

The costs are divided into two:

1 **costs of metal bars, angled and flat** and
2 **costs of electricity and rent.**

These costs are the *marginal* costs. The *fixed* costs pertain to the costs of purchasing the machinery. The costs are summarized in Table 1.

Table 1 Cost of production

Monthly	**1**	–	*rent*	:	Z$50 a month
costs:	**2**	–	*electricity*	:	Z$30 a month
	3	–	*angled metal*		
			bars	:	1.60m @ Z$1.06 a metre × 40 grates a month = Z$67.84 a month
	4	–	*flat metal bars*	:	1.60m @ Z$1.38 a metre × 40 grates a month = Z$88.32
	5	–	*10mm diameter bars* :		1.95mm @ Z$0.54 a metre × 40 grates a month = Z$42.12 a month
	6	–	*smaller bars* : 140m	@	Z$0.312 a metre × 40 grates a month = Z$17.472
			total cost per month		= Z$295.752

fixed costs of purchasing

machinery:	**1**	–	*abrasive cutter*	= Z$500
	2	–	*welder*	= Z$450
		Total		= Z$950

Benefits and costs to consumers

There is no doubt that consumers benefit from the metal grate cooking system, despite the costs of using it. The open hearth system is a health hazard, in that it smokes and has the potential of burning people. The hazard of people receiving burns from open fires was the biggest concern expressed with 34 per cent of respondents mentioning this. There is also a danger of the open fire burning the kitchen hut or a whole village if uncontrolled.

Some households felt that the smoke produced by the open fire affects eyes, chest and nose. The smoke does not cure thatch, as is usually specu-lated. Users of open fires revealed that they replace the thatch of the kitchen hut every three years, while the thatch of other huts is replaced every 10 years. This means that with open fires, kitchen thatch ages three times faster than normal. This is a cost to users, as grass is a scarce material in this deforested region.

Some users (30 per cent) feel the grate uses more wood because it accommodates more pots. Chopping wood is viewed as a problem by 24 per cent of users. About 14 per cent of users feel the grate does not fit pots of all sizes, but most feel it cooks faster. Only a few users feel it is slower

(20 per cent), does not give warmth (6 per cent) and takes up space (6 per cent).

The disadvantages of the grate are outweighed by its advantages. These advantages have been responsible for its resilience to replacement by appropriate rural stoves. Not only does the grate cook faster, it also keeps the kitchen clean and there is less danger of burning children and the hut, compared to the three-stone fire.

Knowledge and skills acquisition

In metal grate production, training is on-the-job. It is basically learning-by-doing. Mr X, referred to earlier, was one of the earliest producers of the grate and has trained about 15 metal grate producers in the past 16 years.

All incumbent trainees come with no knowledge of metalwork from school. Mr X trains them in the basic skills, especially cutting and welding. It takes about six months for a trainee to qualify in basic metalwork, after which time they are able to produce a grate unassisted by more experienced colleagues. The trainees therefore learn by doing.

After spending some time, about three years, with a more experienced metalworker such as Mr X, qualified metalworkers break away. They establish their own small industries or go back to the formal sector as employees in engineering metalwork companies. Of the 15 workers that Mr X has trained, five have left and acquired jobs in Harare-based metalwork companies. The remaining 10 have established their own small metal workshops in the busy area of Mbare and other high density suburbs.

Self-management prevails in the production of the metal grate, with the exception of Mr X. Asked how they felt about modern techniques of management, producers felt it was inefficient because it slows down information from one decision-maker to another. For a small workshop the concept of separating the manager and the artisan worker does not apply. The organization of production is too small to have a stratified system, hence the self-management approach.

In a set-up where artisans work as a group, team-work spirit and encouragement amounts to production management. The division of labour between cutting, welding and smoothing keeps every member busy as their work is an input into the next stage in production. As such, there are no managerial skills required in the way we know them. Any form of management imposed could prove inefficient by slowing down information flow in the production process.

Producers like Mr X are slowly acquiring modern management techniques because of their ability to employ workers in relatively extensive product diversification. Mr X acts as the manager and the four workers he employs report to him. He holds portfolios of general manager, chairman, employer, owner, financial manager, marketing manager, and all management positions we can imagine in a modern formal sector set-up. Such duties are acquired over time and basically learnt on-the-job.

Bottlenecks

The metal grate cooking system is a people's technology. It is popular and blends into the socio-economic environment of the rural population, including about 70 per cent of the Zimbabwean people. The technology is widely diffused and will continue to diffuse quite rapidly.

However, the development of the technology is experiencing some bottlenecks, both in supply and demand. On the supply side, producers face problems pertaining to lack of credit facilities, power costs, space, labour regulations, city council regulations and total lack of support from government. On the demand side, the problematic factor is the nature of the commodity.

Lack of credit
Access to credit facilities is often determined by the ability to raise collateral. The paradox is that those who need credit facilities most have least access because of their low economic status. The metal grate producers have this problem. All the producers interviewed thought this would inhibit the future growth and development of the technology. Producers described the difficulty in raising capital to buy machinery for cutting and welding iron bars. Banks are not keen on giving credit to producers because of lack of collateral in the form of property or money.

Electricity costs
Electricity costs on machinery are quite high for the producers. For instance, Mr X pays Z$150 a month for electricity and this contributes to a profit squeeze. There are no differential tariff rates for different scales of industry.

Space
Producers unanimously described the space shortage problem both for working and storage. Iron bars are ordered in bulk and therefore have to be stored.

Labour regulations
For producers such as Mr X who employs four artisans, labour regulations imposed by government become a problem. There are minimum wage regulations which result in each artisan being paid Z$210 a month. This is too high for the employers' profit levels. Laws against retrenchment of workers whose marginal productivity is below the remuneration contribute to inefficient production.

45

City council regulations

City council regulations pertaining to rent, rates payment, and security payments are bottlenecks to the development of the technology. Producers in Mbare are paying about Z$200 a month in rent and rates and, for Mr X, payment for a security guard is $70 a month. These high costs to producers inhibit further development.

Nature of product

The metal grate is a durable commodity and a capital good in nature. Some of the grates have been in use for the past 15 years and are still intact. The current market for the grate is limitless and will grow as rural incomes grow. But the problem may lie in the future when the market is filled with such a long-life commodity. Producers may find it difficult to sell to an already saturated market.

Lack of government support

Producers felt the government was not giving them support in all their endeavours. In fact, the producers are viewed as a nuisance rather than an alternative to formal sector employment. This is in an environment plagued by unemployment which is growing at a rate of 0.5 per cent each year.

Recommendations for supporting the metal grate

The government, non-governmental organizations, scientific research institutions have a role to play in supporting the development of the metal grate. Such concerted effort from three sides should address itself to bottlenecks facing producers.

Land and space

The metal grate producers would benefit from changes in government laws on procurement of title deeds to land. We submit that the government through the city council and Ministry of Local Government should leave land aside for occupation by the informal sector at lower than market rents. This would solve the rent and space problems of the metal grate producers.

Differential electricity tariffs

One of the high input costs in metal grate production is electricity tariffs, which are uniform for all industrial users. Because of an ability-to-pay problem, a differential tariff structure for electricity on the basis of turnover would be beneficial to small-scale and cottage industries. In this dichotomous tariff structure, small cottage industries would pay less than the big industries. This recommendation should be considered by the government through the Zimbabwe Electricity Supply Authority (ZESA).

Non-governmental support

Non-governmental organizations (NGOs), national and international, should complement government in supporting the cottage industries. NGOs should provide finance capital and physical machinery for the producers. Financial capital is one major bottleneck in the informal sector. Such financial capital could be in the form of both grants and loans, but mainly grants.

Scientific and training institutions

The importance of scientifically-designed products cannot be over-emphasized in this world of technological advancements. Scientific institutions could offer support in improving the design of the peoples' metal grate technology. Already institutions such as the Development Technology Centre (DTC), University of Zimbabwe, Zimbabwe Energy Research Organization (ZERO), Glen Forest and Ministry of Energy exist. Their efforts have been to develop appropriate energy technologies for the rural population. Rather than developing parallel technologies in the cooking system, these institutions should aim at developing the existing metal grate stove. Institutions such as Glen Forest would assist in metalwork training which would be more advanced than the on-the-job approach. Training has to extend to management and industrial planning techniques, which are necessary for the success of the cottage industries.

Salt from silt in Sierra Leone

J.G.M. MASSAQUOI

Background

Sierra Leone is a small nation of four million people located on the west coast of Africa. The country has a reasonably long coastline to facilitate salt production from sea water. However, various studies and surveys in the past have shown that large-scale solar salt works are not commercially viable because of the shortness of the dry season and the high relative humidity of the air. Therefore, Sierra Leone has no organized salt production industry. Most of the salt consumed in the country is imported from Senegal as rock salt and then crushed by the Sierra Leone Salt Manufacturing Company before distribution. The little salt that is produced locally is usually made by small-scale producers in the informal sector who rely on traditional technology for salt manufacture. The solar salt field established in the late 1970s has ceased operation.

Previous studies on the salt supply problem in Sierra Leone have commended strongly the role played by traditional salt manufacturers for their contribution to the supply. As the foreign exchange crisis in the country deepens, thereby inhibiting the importation of salt, the demand for traditionally produced salt will increase. Hence the need to explore the potential of this technology.

In the past, the study of salt production in Sierra Leone has focused on the potential for solar salt fields. It was only recently that a comparative study of the various salt supply sources in Sierra Leone revealed the potential of the traditional salt production technique. However, even this study did not reveal the extent to which the salt processors have consistently applied their knowledge to innovate. The level of skills involved, the changes that have occurred in the operational techniques and the hardware used were never examined. In this study, therefore, the focus has been on innovation in the traditional salt processing industry and the role of the producers, mainly women, in the innovative process.

DR J.G.M. MASSAQUOI (Sierra Leone) is Dean of the Faculty of Engineering at Fourah Bay College, University of Sierra Leone, Freetown. He has nearly 15 years' research and teaching experience in Energy, Appropriate Technology and Technology Policy and has published over 25 papers.

48

Evolution of traditional salt processing

The evolution of traditional salt processing technology in Sierra Leone has been helped by two main factors: the isolation of some coastal rural communities and the inability at some time to import quality salt from abroad. The latter factor has arisen because of conflicts such as the Second World War when it was very difficult to import anything. More recently, importing salt has been a problem because of lack of foreign exchange.

Traditional salt processing technology in Sierra Leone has evolved on three fronts: the evolution of the processing activities, the evolution of the hardware and the evolution of the skills. The evolution process has occurred in almost a perfect sequence without much overlap, starting with the evolution of the process and ending with the evolution of the skills. In this chapter we shall examine all three evolutionary changes.

Evolution of processing activities

Centuries ago, salt was made simply by boiling sea water. Traditional three-stone fireplaces were set up on beaches to boil the brine which was collected using large water gourds. The operation was usually carried out in the dry season by women who normally set up temporary homes in huts built on the beach. The boiling was followed by drying the salt in the sun.

In coastal areas with tidal estuaries, the collection of sea water can involve long walks at some times of the season. Most of those interviewed believed that the idea of collecting the brine in ponds evolved from the need to overcome this problem. At the start of the season, boreholes are dug in the path of the tide. And at high tide the holes are naturally filled with the brine. When the tide recedes, the brine is then processed to give salt. This modification to the processing activity was carried out in all coastal areas with tidal estuaries and mud/clay type of soil. Other coastal areas still continued to operate with fresh sea water.

Traditional salt operation always increases at times of economic hardship. There was a high level of traditional salt production in the 1940s, 1960s and the late 1980s. At the end of each economic depression period, the first group of salt operators abandoning the activity are those who use fresh sea water — not those operators using brine collected in boreholes. The reason often given for abandoning the operation is the high wood consumption which makes it practical only in times of scarcity when salt must be made.

The research team was prompted to find out if there was any difference between the concentration of salt in fresh sea water and that collected in the boreholes. It was discovered that there was indeed a difference resulting from the seepage through saline silts and solar evaporation. Although no one was able to establish the origin of the present traditional technique of producing salt from salt-laden silts, it is felt that it may be connected with knowledge of the fact that seepage of brine through silts into the boreholes had increased the concentration of the brine. Hence there were efforts to actually organize the percolation of salt from silts.

The salt-from-silt process

The production of salt from salt-laden silts is the last stage in the evolution of salt production processes. The technique involves producing a highly concentrated brine from salt-laden silts which are collected from tidal flats and creek beds. The salt is leached from the silts by a percolation process. A filter funnel is made with sticks and lined with wood and leaves. The filter medium at the bottom is a collection of rice straw resting on small sticks. During the peak season several of these filters will be used simultaneously. They are usually placed over a wooden collecting trough. After filtration, the filtrate is poured into enamel pans and heated over stoves. The water evaporates and the salt crystallizes. The wet salt is sprayed with a small quantity of water to wash away the bitter magnesium salts. The salt is then allowed to drain and dry in the sun.

Evolution of skills

During the investigation the processors were asked to identify the activities requiring some skill, a significant amount of skill and no skill at all. The activities in the first two categories were examined. These include the operation of the percolation bed and the boiling of the brine. These two processes were also considered to be the most important activities affecting the quality of the salt. The operation of the percolation unit involves lining the walls of a large funnel with a four-inch thick mud/silt paste and allowing sea water to seep through it. In the operation of the processors, a skilful percolation operator is one whose brine is very clean, resulting in white salt. Similarly, a skilful boiling operation will result in salt and is not bitter.

The main skill involved in boiling is that of controlling the fire to prevent burning or charring of the salt. It is also important to know when to stop boiling and when to discard the bitter solution. There have been no significant changes in the skill either in nature or in level. A large fire can lead to poor quality salt and thus fires are reduced as soon as they are considered to be too large. A skilful operator must have several years' experience, after which time she will have an 'eye' for a large fire. The ability to decide when to discard the bitter relics depends heavily on the taste of the solution at the appropriate level.

Evolution of the hardware

The following pieces of equipment were identified and investigated in order to find their origin: percolation funnels, stoves, spray/drainage units for washing the salt crystals, and wooden troughs for collecting the brine in the percolation process.

50

The percolation funnel came into existence at the same time as the salt-from-silt process. The technological hardware of the percolation process has undergone little change since its inception. When the size of the operations increased, the operators responded by increasing either the size of each unit or the number of units. One possible reason for the lack of innovation with this particular hardware lies with the fact that no salt-operator expressed dissatisfaction with its performance. The percolation process always generated enough brine for the boiling operation. This was probably due not to the rapid rate of the percolation but to the fact that the operation can go on throughout the day and night with minimal supervision. Thus it was discovered that the some of the brine from the percolation process was always collected at night.

The stoves have undergone several changes. During the investigation three categories of the hardware were identified. These included the traditional three-stone open fire, another stove which was basically a fireplace protected by short walls and the fuel-saving mud-brick stove.

The protected fireplace evolved from the three-stone stove because of the need to conserve heat and hence save fuel. This innovation actually came from the salt processors themselves and has occurred only recently as firewood, mainly from mangrove swamps, has become harder to find.

The other stove innovation was introduced four years ago by Plan International (Sierra Leone) in collaboration with the Department of Mechanical Engineering, Fourah Bay College. This improved stove technology, which is now fairly well diffused in one salt-processing community, was also intended to save fuel and time for the women so they could increase their productivity.

The hardware used for washing off the bitter material from the product is a perforated basket supported by wooden legs. This technology has not changed over the period.

Viability and the economics of the technology

The viability of the technology can be evaluated using several parameters, among them the extent of diffusion (the number of users involved), production costs, the cost/benefit to the producer, the consumer and other entrepreneurs (e.g. distributors). In this chapter we show data to support the viability of this technology.

Extent of diffusion of technology

During the study it was discovered that salt is produced in most settlements along the entire cost of Sierra Leone. However, few communities actually use the traditional process of salt-from-silt. Most areas, especially in the southern part of the country, still produce salt using fresh brine collected from the sea. The map shows the main traditional salt-producing villages

51

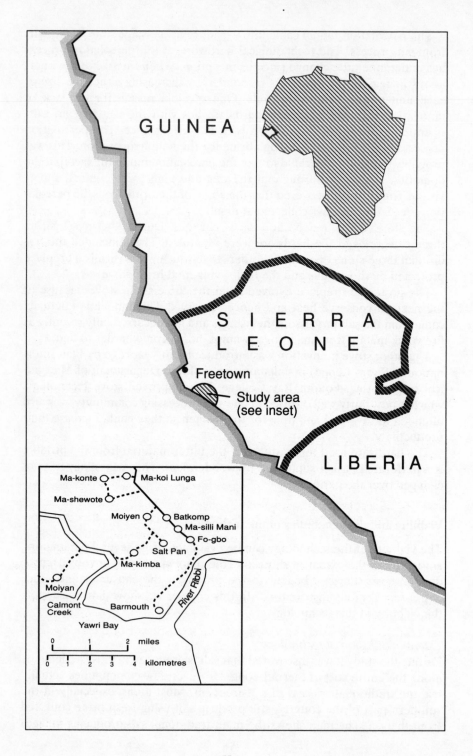

GUINEA

SIERRA
LEONE

• Freetown

Study area
(see inset)

LIBERIA

Ma-konte ○--○ Ma-koi Lunga
Ma-shewote ○
Moiyen ○ ○ Batkomp
○ Ma-silli Mani
○ Fo-gbo
○ Salt Pan
Ma-kimba ○
Moiyan ○
Calmont
Creek
Yawri Bay
Barmouth ○
River Ribbi

0   1   2 miles
0 1 2 3 4 kilometres

where salt is made using silts. It is immediately obvious that most of the salt-from-silt operation takes place in an area about 30km south-east of Freetown (see inset on the map of Sierra Leone). However, a few activities were spotted on Tasso Island north of Freetown, the Sherbro Island, the Shenge Coast and on the estuaries of the Scarcies river.

It was discovered during the study that in the salt-producing areas, during the peak season, every household was engaged in the operation. Using extracts of information from the national population census, it was possible to estimate the number of people engaged in the operation. It is estimated that over 1,100 small-scale salt production units exist in the country. These units produce approximately 3,400 tons or 30 per cent of the local salt consumed. This figure is on the low side since it does not take into consideration the salt produced by seasonal inhabitants of the area who move in only to process salt. It was estimated from a sample survey of two villages that 10 per cent of the silt processors were temporary inhabitants of the area who would not feature in the census statistics. Thus a more realistic estimate of the extent of the contribution of traditional salt-from-silt technology to the supply is about 4,000 tons or 35 per cent of consumption. This was also apparent from the markets in Freetown and the provinces where most salt now sold is from the traditional processors.

It is possible to extend the operation to other coastal areas where deposits of the silts can be found. However, only about one quarter of suitable areas are presently being utilized. In this respect, it may seem as if the technology is not widely diffused. This is explained by the fact that most of these areas are either very far from the nearest major market or no good road communications exist between the market and the resource site.

The study revealed that most of the salt-making activities were done by women. The men were involved only in setting up the operation. Thus the men would normally build the filter/percolation funnel, the wooden trough to collect the filtrate and the stoves. The women carry out the day-to-day operation of the technology. They collect the wood and silt, as well as supervising the boiling and filtration. Thus, any technological evolution that takes place arises out of experiences of the women. The seasonal nature of the operation and its effect on the diffusion process was also examined. It was found that the peak season for the salt operation always coincided with a lull in agricultural activity during the dry season. This coincidence was considered very helpful in the diffusion of the salt technology within the community.

Production economics

The viability of any production technology is dependent on the unit profit of the products. Hence it is essential to establish the magnitude of the profit from the salt produced. In this section, we have computed the capital cost involved in starting the operation, the production cost, and the profit from the operation. For the purpose of this exercise prices have been put on the labour and wood used in the operation even though the salt processors consider these as free goods.

The total fixed capital required in the operation consists of the costs of the boiling pan, the stove (if an improved stove is used), the wooden trough used for collecting the filtrate, the filtration/percolation unit and the hut to house the operation. The boiling pan, the wooden trough and the improved stove involve cash transfer in all cases. In some cases, where the operation is set up entirely by the women, some cash transfer will be involved also in acquiring a filtration system and the erection of the hut.

On the basis of information provided by the processors, the fixed capital involved in traditional salt extraction from silts is 3,900 leones if a mud brick stove is used, and 2,460 leones if the traditional three stone open-fire is used. A breakdown of the costs is given in Table 1. A 20 per cent contingency has been added to account for the cost of assembling the items and clearing the production sites. The costs of the production huts, the filter funnel and stoves have been estimated from information on the labour involved in construction and the local cost of labour. All capital items except the wooden trough are replaceable at the end of each production season.

The fixed capital has increased seven-fold since the last survey. However, more people still engage in the production process because of the high demand for salt. Working capital has also increased considerably. A small working capital (typically around 2,100 leones) is required to feed the producers and their families for the first two weeks of the production season while they wait for the proceeds of their first sale. Much of this capital, such as foodstuffs from a family's farming operations, may be available in kind, which reduces the cash requirement.

Table 1 Fixed capital involved in salt extraction from silts

Item	cost if using traditional stove	cost if using improved stove (mud brick stove with chimney)
boiling pan	850	850
stove	–	1 200
* filtration unit	100	100
wooden trough	800	800
* temporary hut	300	300
contingency 20%	410	650
TOTAL FIXED CAPITAL (in leones)	2 460	3 900

* This item does not usually involve cash transfer

The case equivalent of the total initial input into the production process (i.e. the total capital) is 6,000 leones for the operation using improved stoves and 4,560 leones if the open fire is used.

A typical batch size for the boiling operation results in 30kg of salt. At the start of the boiling operation the pan is loaded with the brine and each time the level goes down more brine is added until salt crystals fill the pan. Six 30kg batches of salt are produced in a week.

In estimating production costs, the following assumptions have been made:

1 Cost of wood at the time of the investigation was estimated to be 50 leones per 50kg bundle, and the cost of labour was 40 leones per working day (eight hours).

2 Overnight rate for supervision of the operations is taken as one-and-a-half times the daytime equivalent.

3 Little labour is involved in the filtration/percolation process.

4 Although not much physical labour is involved in the boiling of the solution, it is assumed that supervisory labour is involved to maintain the fire and prevent an overspill of froth into the fire.

5 Estimates of the boiling times and quantity of wood used are based on the results of a study by Kamara (1985).

In Table 2, production costs of a batch of salt using different stoves are compared. The stoves are: a three-stone open fire, a single burner woodfuel stove and a two-burner woodfuel stove. These costs represent the estimated commercial value of the inputs (labour and wood) into the production process. It should be added, however, that the labour input does not involve cash transfer. Where the wood is collected by the processors, wood acquisition does not involve a cash transfer either.

An examination of the production costs shows that the highest cost is incurred by those processors using the open fire and the lowest cost is experienced by those using the two-burner improved stove. These figures justify the additional cost involved with the improved stove because the production cost is halved as soon as the stove is changed.

Table 2 Energy costs of salt production

type of stove used	hours worked	wood used	total cost per batch (leone)	production cost/kg (leone)
trad 3-stone open fire	16.5	400kg	482.5	16.08
single burner improved stove	11.5	200kg	262	8.60
double burner improved stove	17	200kg	285 (2 batches)	4.75

A final step towards the estimation of profit is determining the amount of salt produced by an average producer in a season. It was established during the study that even though the salt leaching operation can be organized throughout the year, nearly all processors produce salt only in the four months of the dry season. If silt remains at the end of one dry season it is stored until the beginning of the next because the producers engage in subsistence farming when the rains begin.

The average annual production of salt, based on a rate of one 30kg batch per day six days a week for four months, was estimated at 2,880kg. It was surprising that those using the improved stove did not take advantage of the saving in the boiling time to increase their production. It is quite possible that the collection of the silt and the filtration took too much energy and time respectively.

In order to estimate the profit from the operation, the following assumptions about the sale of the salt and the depreciation of the fixed capital were made:

1 The price paid for the salt to the producers is 13 leones per kg. The salt is usually sold by volume and is loosely packed in four-gallon aluminium cans which each go for a price of 250 leones. In the market the salt is sold for approximately 16 leones per kg.
2 There is no sale cost incurred by the producers. All the salt produced is sold at the site within two weeks of production.
3 The annual depreciation of the fixed capital is equal to the total initial cost of the capital except the wooden trough which has a much longer life and hence a very low depreciation rate.

Table 3 Annual profit from a production unit (3–4 persons)

	(a)	(b)	(c)
production cost per kg (Le)	16.06	8.73	4.73
average annual production (kg)	2 880	2 880	2 880
annual production cost (Le) (A)	46 252.80	25 142.4	13 680
annual depreciation of fixed capital (B)	1 860	3 300	3 300
Total annual sale (C)	46 080	46 080	46 080
gross annual profit C – (A + B) (Le)	(+2 032.80)	17 637.60	29.100
loss/profit per kg of salt produced (Le)	(+0.70)	6.124	10.10
profit as % of sale	–	38%	63%

Legend
(a) operation using the traditional three-stone stove
(b) operation using the single burner wood-saving stove
(c) operation using the double burner wood stove

The steps involved in the computation of the profit are tabulated in Table 3. It is immediately obvious that those using the open-fire stoves are really not making any profit when all factors are valued at the commercial rate. This is different from previous observations which were recorded in 1986. At that time all processors extracting salt from silt, regardless of the type of stove used, returned some profit. However the increase in the cost of fuelwood in the area has made the traditional stove uneconomic. It is therefore not surprising, in the light of the lack of profit in the open-fire stove, that nearly all salt processors in the main salt processing area use a chimney-less mud brick stove.

Profits of about 38 to 63 per cent of sales can be obtained when different types of improved stoves are used. Furthermore, when one considers that the costs of labour and wood do not involve cash transfer, total sales revenues are really the net income from the operation. However it is important to look at the profit rate based on the commercial value of the services because salt production has to compete with other activities. It is possible that most people are reluctant to engage in an all-year-round salt extraction process because subsistence farming is more profitable, considering the cost of buying food.

Costs and benefits

In the previous sections we have evaluated the profits from a typical salt-from-silt operation and the benefits to the producers are related to this profit. The average actual income of a salt processor is now about 46,080 leones per season, which is much larger than the average annual wage of a government worker. In general, one would expect that the additional income from salt would enable people to improve their living standards. Indeed, it was observed that there is a better quality of housing in the salt producing area than in other villages.

There is also an enhancement in the status of women in the salt producing communities. Women obtain at least 50 per cent of the proceeds from sales of salt and use this money to provide food and clothing for themselves and their children. The income also contributes towards children's school fees.

The costs to the producers are in the form of health and safety hazards arising from the operation. During the boiling operation some processors sleep by the fire whenever the evaporation extends into the night. They have to be by the fire to supervise and to add to the brine when the level drops. Thus, on occasions, some processors go without sleep for a long time. This is very hazardous to their health. Since most of the operators are women, there is also the problem of the neglect of young children as a result of this continuous round-the-clock supervision of the operation.

The main safety hazard is that fires could break out because the huts under which the boiling occurs have roofs made from elephant-grass. During the night, if the fires are left unattended, the roofs could catch fire.

For the consumers, the benefits are of two types: savings in the amount they spend on the salt and security of supply. From a survey of prices in the markets, it was discovered that there is a saving of more than 20 per cent if local salt is purchased instead of the imported salt. Furthermore, local salt was freely available in the markets whereas imported salt was very scarce. In fact, most consumers who did not like the local salt ended up buying refined table salt for cooking purposes because of the scarcity of imported cooking salt.

The main cost to the consumer is in the form of the shortfall in the quality of the salt. Analyses show that the purity of the local salt is only 96–97 per cent compared to 99 per cent for that of imported salt. Furthermore, it was observed that the local salt was not very white and lacks the vital nutrient, iodine, which is normally added to most refined salt.

The main entrepreneurs involved in salt production are the distributors/wholesalers and the retailers. The wholesalers collect the salt from the production site and transport it to the towns where salt is sold to retailers by volume in 20 litre cans. The wholesalers make about 20 per cent profit on sales and the retailers make about the same. Transport owners within the community also make some additional profit due to the increase in traffic during the salt-processing season.

The salt business also helps to slow migration from rural to urban areas and there was even some evidence of a migration in the reverse direction. One man who had gone to the city in search of a job later returned to the village to engage in salt processing. There was also the advantage of technological skills accumulation amongst the inhabitants of the area. Masons were needed for the construction of the improved mud-brick stoves, blacksmiths for the fabrication of chimneys and wood-cutters for the shaping of the wooden troughs.

Comparison with other technologies

In the previous sections we have shown that the salt-extraction technology is economically viable. However, it will be useful to compare this technology with other conventional salt production technologies.

The conventional technology for marine salt production is the use of solar salt fields. The only salt works that used to operate in the country has been closed now for over three years. Throughout its operation it never returned a profit. Several studies have indicated that the main problem with this technology is the climate. Sierra Leone's dry season is very short and its relative humidity is high throughout the year. In short, the conventional technology is not viable in Sierra Leone. Even if the climate were favourable there would have been the problem of the availability of the technical staff for the operation in the rural environment. Previous studies had shown that while the climate affected the productivity of the solar salt field at Suen, the lack of careful control over the density of the brine at various stages of the operation, especially in the crystallization pond, contributed to the poor quality of the salt.

The conclusion to be drawn is that traditional technology for salt production is superior to conventional technology on the basis of both productivity and salt quality.

Knowledge/skills development

Several types of knowledge and skills are involved in the production of salt from silt. The knowledge and skills can be classified broadly into two areas: what is involved in setting up the operation and what is required to operate the facilities. During this study we tried to establish the sources of the skill as well as the method of transfer of the skill and knowledge. We also made comparisons with the scientific method of skill acquisition through formal training.

Skills for establishing the production facilities

The following skills were identified for setting up the operation. Masons are needed for the construction of stoves when mud brick stoves are used, blacksmiths for metal chimneys, wood-carvers for the shaping of the brine container, basket-weavers for preparing the percolation funnel and the basket for spray-washing of the fresh salt. These are all specialized skills which are available in nearly all rural communities in Sierra Leone.

The method of skill transfer is by apprenticeship. Trainers learn by doing. No formal instruction is given. The trainees observe the trainer carrying out the various activities and from this observation trainees gradually understand the procedure. Questions are asked to establish the reason for a particular activity. Answers to these questions help to transfer knowledge.

The skills listed above are not used solely by the salt processing industry. Other activities in all rural communities require these skills as well. Therefore, a lot of those who apply their skill in the salt-extraction process may have moved into this from other community work. This in effect represents another mode of skill transfer through the movement of people. It is, however, different from the transfer of technology/skills between people.

Skills for operating the salt facilities

The investigating team was able to identify three major skills in the operation: the control of fire during boiling, the ability to discern the appropriate time to stop boiling and drain off the bitter solution, and the lining of percolation walls with leaves and mud to provide clean brine solution. All other activities require unskilled labour. Each of the skills mentioned above have direct effects on either the quality or productivity of the operation.

The method by which the skills are acquired depends on whether the person receiving the knowledge is from within the community or resident outside. This distinction arises because of the time available for the training in each case.

Those candidates for training in salt processing who come from outside usually acquire their skills in a more scientific manner. In other words, they receive instructions on the theory and principles and they observe practical demonstrations. The procedure for training is as follows. Candidates usually arrange with someone to provide the training. The trainer then explains all the operational techniques including the nature and purpose of all equipment. This instructional stage will take a few hours. After the explanation, the candidate will then observe the trainer carry out demonstrations of the various operational techniques. This will normally take a few days. During the demonstration, the trainee will from time to time be asked to participate by repeating some of the activities. Any error noticed in her participation will be pointed out to her and the significance highlighted.

After the demonstrations the trainee is expected to acquire her own facilities, or rent these from someone, to use for repeated practice. During this practice, the trainer will supervise and any salt produced will be shared by the two. In other words, the trainee's first batches of salt will be used to pay the trainer.

For those in the community, transfer of skill is through an informal type of apprenticeship. Since they have grown up in a community where nearly everybody processes salt, the skill is acquired as people grow up. Learning is through observation. The period of training stretches over a much longer time.

Constraints on the industry

The small-scale salt industry produces 4,000 tons of salt a year with a revenue of over 80m leones. As pointed out earlier, this industry makes a significant contribution to various sectors of the economy and society. However, the contribution is far less than its potential. In this chapter we shall examine the potential of the industry and highlight the constraints that hinder its development.

Potential and achievements
Before we examine constraints on the industry, we need to know the size of the potential capacity being hindered and the gap between this potential and the existing level of activity.

Existing facilities for salt production from silt are concentrated mainly at the estuaries of the rivers Rokel, Ribbi, Kukuli and the Great and Little Scarcies. However, other coastal areas also have silt deposits and therefore could serve as a salt-from-silt production centres. These areas are located in the estuarine swamps of rivers Kagboro, Thanka, Bagra and Jong as well as the northern area of the Sherbro Island. The soil types in all these estuaries are weakly developed mud and hydromorphic clays. The total area suitable for deposit of salt-laden silts is estimated at 2,347km². Only about a quarter is being utilized at present. Thus, from the point of view of availability of silts, salt production could be extended easily to other areas and increase its present level four times. Furthermore, there is plenty of silt for additional production facilities at the existing production sites. In effect, all this means that the potential is at least 20,000 tons per year.

Even with the present low-level of production, the industry makes a significant contribution within the economy. Salt-making provides employment for the rural population, savings in foreign exchange, security of salt supply and a low-cost product. With the correct policies, the present contribution could be quadrupled with significant effects on rural life all along the coast.

Constraints
There are all types of bottlenecks which affect the growth of the industry. These problems include those that hinder the expansion at existing sites and those that affect the diffusion of the technology to other locations. As far as expansion at existing sites is concerned, three major problems were identified: social, technical and economic. The social problem was the size of the population in the salt areas and the number of non-resident salt processors that can be accommodated. There is an acute shortage of drinking water in salt producing areas and houses are few. Water in boreholes is usually saline and migrant salt processors tend to sleep in huts in the field. This hostile environment makes it difficult for more people to engage in the operation, thus keeping the production level very low.

The technical problems are connected with the boiling of the brine. The resources utilization efficiencies at this level are very low. Woodfuel is used in large quantities and the period of supervision is very long. Better management of resources, in this case wood and time/labour, would greatly enhance the productivity. It would be possible to increase the level of production without any increase in population. One way forward is to introduce wood-saving stoves. Previous efforts in this direction have shown that some wood and time are saved by using these stoves. Furthermore, it has been revealed that even though the Sierra Leone climate may not be suitable for solar evaporation of sea water, the evaporation of solution obtained in the percolation of silts can be managed with solar energy.

Indeed, experiments at the University of Sierra Leone have shown that the brine obtained from the percolation is very nearly saturated and that the solar crystallization can be completed in a black metal trough in about 30 days. Thus it will be possible to run three batches of solar crystallization in a single season.

The technical problem highlighted also has another effect on production levels. The high level of wood utilization coupled with the scarcity of wood during the rainy season prevents an off-season, or all-year-round, operation even though large quantities of silts may be in storage. The situation is not helped by the fact that in the rainy season there are several competing economic activities in the agricultural sector. If the woodfuel utilization efficiency were to improve to the level where the operator notices considerable increase in productivity and income, then an all-year-round operation could be feasible. Such a situation is likely to increase considerably the overall annual production of salt.

The economic problem highlighted was mainly the lack of working capital. As mentioned elsewhere in this report, the working capital really represents the cost of food that will be consumed while the proceeds from the first sale are awaited. Some people also mentioned the difficulty of obtaining enamel pans which are normally used in the boiling operation. However, this problem has been overcome by the use of locally fabricated galvanized iron pans.

With regard to the diffusion of the technology to other areas, the biggest problem identified was infrastructure. Most of the other suitable areas were located away from the major market towns with no road communication to the site. Thus it is impossible to employ this technology at the other sites unless roads are built in the area.

Conclusions and recommendations

It has been established in this report that the salt-from-silt technology is viable especially as a small-scale industry. However, it has been shown also that there are some bottlenecks which hinder the full development of the potential of this industry. In this chapter we shall make some recommendations of actions to be taken by government, scientific and other institutions and non-governmental agencies.

Recommendations for government
The following are specific recommendations for governmental action:

1 Efforts should be made to register small-scale salt processors with a view towards organizing them and facilitating the provision of any aid/grant or loan. The Ministry of Industry could administer this in much the same way as they currently support other small-scale industries. Since the

processors are all concentrated in a few locations, the registration should not pose too much of a problem.

2 Government should employ extension officers to provide advice on marketing, new technologies and any government policy relating to salt trade and manufacture.

3 Once a register has been developed it would be possible for government in collaboration with some commercial banks to guarantee loans for use by processors as working capital. The administration of such loans can be difficult and a lot of thought would need to be given to such a system before implementation.

4 The provision of certain facilities and infrastructure, especially water and roads, is extremely important. Boreholes for drinking water are required urgently to allow more people to engage in the operation. Roads linking the production sites with major markets should be improved as well.

Action by scientists and R&D institutions
Scientific research can concentrate on the strengthening of the small-scale sector or the development of large-scale industry based on the people's own technology.

Scientific research on the strengthening of small-scale salt production units should concentrate on the development of wood-saving stoves and/or the substitution of stoves by solar ponds. Research should concentrate also on percolation tanks. At the moment, given the size of the capital available to the processors, it seems that the existing percolation systems are adequate. Where large solutions are required, more units can be used. Perhaps the need is really for percolation systems giving cleaner brine rather than a faster rate of percolation.

Actions to be taken by NGOs
These agencies are involved with several rural development projects in the country and it would be very useful if they were to develop projects to enhance the coastal rural areas through a development of the salt industry. An action-oriented project in which salt producers are assisted with inputs such as boiling pans would be useful. Commercial banks should look also at the possibility of giving loans to salt processors.

Cassava processing innovations in Nigeria

R.O. ADEGBOYE and J.A. AKINWUMI

Evolution of cassava processing machines

The earliest mechanical grater developed in 1931 when Mr Busari Ogundokun, a blacksmith in Oyo town, pondered about the drudgery of grating cassava by hand. He then produced a hand-operated grater that rolled round a circular wooden drum. It grated more cassava and was less labour-intensive. Mr Ogundokun placed one of these on the roadside in Oyo where some expatriates working for the United Africa Company (UAC) noticed it and showed interest. They were directed to Mr Ogundokun and later took him to Ibadan. He worked with the expatriates to develop the first powered cassava grater to which a motorized engine was attached. The principle had been applied already to corn mills, pepper grinders and yam flour grinders. The idea involved a power take-off belt attached to a petrol engine to roll the cylindrical grater, which had a wooden housing.

Several cassava graters were fabricated and distributed to the UAC through its network of distributors. Mr Ogundokun was paid £100 for his innovation. He returned to Oyo town and continued to make graters and several other machines. He produced feed-mixers, bone-crushers and some special bellows that reduced labour drudgery.

In 1965, Mr Ogundokun made two bailers for the Premier Tobacco Company at Oyo. The principle was later employed to develop the cassava pulp de-waterer now commonly used in *gari* processing. He made and sold several of these pressing machines to order. The system of pressing was later modified to take advantage of locally available materials.

Ogundokun was so versatile that he was nicknamed 'Ologbon Ori', meaning 'the man with creative thinking'. Many of his apprentices are no longer alive but we were able to trace a very old man at Feleye, Ibadan, who had graduated from Ogundokun's workshop. We also traced another man aged about 80 Abeokuta who learnt blacksmithery from his father. This man claimed to have travelled to all parts of Nigeria to inspect and learn from other outstanding blacksmiths, including Ogundokun in Oyo town.

PROFESSOR R.O. ADEGBOYE and J.A. AKINWUMI (Nigeria) work in the Faculty of Agricultural Economics at the University of Ibadan.

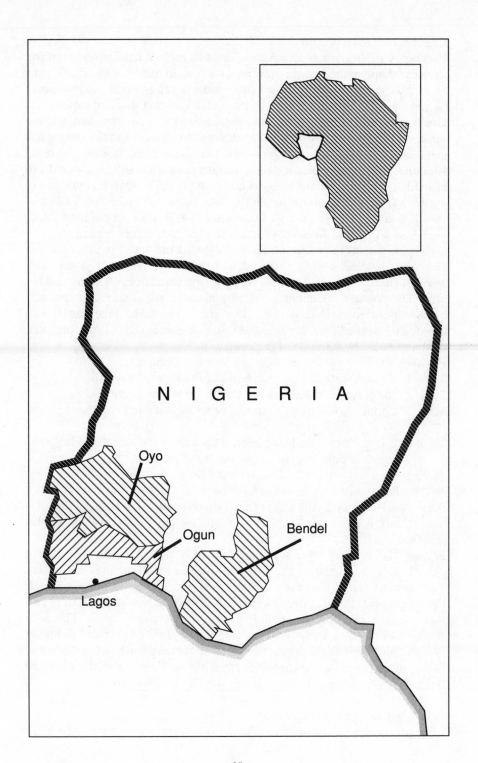

NIGERIA

Oyo

Ogun

Bendel

Lagos

Changes that have occurred:

Peeling: A peeling machine was developed to replace hand peeling but the irregular shape of the cassava prevented success. In order for this machine to be useful the cassava breeders/scientists must develop round cassava tubers or make machines that will be sensitive to the tapering shape of cassava.

Grating: Hand-grating has become mechanized to save time and remove drudgery. The wooden structure has changed to all steel and the grating flat metal sheet remains. Several variations have been introduced to the body structure. The metal grater is nailed round a cylindrical solid wooden drum in Ibadan, or a set of hard wooden plates in Oyo. The Oyo manufacturers use mainly all-metal guards inside the four-sided bowl into which the cassava is poured prior to grating. Meanwhile, the Ibadan people have introduced an adjustable wooden guard. The Oyo fabricators argued that the metal guard leads to greater efficiency, allowing the grater to process three pick-up van loads daily, compared to one for the wooden grater. The wooden guard is also said to wear away, giving wooden chips in the cassava pulp. The counter argument is that the metallic guard corrodes and may become poisonous when it rusts. The grater has to be taken apart and thoroughly washed each day to avoid this. Sometimes it is painted, but even the paint could be a source of impurities.

Pressing: Pressing passed through the four following stages:

Stage 1   Stones were placed on a basket full of grated cassava;

Stage 2   Bags replaced baskets but the use of stones continued;

Stage 3   Stones gave way to hydraulic or screw jacks and bags were placed neatly within steel frames;

Stage 4   Steel frames are being braced up with wooden slabs to keep the cassava pulp bags in shape under the press.

Sieving: This was originally done by hand on woven cane sieves but a few electrically operated metal sieves have been introduced. Some users return the de-watered pulp to the grater for sieving. If palm oil is being added, it is best to mix it in at this stage of *gari* processing. Better hygiene is also achieved.

Frying: The original fryer was made up of a clay or round metal bowl placed on a mud tripod with firewood introduced from three directions. The operator was exposed to the direct heat of fire as well as smoke. Later, the 44 gallon (210 litre) drum was split into two halves and placed over a long furnace carefully finished (plastered) to conserve heat. The heat source was directed away from the single operator. To respond to higher demand and large-scale production, a large rectangular bowl operated by two or more people was introduced. Here, the furnace is placed outside the building while the operators are inside a well-ventilated room.

Why have the changes occurred?

Changes occur as a result of feedback from users and partly as new ideas are being tried by producers. It is the duty of the producer to satisfy his customer, the user of the product, in terms of machine efficiency and affordability.

Who made the changes?

Sometimes the original innovator may go on making new changes in response to further ideas for possibilities of improvement. It also happens that apprentices introduce changes. These may be brought about during the process of making repairs or responding to complaints from users.

Research methodology

Area of study

Two states, Bendel and Oyo, were chosen because they are major processors of *gari*. In Bendel, the following towns were chosen: Umunede, Isele-Uku, Agbor-Alidinma, Owa, Ndinili, Abavo, Asaba and Irrua. In Oyo state, Oyo town and Ojoo, Mokola, Apata, Agbowo, Omi-Adio in Ibadan were chosen.

Questionnaire administration

Structured questionnaires were administered by enumerators. Two types of questionnaires were designed. One questionnaire was for users who grate for their own use and for others, charging a fee. Another questionnaire was for producers of cassava processing machines such as the grater, frier and de-waterer. In the two types of questionnaires information was sought on the evolution/history, economics, diffusion and bottlenecks associated with the design and use of cassava processing machines.

In both states, medium-scale production factories were visited only for general information. Two major towns in Ogun State (Abeokuta and Ijebu-Ode) were also visited. In the analysis of data descriptive statistics, averages and percentages are used.

Limitations of the study

The costs and returns to fabricators of machines spanned over a long time and rapidly-rising prices made calculations complex. Besides, many fabricators regard costs and returns as business secrets which should not be revealed to strangers who could turn out to be future competitors in the trade.

Viability and economics of technology

Technology diffusion

All the 37 users interviewed in Bendel State and 19 out of the 20 interviewed in Oyo State reported that the cassava grater and the accompanying machines are widely used by other people apart from themselves. They pointed out, however, that certain operations are still being carried out manually which they would like to see mechanized. These include cassava harvesting, peeling and frying.

Our investigations showed that frying is about 40 per cent mechanized, sieving 50 per cent, pressing or de-watering 90 per cent and grating 95 per cent. Several types of petrol and diesel engines were used to supply power to the grater. There were electric motors especially in cities where electricity was supplied regularly.

The users were asked how long they had been using the machines for processing cassava. Twenty-one per cent in Bendel State and 80 per cent in Oyo State said they had operated the machines for one to five years. Another 32 per cent in Bendel and 15 per cent in Oyo had used them for six to 10 years. Thirty per cent and five per cent respectively had operated the machines for 11 to 15 years while 16 per cent in Bendel had used them for 16 to 20 years. The processing of cassava with mechanical graters started earlier in Bendel State from where large quantities of *gari* were transported to Lagos, Enugu, Jos and other parts of the north in the early 1970s.

Most users, 76 per cent in Bendel and 70 per cent in Oyo State, reported that they had been using the same type of machine since they started. The few who changed did so when the old machines either broke down or lost efficiency. They usually took the old machines to producers to repair damaged parts. In the process, slight modifications were made to improve efficiency. The fabricators then seized the opportunity to incorporate the changes in the newly-manufactured machines. Most users showed that they were satisfied with the machines and were not in a hurry to change to new types. There was, however, clear evidence of innovation in Oyo State where 30 per cent of the processors had been using different machines and 45 per cent said they hoped to change to something new. There are many more machine fabricators in Oyo, each modifying existing graters and de-waterers to improve the efficiency. On the other hand, the Bendel users contact carpenters to help build the wooden parts to replace those worn out.

A few users interviewed (13.5 per cent in Bendel and 35 per cent in Oyo) said that they had found better machines and there are claims of superior workmanship by various manufacturers. One fact was clear, the machines produced for the government under contract were invariably of lower quality due to the use of cheaper raw materials. Several of these had been abandoned or taken to other manufacturers for repairs.

The users were asked how they first became aware of the cassava grating machines. Their responses are shown in Table 1. This shows that most cassava grater users came to know about the machines through other users operating within their area. The pattern of establishment of graters follows closely the cassava supply pattern. In Agbor Alidinma, Bendel State, there is a periodic fourth day market to which over 500 women cassava farmers

68

Table 1 Awareness of processing machine

source of awareness	BENDEL		OYO	
	no. of resp	%	no. of resp	%
friends	10	27.03	1	5
people from town	14	37.84	15	75
relations	8	21.62	2	10
others	5	13.51	2	10
total	37	100	20	100

Source: Field Survey, 1989

bring peeled cassava tubers for sale. The *gari* processors buy the cassava and immediately take it to the graters who set up their operations near the market. In a similar way, the processors at Isale-Oyo set up over 40 graters to whom pick-up loads of cassava are brought daily. Women and children can be seen peeling heaps of cassava in adjacent locations.

The grated cassava pulp is bagged and held for a few days to allow fermentation before being pressed (de-watered) prior to frying. The frying takes place in sheds behind the grating-pressing centres. There are a few large-scale *gari* processors who own the graters, the pressing equipment and the friers. They often scout round the farming areas to purchase cassava which they deliver to Oyo in their own pick-up vans.

They employ graters, pressers and friers. They gather the fried *gari* for bagging and supply to their customers in distant cities like Lagos, Abeokuta and Ibadan. One such business owner reported that she employed over 40 workers, purchased matured and immature cassava farms and used her own harvesting gangs and transport facilities. She had a bank account and often borrowed money from the bank for her operations.

Importance/receptivity of technology
The old method of grating cassava by hand on a flat grater is very labour-intensive and slow. It involves risks of injury and has been virtually replaced now by the motorized graters. Only in very remote villages with few *gari* processing women can the old practice be found today. Many women carry their cassava by lorry or bicycle over 5 to 10 kilometres to have it grated, as this has reduced labour drudgery. This has remained a relatively cheap operation since one bag of pulp is still commonly grated for 50 kobo. The same quantity would take four to six hours to grate manually. The de-watering of cassava pulp is still done with heavy stone loads in those remote villages where there are not sufficient *gari* processors to warrant the establishment of a grating-pressing centre. The need to hold grated pulp

69

for three to four days to allow fermentation means that women may not press off the water immediately after grating the cassava on market days.

However, in Bendel State, there is a modification in which the grated cassava is immediately de-watered, sieved and fried. Such 'instant gari', as it is called, is immediately sold for transportation to large cities such as Benin, Ibadan, Lagos and Kaduna. Lime juice is sometimes added to obtain the sour taste of the properly fermented *gari*. This is risky, however, in view of the higher concentration of hydrocyanic acid (HCN) which causes various disabilities for heavy *gari* eaters. There is a need for a standards organization of Nigeria to test *gari* for residue levels. The claim that the addition of palm oil neutralizes the poisonous effects of cyanide should be verified so that specific policies can be formulated to guide *gari* processors.

Gari frying has not been sufficiently mechanized and remains the most labour-intensive and inconvenient stage of the operation. Machine producers are currently attempting to reduce the drudgery at this level. Larger open bowls that can be worked by two or three women at the same time are being fabricated. Mechanized stirring is being contemplated, but the slow rolling motor needed to turn the frying *gari* is yet to be developed. Also, various alternative sources of heat are being investigated to replace the smoky firewood method. There are gas friers and a few electrical friers in the testing stages now. The large kilns and ovens developed by the Federal Institute of Industrial Research (FIIRO) and Project Development Agency (PRODA) are not within the each of active small-scale *gari* processors in rural Nigeria.

So far the best technologies, the most effective and economic, have been those developed by the people in response to their local needs. The rough and ready machines have been made from locally available raw materials. These machines are far more economical than imported, sophisticated technology. We can best call on our scientists and trained technologists to help improve on efforts by local people.

The greatest bottleneck observed in the field was the lack of locally manufactured engines to supply power takeoff. Apart from simple repairs and replacements of worn-out parts, no Nigerian manufacturer has been able to make an engine or motor such as the Lister or electric generator. Since these have to be imported, they raise the costs of *gari* processing machinery, especially now that the devaluation of the naira has forced up the prices of all imports.

Centrality of product in diet

In recent times, *gari* and associated cassava products have become universal food items in the diets of virtually all Nigerians. Prior to the Structural Adjustment Programme (SAP) bread was used as a major source of cheap food energy. But when wheat was banned, the people turned to *gari* as a staple food for energy and a universal snack. Even affluent Nigerians now include *gari* in their regular menu. *Gari* is now ground and added to fresh milk to make *fura da nono* by the Fulani.

The relatively high yields of cassava and the fact that its cultivation requires fewer purchased inputs and less labour have combined to raise its production relative to other starchy foods such as yam, Irish potatoes or the cereal grains. The survival of people during hard times has been aided by the production of cassava and *gari*. This has resulted in a rapid proliferation of cassava processing machines particularly in the southern states where cassava grows very well.

A good guess at the percentage of people consuming foods such as *gari*, *foofoo* and *cassava lafun* is about 85 to 90 per cent. There is hardly any household in Nigeria today where cassava is not used in one form or the other. Cassava flour is steadily entering the biscuit and bread composite-flour market in Nigeria.

Production economics

In this section we examine two sets of operators, namely the users of cassava graters and the manufacturers of the machines. The users either own and process cassava into *gari* for sale or help to grate cassava, press (de-water) and sometimes sieve for a fee. All users interviewed provided information on their initial capital investment and the operating costs. They gave the quantities of cassava grated per month and the prices. From these, the average revenue and costs were calculated. Table 2 shows the range of initial capital investment in cassava processing equipment.

As shown in the Table, most users invested 3,000 nairas or less. The largest investors were in Bendel with an average of 26,250 nairas. The average overall investment per user was, however, higher in Oyo State at 5,020 nairas while that of Bendel State was 3,645 nairas.

Low investment was due to the fact that very simple sheds were built for operations while most operators carried out the pressing in the open air. Those who invested much more money provided cemented floors, roofed

Table 2 Initial capital investment in cassava processing machinery

range in nairas (₦)		BENDEL			OYO	
		no. resp %	average ₦		no. resp %	average ₦
0–2 000	16	43.2	1 176	3	15	1 288.33
2 001–4 000	13	35.2	2 633.62	9	45	3 022.20
4 001–6 000	6	16.2	4 887.17	2	10	4 966
above 6 000	2	5.4	26 250	6	30	9 903.38
total/average	37	100	3 645.48	20	100	5 020.85

71

buildings and several facilitating gadgets which made the workplace neat, attractive and convenient. The relatively small capital investment involved in starting the business has made entry very easy and is now causing some friction since processors in certain locations no longer have enough cassava to grate and press.

Table 3 Income estimate (Bendel State users)*

average number of bags grated	= 25.98 per day
average price per bag	= 1.09 nairas
revenue per day	= (25.98 × 1.09)
	28.32 nairas

* The average user in Bendel State takes cassava processing as a part-time job, usually carried out in the evenings and on market days.

Operating costs per month and per year
The range of monthly operating costs shown in Table 4 is from 100 nairas to over 600 nairas. The costs in Bendel State are 262.91 nairas (29.7 per cent of processors) and the highest costs are 692 nairas. In Oyo State, the lowest costs are 90 nairas per month while the highest are over 1,000 nairas per month. Operating costs include fuel or electricity, repairs and main-tenance of equipment, and labour costs. The operating cost may increase if the volume of cassava processed is increased.

From the estimates presented in the two tables, it is possible to calculate the total cost of processing cassava with simple technology using the aver-age quantity of cassava grated per month and per year.

Average yearly net incomes, based on grating between 26 and 46 bags of cassava per day, vary between 4,200 nairas in Bendel and 16,300 nairas in Oyo.

Analysis of data from grater producers in Bendel and Oyo States

The manufacturers of cassava grating machines were very few, though many apprentices and journeymen were employed to help increase their output. Only two producers were identified in Bendel State during the field survey. Five producers were identified in Oyo State. All the seven pro-ducers make cassava graters and cassava pulp pressing frames. Two of the Oyo State units also make yam flour grinders and all five make pepper-grinding machines as well as *gari* friers, block moulding machines, maize shellers, bone-crushers and stone-crushers.

Four of the Oyo State producers indicated that they had been operating for up to 10 years while the fifth, and the two in Bendel State, stated that they have been in the business for between 11 and 15 years.

The idea of making cassava graters was acquired from Ibadan by two of the Oyo producers while two others learned it from Oyo town. The fifth did

Table 4 Operating costs per month and per year of cassava processing in Bendel and Oyo States

range (naira)	no.	%	average per month	average per year
		BENDEL		
0–100	2	5.41	57.07	692.64
101–200	2	5.41	190	2 280
201–300	11	29.72	262.91	3 154.92
301–400	9	24.33	339.44	4 073.28
401–500	2	5.41	460	5 520
501–600	5	13.51	562.80	6 753.60
above 600	6	16.21	692	8 304
total/average	37	100	387.25	4 647
		OYO		
0–100	2	5	90	1 080
101–200	4	20	160.75	1 929
201–300	4	20	262.67	3 152.04
301–400	5	25	344.10	4 129.20
401–500	1	5	460	5 520
501–600	3	15	578	6 936
above 600	2	10	1 016.67	12 200.04
total/average	20	100	363.58	4 362.96

Source: Field Survey, 1989

not specify his source. One of the Bendel producers indicated that the idea came to him from Japan while the other learned from Umunede in Bendel State. Only one of the producers reported that he had been to technical college; the others studied as apprentices under blacksmiths, welders or iron-benders.

The producers indicated that they were satisfied with the work and had no plans to change to other occupations. One of the Oyo State producers highlighted major changes in the pattern of production. He pointed out that he used to place an eight-inch diameter wood at both ends of the cylindrical grater sheet leaving nothing in between. Later he noticed that it led to rapid wearing out and low efficiency. He then replaced the wood with metal, thus raising the efficiency from 20 to 60 bags a day.

The two Bendel producers and two of the Oyo producers said that they could diversify their business to include fabrication of spare parts, making bolts, nuts and engine parts. They could also maintain tractors and carry out general welding. They were confident that they could copy any spare part.

73

The products are custom-made on request. This was because sales were uncertain and the costs of raw materials have risen beyond their means. This is indirectly limiting their scope since many buyers would like to inspect the fabricated machines before deciding whether to buy or not.

Most producers considered that raw materials were easily available. In Oyo State producers purchase their raw materials in Ibadan or Lagos while those in Bendel go to Onitsha. Lack of record-keeping prevented the accurate estimating of the quantities of raw materials used. Furthermore there were no standard raw materials as most producers employed scrap metals to reduce costs.

Constant changes in prices were identified as one of the main problems of the trade since it was difficult to set prices of the fabricated machines a week ahead. Such prices would be overtaken by price rises.

The producers in Bendel State stated that it took an average of two-and-a-half days to fabricate one cassava grater. The Oyo State average was four-and-a-fifth days. Most small producers sell between 7 and 20 units per year. Large producers may sell up to 150 units per year. The number of workers ranged from 2 to 15 in Bendel State and 1 to 8 in Oyo State. All workers were male.

The producers in both States considered the market for cassava machines to be growing. The Oyo producers have had customers from Ile-Ife, Iwo, Ibadan, Ijebu-Ode, Kwara, Lagos, Kaduna, Ado-Ekiti, Ondo, Ogbomosho and Iseyin. Those in Bendel indicated a concentration of customers in the area of Umunede, the biggest cassava processing centre.

The bottlenecks identified were finance, non-availability of raw materials, high prices of purchased inputs and government intervention. A few producers were worried about increasing competition from other fabricators. The effect of Structural Adjustment Programme (SAP) is clearly being felt because the cost of imported motors is rising daily. While the fabricated graters are sold for between 300 and 500 nairas, the engines that supply power to run them cost between 3,000 and 15,000 nairas. This is limiting the sale of graters as most processors cannot afford the engines.

The rising costs have compelled fabricators to use any type of metal sheet for the graters, some of which wear out rapidly. The producers make brisk business helping to repair or replace them while the processors frown at the frequent need to replace the graters. The problem with the pressing frame is that it rusts and becomes less efficient.

Knowledge/skill development

Most producers of cassava processing machines served varying periods of apprenticeship under their fathers or masters. A minimum of three years of apprenticeship occurs. Younger people take more time. There are no

74

prerequisite qualifications, though the literate apprentices are quicker to grasp measurement units.

How training occurs
Training occurs through
1   blacksmith: father-son relationship
2   blacksmith: trainer-apprentice
3   technical colleges, craft villages mechanic workshops, polytechnics and short courses in universities
4   welder/iron-benders workshops
5   company affiliation trainer of employees
6   user/promoters such as RAIDS — Rural Agro-Industrial Development Scheme
7   government institutions such as the Federal Institute of Industrial Research (FIIRO), Oshodi and Project Development Agency (PRODA) and
8   international organizations such as UNICEF, FAD, and IDRC.

How learning occurs
Learning occurs through Research and Development. People say that practice makes perfect. Any machine intended for fabrication is first dismantled, studied and then duplicated. This is a kind of technology transfer. The producers of cassava processing machines are always looking for alternative inputs and trying to improve the efficiency of the various machines.

In some cases, problems arising from the use of one machine are taken to experienced blacksmiths or welders who use the occasion to learn more about the technical structure and functions of the machine. Many spare parts are improvised. There are occasional gatherings to brainstorm and find solutions to knotty problems.

Apart from cassava processing machines, users of various equipment submit damaged or worn out parts for remoulding. This is common with motor spare parts and especially now that Structural Adjustment Programme (SAP) measures have raised the cost of imports considerably.

Relating the processes to scientific methods
First the welders and blacksmiths move from the known to the unknown. They attempt to solve real problems and ease bottlenecks in the cassava processing operations. To achieve their aims, the problem is studied carefully. Goals are set and methods of achieving the goals outlined. The low level of literacy and formal education, however, makes record-keeping uncommon. Even the methodology is not written down but whatever is achieved through trial-and-error is made part of acquired experience.

The products developed by this method are tested and their defects are identified for corrections. Sometimes the fabricating group waits for the

75

users to report defects. But in at least one case, the fabricator was a user who refined his product as necessary whenever he noticed defects during use.

How managerial skills are acquired

Managerial skills involve being able to plan the business for profit. They cover understanding the product, its market potential, the raw materials needed, their acquisition, judicious use and inventory management. A good manager thinks ahead and innovates. He ensures that there is sufficient capital for his business. He is able to forecast supply and demand, identify his competitors, study government policy interventions and adjust accordingly.

Most cassava processing machine producers were limited with respect to the above listed managerial skills. This was due partly to limited education and lack of exposure to workshops where they could acquire such skills. No matter how long the period of apprenticeship, if the trainers themselves are not well-equipped with managerial skills, their apprentices won't develop the skills either.

The skills can be acquired through regular participation in trade fairs, workshops and seminars. It is recommended that government and donor agencies should assist in establishing modern workshops with appropriate tools and equipment as well as organizing short-term training programmes. Some of the very experienced blacksmiths and welders should be invited to help teach practical knowledge even at the polytechnic level. This will permit cross-fertilization of ideas and skills and the nation stands to gain from this kind of investment.

Potential of peoples' technology

The high cost of imported machines and raw materials has forced Nigerians to look inward for new technology and products. For example, bone-crushers have been designed now to produce bone meal locally. Feed mixers have been manufactured as well. Mechanical *gari* sieves, friers and cassava harvesters have been fabricated. Palm kernel crackers and kernel oil extractors, fruit juice presses and palm oil presses have been made. There are soya bean oil extractors, groundnut shellers, grain planters and hand ploughs — all in crude form but ready for refinement.

There is no limit to the potentials of these intermediate mechanical technologies. Interviews with a few of the machine producers indicate the possibility of developing a lot more ideas if some key equipment such as turning and bending machines could be acquired.

Major obstacles

1 Limited education means limited technology innovation/adaptation and hence low output results. There is a lack of communication between polytechnics/universities and roadside workshops.

76

2 Increasingly exorbitant prices of machines, equipment, spare parts and input materials cause prices of products to rise beyond the reach of users.

3 There is a lack of communication between individuals trying to establish workshops. Establishers also face inadequate funding, lack of credit and other problems.

4 There is a lack of standardized markets for inputs and products.

5 There is a lack of good-quality water at village level thereby rendering the final product unhygienic.

6 The toxicity and perishability of cassava is another inhibiting factor.

7 There is a lack of modern storage technology for matured tubers. (The traditional method is to leave tubers in the ground and harvest when the need arises.) Seed stalks also lack modern storage technology. They perish unless planted immediately.

8 Due to a lack of standard raw materials, and in order to reduce costs, machine fabricators pick up scrap metals anywhere they can be found. The sizes, gauges and thicknesses are varied, leading to a variation in quality, service and durability.

9 Uncertainty in the market for *gari* processing machines is due to a shortage of cassava tubers. The users are no longer placing orders regularly and this affects business planning among machine makers. Many fabricators could not produce the machines unless orders were placed by users. In some locations such as Agbor Alidinma, Bendel State processors now rotate the days to allow each member to have sufficient business (i.e. there are more processors than the available cassava tubers).

10 There is a near total absence of modern harvesting (uprooting) technology. This has left the process as labour-intensive and time consuming. A few years back, the harvesting trend of cassava could be predicted. But with the enforced ban on importation of wheat and rice, there has been a general shift towards cassava not only for human consumption but for industrial use. This has increased the pressure on cassava to the extent that immature crops are now often harvested.

11 Despite government efforts in rural electrification, the irregular supply and general shortages of electricity in rural areas have prevented the even spread of welders into these areas. The blacksmiths/welders thus concentrate their production in urban areas causing additional distribution costs for machines once they have been made. Efforts to convert friers using firewood to make them suitable for electricity have been hindered by lack of electrification in rural areas.

Social and political factors helping and hindering
1 The mass movement into urban areas has led to a large concentration of people that must be fed. There is a need for mass production and rapid processing of food.

2 The ban on importing processed and semi-processed food items has forced Nigerians to process and use local foodstuffs.

3 Prior to the banning on exporting food items, west Africans living in the USA, Canada and Europe were taking advantage of the devaluation of the naira to purchase processed food from Nigeria — especially *gari*. This increased the use of small-scale processing capacity and encouraged the manufacture of necessary machines. However, there has been drought which has devastated a lot of crop fields and livestock in the north of the country. This has encouraged many Nigerians, including northerners, to develop a taste for food items produced in the south, particularly *gari* and other cassava products. For example, *cassavita* made of finely ground *gari* is mixed with fulani fresh milk to make *fura da nono*.

In certain areas, there is an over-concentration of cassava processors leading to an inefficient use of potential capacity. Friction among these processors is becoming common. However some processors' associations have been formed to allocate processing time and thus minimize disagreements.

Supporting peoples' technology

It is our belief that formal education and training would enhance the performances of the cassava processing machine fabricators. They should be able to understand the scientific and engineering principles on which the operations of the machines are based. Machine makers should document their steps, methodology, types and properties of various raw materials and the appropriate materials for specific machines and spare parts. Fabricators must consider the implication of various processes not only on machine efficiency and costs but also on the safety and hygiene of the food processed. Food forms and eating habits of consumers must always be taken into consideration when attempting to develop processing technology and equipment.

So far, the breeders have continued to work towards minimizing the cyanide content of cassava. Their successes may result in the production of sweet cassava which can be consumed directly. This could reduce the need for several steps in the *gari* production process. But as long as the bitter varieties of cassava exist, there is a need for fermentation and proper frying. The producers of processing machinery must continue to refine equipment to reduce drudgery and obtain better quality gari at a lower price.

Government
1 Government should provide loans to producers and users, should strengthen and improve skills through exchange of ideas.
2 Government should improve farming support systems by giving more subsidy on fertilizer to permit increased production of cassava to better occupy the processing machines.

Scientists

1 Manually operated presses should be upgraded to electrically operated ones in order to give the job of pressing (de-watering) back to women. After all, the whole of cassava processing used to be handled by women.

2 Similarly, starting the machine by putting rope around the pulley and pulling should be changed to a winding handle or press button switches like those used on vehicle kick starters.

3 More work should be done on the frier to fully mechanize it.

4 Peoples' technology should be waste-free, i.e. peels, central fibre and starch in the cassava tuber should be salvaged for use as animal feed and industrial starch.

5 Peoples' technology should include awareness of environmental concerns such as waste disposal systems to permit drainage, deodorization and machine cleanliness. For example, a user in Asaba, Bendel State, collects water from the pulp, allows it to settle in order to separate starch from water. He sun-dries the starch which removes the odour and provides additional income through the sale of starch. Peels are also sun-dried and fed to goats and pigs.

6 The fuel tank should be enlarged to allow for a longer operating period and reduce refuelling time.

7 Producers should develop engines with less noise.

8 Scientists should develop more gas-operated friers. It has been demonstrated that 30 nairas worth of gas lasts one week, i.e. the same time a 30 nairas worth of firewood lasts. This encourages forest preservation.

Non-governmental organizations

1 Non-governmental bodies could help with the introduction of local engine-making capacity into Nigeria. For example, NGOs could work with an organization like the African Regional Centre for Engineering Design and Manufacture in Ibadan.

2 Short training workshops or attachments could be arranged to upgrade the skills of artisans in repair, maintenance and fabrication.

3 NGOs, particularly religious groups, can perform useful roles as extension agents by motivating their followers to adopt the use of peoples' technology. Business firms, including banks, can supply the finance to establish training centres on long-term loan interest and partnership arrangements in order to supplement government efforts.

The Nigerian cassava grater

SELINA ADJEBENG-ASEM

Introduction

A great deal more emphasis needs to be put into the development and diffusion of affordable technologies that help to raise the standard of living of the average Nigerian. There is a special need for technologies that are targeted at rural and urban small-scale producers. These must be technologies that step up food production, ensure food security and reduce the drudgery of food processing for women, the main workers in rural and urban small-scale food processing.

This article focuses on the evolution, viability, diffusion and utilization of 'the peoples' cassava grater' produced in the informal engineering sector. This equipment deals with one of the critical and labour-intensive stages of the processing of one of Nigerian's local staples derived from cassava — *gari*.

Cassava in Nigeria's economy

In Nigeria and many parts of the world, cassava (*manihot esculenta*) plays a major role in the economy both as source of food and as industrial raw material. In the western and eastern parts of Nigeria, cassava occupies an important position in the agricultural economy. The root accounts for over 50 per cent of carbohydrate intake when processed into various foods.

Cassava must be adequately processed before it can be consumed as food. Raw cassava is known to contain *linamarin* and *lotaustralin*, which, when acted upon by *linamarase* (the enzyme released when cassava root cells are ruptured) are converted to hydrocyanic acid (HCN). The HCN is converted to thiocyanate, a sulphur-containing compound, when it enters the bloodstream. Thiocyanate is detoxified using body sulphur after which it is excreted in urine. Thiocyanate is known to poison the body by using up the body sulphur during detoxification, thereby interfering with the thyroid gland's uptake of iodine resulting in goitre. Chronic pancreatic

DR S. ADJEBENG-ASEM (Nigeria) is a lecturer/research fellow at the Technology Planning and Development Unit, Obadfemi Awolowo University, Ile-Ife, Nigeria. Her research interest and focus has been on development of indigenous technology, technical innovation and entrepreneurship, appropriate technology and women in technology.

calcification and neoropathy have also been linked with cyanide poisoning in certain parts of the world.

The most common species of cassava tubers in Nigeria are known to have high cyanide concentration. Processing cassava into *gari* is known to reduce the cyanide content of cassava quite considerably. This is a reduction of 98.17 per cent as compared with a 69.85 per cent reduction of boiled tuberous root.

Cassava is produced in varying quantities all over the eastern and western parts of Nigeria and consumed mainly in the form of *gari*. Thus the importance of *gari* processing equipment in cyanide reduction and higher output of food can hardly be over-emphasized.

Gari in the dietary pattern of Nigerians

Gari is one of the commonest and cheapest local staples available to Nigerians. The staple constitutes over 70 per cent of carbohydrate intake for rural dwellers and low-income urban workers. *Gari* also offers a type of 'convenience food'. It needs little preparation and is helpful in particular to working mothers and wives who are often preparing meals in a short time.

Gari is a very versatile product which can be prepared in a variety of ways. It is usually made into a thick paste called *eba* for a main meal and eaten with leafy green or okro sauce with meat and fish. When eaten as a quick food or snack, *gari* is mixed with water and occasionally sugar and milk. It is taken with various groundnut or bean preparations.

Gari is also an important product with regard to food security at the household level. The shelf-life of well-prepared *gari* is estimated to be up to two years.

This introduction is an attempt to underline the importance of *gari* in the Nigerian economy, and, consequently, the importance of *gari* processing equipment. This study analyses one of the critical stages of the processing activity — grating.

Gari preparation

Gari preparation from cassava is one of the most popular food processing industries at household and community levels in the eastern and western parts of Nigeria. Traditional *gari* processing consists of a set of laborious and labour-intensive activities, with rural or urban poor women at the centre. This processing normally involves the following set of activities: peeling, washing, grating, fermenting, pressing or de-watering, sieving, frying, cooling and storing.

Some of these sets of activities, particularly peeling, pressing or de-watering and frying are highly labour-intensive. This labour-intensiveness has the effect of reducing output levels considerably, creating shortages on

81

the market, raising the price of *gari* beyond the reach of the poor and reducing the overall income of the majority of women who engage in these processing activities.

However, present political economic factors have led to foreign exchange restrictions and a consequent ban on importing food alternatives such as wheat flour and imported rice. Therefore, *gari* has assumed important status as a food item in Nigeria. A great deal of research attention is being turned to efficient ways of *gari* production. Several attempts have been made by research and teaching institutions and other large-scale formal engineering organizations to mechanize either the entire *gari*-making process or some sub-processes. However, these attempts have not culminated into successful innovations, particularly in the case of cassava peelers.

Over 80 per cent of *gari* on the markets in the eastern and western parts of Nigeria is processed either traditionally or using machinery developed in the informal engineering sector of the economy. Indeed, none of the randomly sampled respondents for this study was using any of the large-scale formal engineering based equipment. More engineering innovative efforts in *gari* processing are concentrated on cassava grating than on other steps in the processing chain. Reasons for this include the fact that these graters have gained wide market acceptability and are much cheaper. The graters compete very well with formal sector engineering efforts and have attracted a considerable number of carpenters and metal fabricators to work on them.

Method of research

The data base for this study was collected with a detailed interviewee guide from interviews with 50 informal sector engineers, 50 cassava grater and press operators and 50 *gari* processors sampled from various *gari* factories or processing centres. Commercial *gari* processing is rarely undertaken in isolation. Usually a number of individual processors congregate in a particular spot with close proximity to mechanical grating and pressing machines. The processors usually form mini associations that render mutual assistance when necessary. The stratified proportional sample was used to sample the target groups from four major *gari* producing areas in Oyo, Ondo and Bendel States. In Oyo State, Ife was selected. In Ondo State, Akoko was chosen and Benin-City and Urohubo were selected in Bendel State. Thirty informal sector engineers in Bendel State and 10 engineers each from Oyo and Ondo States were interviewed. Twenty machine operators and 20 *gari* processors were interviewed in Bendel State while 15 machine operators and 15 *gari* processors were interviewed from Oyo and Ondo States respectively. Ten *bukatera* (restaurant) owners, four in Benin and three each in Ondo and Ife were also sampled to provide the large-scale users' perspective.

Evolution of the cassava grater

Based on oral history, it was difficult to date the beginning of *gari* making in Nigeria. Two of the oldest interviewees, 70 years and 75 years respectively, grew up with *gari* being produced traditionally in their family compound. This puts traditional *gari* production as older than the 1920s.

Traditional method of grating
Traditional grating involved the use of a sheet of perforated metal usually 3.6 × 4.6cm or 3.6 × 5.6cm. The most commonly used metal was from the sides of imported kerosene containers. The women involved in grating ran the peeled cassava over the perforated metal sheet until the cassava was reduced to an ungratable size. This end piece was discarded. The basic method has passed through various stages of development, some radical, others incremental.

Developmental stages of the grater
The grater seems to have passed through three major stages, completely manual to semi-mechanized to fully mechanized.

From the traditional method which is fully manual, there was a radical change to mechanized grating. This was in response to three basic social demands: women's intensive search for less laborious techniques of grating cassava, the need to increase the output of *gari* production and the desire by entrepreneurs to sell more graters.

The demand for changes resulted in two basic improvements: the semi-mechanized graters, either hand or bicycle-driven, and the fully-mechanized grater. At the people's level, the grater moved from being completely manual to being completely mechanized. Virtually all the respondents of the study, 95 per cent, had nothing to do with the semi-mechanized systems. The common response is 'we are either grating by hand or by machine'. The fully-mechanized system was said to have been developed in the 1940s.

One of the oldest carpenters in Benin was said to have built the first machine based on his knowledge of imported cornmills. He had great skill in making hand graters and his three wives pleaded for more efficient equipment. He is known to have modified the manual grater into different shapes. The longer-framed grater enabled women to stand while grating while shorter ones allowed for grating in a sitting position. The use of these spread quickly.

Later, the same carpenter attempted to make a wooden grater that operated on the principle of hand-grating and a mechanized cornmill. The first prototype was not significantly different from the modern grater. Though attempts were made at this time to hand-drive the original prototype, these did not succeed until the machine was motorized five years later. The fully mechanized graters became popular in the 1960s in Benin. Gradually but systematically, metal- and wood-workers copied the design and sold machines to entrepreneurs who commercialized their use. Production relations began to change. *Gari* processing, which had been predominantly a woman's task, began to be infiltrated by men, primarily because women lacked the capital to purchase the new machines. The development of capitalism in Nigeria at this point was tending to place productive resources in the hands of men, and this tendency is underlined by the present study. Nowadays, men plant the cassava and sell to women who make the *gari* but in 75 per cent of cases men own the grating and pressing machines while hired women operators sell their labour.

The semi-mechanized machines were later attempts, mainly by learning and research institutions, to produce equipment at a cost lower than that of the fully mechanized machines. This was meant to bring technology into the reach of women processors. The attempts were not very successful and the semi-mechanized graters hardly spread ino use.

Diffusion

The traditional manual grater diffused rapidly throughout every *gari*-making community. Information about this new technique was passed quickly from one woman to another. If one woman saw it in a neighbourhood she described it to her husband or son who then made one to her specifications. Further suggestions were provided by the women until the right standard of equipment was achieved. These traditional graters cost virtually nothing — one or two pieces of wood, a piece of scrap metal and a few nails. The grater was used mainly by women and was easy to maintain. Corrosion, one of the greatest problems of the grater, was minimal since the hand equipment could be washed and dried easily. However the grater's efficiency rate was low due to its slowness in use. It took from 8a.m. to 4p.m. for a woman to grate 50kg (1 bowl) of cassava, which is obviously a large part of the day. Besides cassava grating, women have maternal and domestic tasks to perform as well as responsibilities towards husbands, kin, other wives and the community at large.

Besides adding to the overload of work for women, the grating process itself had its problems. A little-known fact is that women who use the traditional method of grating sustain degrees of hand injuries. Some neglected wounds have led to tetanus infections in a few cases.

The hygiene of traditional grating is also an issue. In particular, many women have a number of small children and operate in an environment where basic facilities for washing are absent. Thus, the *gari* can become dirty and unwholesome. It should be added that this is only a recent phenomenon. In the 1920s, where families lived in the same compound there were supportive social systems to take care of the young ones separately while mothers busied themselves with grating.

These disadvantages and the increased demand for *gari* led to eventual rejection of the manual grater. By 1970 in Benin every woman was using the fully-mechanized machine to grate her cassava, even for home consumption. In Ife and Ondo, the traditional method of grating persisted until the 1980s but totally left the cassava-processing scene by about 1981.

Semi-mechanized graters of the hand-driven or bicycle type were more of a technology push than a demand pull innovation. Thus they were considered inappropriate in several respects. The bicycle type brought a role reversal since bicycles are normally ridden by men and grating is a woman's occupation. It was gathered that men wanted to establish exclusive operational rights. This generated role conflicts and led to eventual rejection.

The hand-driven grater, though estimated to be 50 per cent faster than the traditional model, was considered laborious in operation and its output was inadequate. It was seen as doing very little by way of eliminating the drudgery element of women's work. As a result of these disadvantages, the semi-mechanized graters were not successful.

The fully-mechanized informal engineering sector grater has achieved a high rate of diffusion. It can be considered a very successful people's innovation. The diffusion trends can be explained not only in terms of the efficiency of these machines but also by cultural factors. There has been a more rapid diffusion of the grater in eastern Nigeria, which can be explained by the fact that *gari* to the easterner is an acceptable staple. Among the Yorubas of western Nigeria, this has not been so until recently. A common adage in Yoruba underlines this point:

'Iyan lonje;
Oka loogun,
airiye rara la nje ko
kenu madile lanje guguru.'

which translates as:

'Yam is food; that is what I eat. I eat yam powder
as a restorative food.
I eat *eko* (made from maize) when there is absolutely
nothing to eat.
When I need to nibble, that is when I chew roasted
corn.'

In this Yoruba adage 'cassava' is not mentioned at all. It is, in fact, not considered food. Recent social changes and economic conditions are the factors that have placed *gari* on the Yoruba dining table.

From the 50 processors interviewed in the four study areas, it was gathered that few people grate cassava by hand these days, particularly when the cost of grating 50kg of cassava is as little as 50 kobo (100k = 1 naira). It was pointed out that machines abound in almost all parts of eastern and western Nigeria, and it was claimed that there is no village with a population of over a thousand people that does not have such a machine. Nowadays women do not have to travel long distances across villages or towns to grate. Indeed, in Bendel State these machines are concentrated in certain areas where the scramble for patronage is very keen. But sometimes machine operators have no patronage at all. In certain wards where there are viable associations, there was a vote to share the operation of machines so that each operator can earn some money. In central Benin, however, where such associations are defunct because of internal rivalries, rules of the market operate and customers are won on a competitive basis. Some of the operators have built up a regular clientele over time.

Graters produced by the formal engineering sector have so far achieved very low diffusion rates. None of the operators in our Ife sample and only four out of 30 operators in Bendel State were using formal sector graters. Although the formal sector graters are known to be well-made, durable and are well finished, their cost is usually beyond the financial means of either individual women or small-scale male entrepreneurs. These graters also have capacities far in excess of the processing needs of a small-scale operation.

The production process

Most Nigerian informal sector metal workers operate under sheds or by street corners. They use scrap metal of a reasonable strength, gauges 14 to 20, which is heated in palm kernel furnaces with simple bellows. The metal is then heated and shaped as required, and quickly cooled by immersion in water or slowly by burying in sand, depending on the material strength needed. A simple cutting tool is used to cut the metal into the required shape and a grinding machine is employed to smooth the surface of the metal. With the aid of a simple drill and welding machine, the parts are standardized and welded together in two separate blocks, the base and the receptor. The machine is then painted. After this, the grating sheet is fixed into the base block and the removable receptor is screwed on. On completion of the metal frame, an electric or diesel motor is fixed to it.

Assessing the production method with a metallurgist, it was discovered that these metal workers are 'scientific' to some extent. They understand some basic principles of material selection and some basic metallurgical principles of heat treatment and handling of materials. In the interviews they provided a rational basis for their present level of operation and skills. It was discovered, however, that their knowledge of sources of alternative materials and techniques of using them was limited.

Systematic efforts are made by all the workers involved to ensure profit

86

maximization. Consequently fabricators will balance the use of the right materials against costs. Cost-effectiveness is the primary motivation of production. They refuse the use of superior material if it is thought that this will unduly raise costs in a competitive trade.

A considerable number of fabricators (30 per cent in Benin, 15 per cent in Akoko, 40 per cent in Ife) identified faults in the design of grating equipment. For instance, they recognize that stainless steel is a better alternative for the grater and that aluminium could be used for the receptor. However, they failed to adopt the first option because of the high cost and the second for lack of the necessary skills and equipment. Most of them therefore continue to use scrap metal for the base design and mild steel to make separate graters as replaceable parts to be sold.

Incremental changes in grater design

The original design of the mechanized grater was said to be an adaptation of imported corn and dough mills. The first prototype was made of wood, but this was found to be not durable as the wood rotted quickly and became mouldy. The women complained that it was difficult to keep clean, especially during the rainy season. As a result, local blacksmiths involved in the making of metal trunks were consulted. Using their rudimentary knowledge of metallurgy, heat treatment, straightening and welding, they made a metal grater comprising a metal receptor, a grating roller of 10 × 13cm, and a casing for the roller.

A few improvements have been made to the basic design. These include changes in roller size from medium (10 × 13cm) to small (10 × 10cm) in response to a call for cost reduction, and the use of stronger imported flat sheets for the grater roller. This raises the cost, however, and is used only when consumers are willing to pay the higher price.

In the east, many users have attached slates of wood to the metal. The justification given is that this closes the gap between the metal casing and the grater roller, and thus ensures finer grating. Also, it is said to prevent extensive corrosion. In Ondo State, 40 per cent of machines had this wooden slate, compared with 10 per cent in Ife. From a metallurgical point of view, the wood slate can be disadvantageous. It may help to seal unwanted gaps in the equipment but it definitely does not help to prevent corrosion. Wood absorbs water easily and accelerates corrosion. In addition, wood also harbours bacteria.

There has been little improvement in the final finishing but this appears to be of less importance to producers and consumers. In Benin City it was stated that a large manufacturer who produces graters to a high standard of finish sells them at prices 40 per cent higher than locally produced versions. However, it is asserted also that the skill level in the formal sector is not higher than that of local artisans who form the majority of mechanized grater producers. What then are the factors which influence the production of innovations at the informal level?

Women have been the major instigators of change. Seventy-eight per cent of producers attributed the changes to women customers' suggestions while 22 per cent attributed alterations to a natural quest for improvement in design. The changes have been geared towards sturdier machines and more durable grater sheets. From interviews with women *gari* processors it was established that women are keen on technological improvements, particularly as they affect their work. Contrary to prevailing myths, women are very active in providing various suggestions as to how designs might be improved, based on their rich traditional store of knowledge.

Ownership of graters

Very few women own graters. Four women owned graters in Benin, and these women were not *gari* processors themselves but entrepreneurs who hired boys to operate the machines. Ten women were found operating graters in Benin, four in Akoko and three in Ife. However, in all cases they were working for their husbands and the money they made went to the men. In six cases in Benin, seven cases in Akoko and eight cases in Ife, men operate their own machines or appoint other men. Men and women operators charge different prices for grating and pressing. On average, men charged between 3 nairas and 4 nairas for grating and pressing 50kg of mash, while women charged between 1.50 nairas and 2.50 nairas. There seemed to be no rational basis for the price differentials. The men liked to give the impression that they were more competent in handling the machines, and it appears that many women customers believed them.

Production economics

Producers of graters and presses, particularly those who depend on it for their livelihood, have said that profit margins have not increased as they should have in recent years.

Production cost has increased astronomically since the late 1970s, by about 80 per cent, while profit margins have not exceeded 30 per cent. Machines in the 1960s were sold at 50 nairas and cost approximately 35 nairas to produce. The motor cost 150 nairas. The metal large-sized grater now sells at between 400 nairas and 500 nairas and costs about 350 nairas to produce. The electric motor costs about 2,000 nairas for 3 HP. The cost of metal sheets has risen enormously. In the 1960s a sheet cost 20 nairas compared with 300 nairas in the late 1980s. A sheet can make only one machine. The costs of welding materials and bolts and nuts have also risen, from 50k to 2 nairas. Most fabricators are thus forced to use metal scraps of

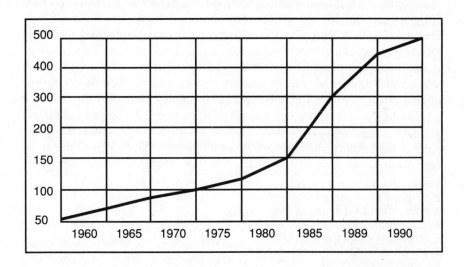

Rising costs of graters since 1960

dubious quality or metals of milder strength for the grates in order to maintain reasonable profit margins.

Nevertheless, the production and operation of graters appears to be a viable enterprise. Average sales in Ife are estimated at six machines per month per technical entrepreneur, while in Benin it was eight machines per month. This rise in demand from two a month in the 1960s in Ife and three per month in Benin indicates that demand is growing. One machine can service a maximum of 20 customers on a 'good day' and minimum of three on a 'bad day.' This relatively high demand for the equipment makes the grater a favourite among metal workers, second only to pepper grinders. Demand for the machine is high, not only because of increased demand for *gari*, but also because the machines create employment for the fabricators, the operators and users.

Costs and benefits to women
The grater has had both positive and negative benefits for women. For the rural or urban woman who depends on *gari* processing as a major source of livelihood, the grater reduces drudgery, saves labour and time, and increases productivity.

Processing *gari* traditionally by hand takes an average of five days from start to finish. Grating takes a complete day. Pressing then takes two days, and sieving and frying take another day each.

With the mechanized grater, grating takes a maximum of 15 minutes for 50kg of cassava. This is a great improvement, 360 per cent more efficient than hand-grating and 120 per cent more efficient than using the semi-mechanized machine.

The extra time gained by women is used for various activities which women previously had little or no time to undertake. Responses as to how processors use the extra time is reported in the following Table:

Table 1 How women use time saved by using mechanized processor

responses	number	percentage
1 cultivate my own cassava	6	12
2 help my husband on the farm	10	20
3 have more time to sleep and or relax	0	0
4 make more *gari*	15	30
5 engage in retail trade	8	16
6 shop for cheaper inputs (cassava and firewood)	11	22
	50	100

A great majority of women used the extra time to participate in the money economy, which eventually results in improved standards of living for them and their children. These activities, though limited, demonstrate the benefits of improved technologies for women.

Costs to women result from lack of access to ownership of graters, and to lack of control over profits from the grating process. In the Ondo and Ife samples, it was made clear that 'women have no money to buy a machine for grating' and that 'the profit made from *gari* processing [not grating] is so small that it can only buy food. It is only in rare cases that it can buy clothing.'

Benefits to consumers
The grater and press have stepped up the output of *gari* at a time of a scarcity of alternative staples. In addition, they have enabled better-quality *gari* which has fine uniform granules and is more hygienic to be put on the market. However, the findings of the study show that the average consumer of *gari* does not appreciate the existence of grating machines. In fact, most people do not understand the impact of grating machines as the price of *gari* has been pushed up by high inflation in Nigeria. It was generally agreed by makers of *eba* that *gari* is simply obeying market laws of supply and demand. They explain that the high cost of *gari* is the result of the added demand made on *gari* production by the lack of cheaper alternatives. In season, a measure of *gari* costs 2.50 nairas, compared to 9 nairas for local rice, 14 nairas for imported rice and 6 nairas for beans.

Benefits to entrepreneurs
Grating machines are of immense benefit to entrepreneurs that buy and commercialize their use, either by operating them themselves or by hiring labour to operate them. For all of them it provides a livelihood. Production capacity is 1,000kg per day at 2.50 nairas per 50kg, and average running costs are 10 nairas per day in diesel or petrol. Most operators run a six-day week and operate graters and presses together. Grating averages 1 naira and pressing 1.50 nairas. Thus the average machine is making 960 nairas a month gross, minus about 160 nairas for maintenance and overhead costs, giving a net monthly income of about 800 nairas. This amount is equivalent to a level 12 officer in the civil service. In addition, some operators collect laundry starch from the grated cassava, and this starch is often processed for sale.

Benefits to the community
Other benefits discovered include new employment for workers out of a job. Of the 50 workers interviewed, six had come to this trade after they had been made redundant. In Benin, some high-school leavers were found to have been employed to operate the machines. Grating machines are said to provide employment for non-farming women in rural areas.

Knowledge/skill acquisition

Three aspects of skill acquisition were investigated: product development skills, product operation or processing skills, and managerial skills.

Product development skills
Training for development of the grater occurs through informal apprenticeship spanning a four-year period. There is no age limitation or entrance qualification but the age of recruits is usually between 9 and 25 years. Their levels of education range from nothing to high-school drop-outs. On average, each fabricator or metalworker has four apprentices, and some have as many as 10. This in itself underlines the employment generation potential of diffusion of the product and associated skills. When the apprentices were interviewed, they almost all agreed that metalwork is a lucrative business. It should be added that these apprentices are not trained only to make graters and presses but also acquire skills general to metalwork. This includes welding and fabrication of other food processors. However, there is greater emphasis on the *gari*-making machine as they sell much more quickly.

Like most apprenticeship systems in Nigerian non-formal sectors, apprentices pay for their training. They are then informally tested and if certified competent are given an official certificate. The criteria for assessment and certification are set by the metalworkers' association of each community.

Processing skills
Acquiring skills for operating the machine or grating the cassava takes about three weeks. This involves learning to fix the belt on the motor and ensuring the grater roll is properly fixed into the machine and can be removed and cleaned. In all cases, particularly with high-powered diesel engines, apprentices learn how to avoid injury during processing, and how to undertake general maintenance of the machine.

Managerial skills
As in all businesses, basic managerial skills such as book-keeping, costing, stock control and marketing are important. These skills were generally found to be inadequate in the survey, particularly amongst the product developers and operators.

Bottlenecks

Various bottlenecks have been identified as impeding the development of cassava graters to a higher standard.

Financial constraints
All the respondents identified finance as crucial to the success of their operations. From the product fabricators to users, everyone needed working capital to purchase raw materials and cover initial operating and running costs. A further financial constraint is the high and rising cost of engines. Three and five horsepower electric motors now cost up to 10 times more than in the 1970s and diesel engines are even more expensive. For the small-scale industrialist, such costs are a serious disadvantage. Similarly, the cost of cassava has risen also. Women normally buy the cassava plants on the farms and later uproot them for *gari*. A single cassava stem that used to cost 1 naira today sells at between 1.50 and 2 nairas. The high cost of cassava reduces the profit of women processors drastically, and raises the price of *gari*. As early as 1987, 1kg of *gari* cost about 70k, but today the same weight costs 3.50 nairas.

Cassava supply
For the grater operators and processors a major bottleneck has been inadequate back-up supply of cassava. This is due to problems such as low yields per hectare, crop disease and transport difficulties.

Lack of inputs
Metalworkers complain about lack of necessary inputs of, for example, flat sheets. If *gari* production is to be increased then such bottlenecks must be removed. Nigeria could even begin to make motor engines.

Lack of knowledge and skills

Lack of managerial skills constitutes a bottleneck for producers and operators because the majority have had little or no formal training. Also, fabricators have inadequate knowledge of selection of materials and of possible alternative materials, such as plastics. Some fabricators were found to be using inappropriate metals and toxic paints. A few makers thought of using aluminium but lacked the necessary handling skills and equipment. There is a lack of linkage between academic and research institutions and the local artisan or technical entrepreneur operating in the informal sector. Local artisans cannot improve or upgrade their skills independently as they lack both theoretical knowledge and contacts with scientific establishments.

Technical problems

A technical constraint noted by all the machine operators is the short life-span of the grater plate, which needs replacing every two to three weeks. The replacement cost is about 50 nairas per plate, which sometimes drives producers to make their own plates from inferior materials. The graters themselves are not very rugged and 'fall apart earlier than expected'. A number of operators were seen supporting their 'shaking' graters with pieces of metal or wood.

A further technical problem is the highly corrosive nature of the grater plate, which women believe can be hazardous to life. Generally, metalworkers use iron, which is not toxic but which looks unsightly when corroded and discourages potential buyers and users. Lack of metallurgical knowledge sometimes leads grater producers to match anodes with cathodes which accelerates corrosion. Metalworkers are aware that corrosion-resistant materials such as stainless steel can be used for the grater plate, but neither they nor their customers can afford it.

Socio-political considerations

There have been a number of socio-political factors which have influenced the development and diffusion of cassava graters. For example, the current ban on imported flour and rice has given a boost to *gari* production. Most people now depend on *gari* and entrepreneurs are seizing the opportunity and demanding more graters.

However, national economic problems and Structural Adjustment Programme measures have had serious repercussions on the cost and maintenance of grating machines. Prices have risen and small-scale producers are no longer able to purchase this equipment. Women are particularly affected as they have less access to capital of their own. They are losing more control over cassava grating as men purchase the equipment and employ women to work for wages.

93

Conclusion

The cassava grater developed from its main users — women. Grating has evolved through three basic stages of development: traditional manual, semi-mechanized and fully-mechanized. At each stage, user input has been critical for modification and diffusion. Graters developed by the informal engineering sector have been more successful in terms of diffusion and market acceptability than those developed in the formal engineering sector.

Informal sector graters have some basic defects due to lack of basic scientific knowledge of metalworkers. Critical among these shortcomings are lack of knowledge of alternative fabrication materials, lack of technical skills to handle alternative materials, and lack of general business and managerial skills.

Artisans need to link up with research institutions of professional engineers in order to upgrade their basic skills and increase their output. The present socio-economic situation in Nigeria is forcing up the cost of all materials used in grater production, so that graters are becoming more expensive. Usually only men can afford to buy graters, giving them control of predominantly women's work, and consequently creating gender conflicts. Women need credit facilities to enable them to purchase equipment necessary to their areas of work.

Policy recommendations

Government

The Nigerian government needs to create socio-economic and political environments conducive to indigenous innovation and local entrepreneurship. Where indigenous capability has been demonstrated (as in the development of cassava graters), government should ban the importation of competitive goods such as hammer mills. Local artisans should be organized into viable co-operatives and provided with the necessary capital to undertake larger-scale batch processing. Instead of pumping all research funds into R&D institutions with little success, the government should earmark a proportion of such funds as venture capital for local co-operatives. The government should also encourage all R&D institutions to adopt some local artisan co-operatives as partners. In this way, the artisans will have access to both the money and technical skills in manufacturing and marketing while the parent institution undertakes the monitoring of allocated funds. There is also the need to identify and encourage inventiveness. The government should create a forum for all inventors and call it 'Inventor's Day'. Deserving creators could be identified and honoured in order to stimulate creativity amongst Nigerian citizens.

Research institutions

There is a need to create new institutions such as the National Innovation

94

and Entrepreneurship Board (NIEB). This is a liaison department that takes prototype/innovations, finds entrepreneurs for them and gives venture capital to these entrepreneurs. A positive policy in this direction would be to identify the innovations, pull them out, package them and sell them on to entrepreneurs.

Government should adopt appropriate measures to support companies and institutions. It is better to start with what is possible and to worry about the impossible later. In this sense it may be necessary to re-structure existing institutions or firms by giving them new know-how, instead of developing new companies.

Special recognition for women

Current government efforts to help women do not touch the grass roots — the very poor women who are really in need of help. From this study, it became apparent that women have the capacity and are keenly interested in owning food-processing equipment of any type. Most women are already organized into associations with able leadership. These women should be assessed and given venture capital to purchase equipment which would give them control over their work. Such investment would also raise the quality of their lives and those of their families.

Building of communicative linkages

Special attention should be paid to the building of communicative linkages between different groups and institutions. An arm of the Ministryy of Science and Technology should be put in charge to ensure that effective co-ordination exists between all engineering institutions, research institutes and the engineering sectors. Research institutions should endeavour to improve communication between the formal scientific and the informal engineering sectors, and should improve communication to users of the innovations as well. For example, research institutes could organize periodic tours for their project personnel, researchers or students. Finished or on-going projects could be inspected, problem areas identified and suggestions for improvements made. This study has led to two metallurgical engineering students from Obafemi Awolowo University linking up with local cassava grater fabricators in order to identify bottlenecks and suggest improvements.

To help the consumer, the government can organize mini-trade fairs based in rural areas where new technologies are displayed and operated.

Alternative raw materials/upgrading of local skills

It is strongly recommended that metallurgical and materials engineers, mechanical engineers and polymer scientists link up with informal sector engineers. This would help education about the use of alternative fabrication materials and techniques. For instance, it is possible that instead of

95

toxically painted iron hoppers for the grater, local artisans could use aluminium instead, or even plastic. If the parts for the grater are standardized, the plastic companies or aluminium extrusion companies can be contacted to produce the hoopers on a large scale for this sector.

For more durable grater sheets, it was suggested that metalworkers be provided with heat treatment facilities and be taught surface hardening of mild steel by introducing carbon and/or nitrogen. The engineers in the informal sector expressed great desire collaboration that will help them acquire new skills and reduce the costs of their production.

PART II

Asia

ASIA — Regional overview

RAKESH BASANT

Background

Four papers were prepared for the Asia region. These covered five diverse technologies: blacksmithy in Bangladesh; a bullock-drawn multipurpose tool bar in Gujarat, India; artificial fishing reef and bait in Kerala, India; and micro-hydro power in Nepal. Case studies from India and Nepal focus on specific technologies and analyse the processes which characterized the generation, adaptation and diffusion of these technologies over a period of time. These studies also evaluate the socio-economic benefits of the technologies. The case study from Bangladesh has a somewhat broader focus. It attempts to compare the socio-economic and technical characteristics of 'more popular' and 'less popular' blacksmiths. On the basis of this comparison, the study assesses the possibilities of transfer of knowledge from the 'more popular' artisans to 'less popular' ones.

Perspective

All the studies share the broad perspective that development in most developing countries has resulted in the marginalization of local knowledge and innovations. In fact, indigenous knowledge is often unknown to, or ignored by, policy makers and development workers seeking solutions to rural problems. While many successful innovations are based on indigenous knowledge, some technologies are not accepted because they do not fit in with local knowledge. All the studies of the Asia region recognize the need to study local innovations to identify their socio-economic and technical elements. These can be incorporated both in research undertaken by the formal R&D sector and in the formulation of development strategies.

Evolution, learning process and motivations

The case studies from Nepal and India provide a detailed account of how

DR R. BASANT (India) works at the Gujarat Institute of Area Planning. Areas of research: agricultural technology, agricultural labour markets and the rural non-farm sector.

the technologies evolved over time. The documentation highlights two basic features of the processes of local innovation:

1 Innovation is a process in which the users and innovators of technology continuously adapt and modify to suit local conditions and to improve efficiency
2 The changes embodied in the adaptation/modification undertaken locally are incremental in nature and do not represent quantum leaps forward. Local innovations develop and diffuse slowly but steadily through a trial-and-error process.

The interaction among users and makers (producers or innovators) of products under study provided a major impetus for the development, adaptation and diffusion of the technologies. Such an interaction continuously transmitted users' experience to the fabricators. In most cases, the fabricators respond to the needs/problems of local users and introduce changes in the technologies. Therefore, the adaptation/modification process is largely demand-induced.

In the case of blacksmithy, the tool bar and the improved ghatta 'users' and 'makers' were two separate entities. In the case of the artificial reef and bait, 'learning-by-using' and 'learning-by-doing' was embodied in the same set of individuals, the fishermen. Thus, the interface between learning-by-doing on the part of makers (fabricators) and learning-by-using on the part of users provided the impetus for the development and the widespread use of the technologies under study. In this sense, the case studies provide instances not only of useful local innovations but also of 'horizontal' diffusion of these innovations.

The role of formal R&D in the development and diffusion of the technologies under study was insignificant. In fact, technical personnel participated in the innovation process to a limited extent only in the case of the tool bar and the improved ghatta. The linkages between the scientific community and the fishermen making artificial reefs are beginning to develop only now.

The motivating factors in all the cases were largely internal to the system. The innovation of artificial fishing reefs and baits was interpreted as a survival strategy. Trawler fishing on the Kerala coast resulted in the destruction of natural reefs which in turn adversely affected the catch of artisanal fishermen. Experiments with artificial reefs and bait were essential strategies to survive.

The issue of survival was not explicitly relevant in the other cases. The technical superiority of products of the more popular blacksmith could not be attributed to his conscious efforts to retain his competitiveness in a shrinking market. Similarly, there was no immediate threat to the survival of fabricators and users of the tool bar and the improved ghatta. These two innovations highlight the continuous quest to improve and adapt existing technologies to suit changing socio-economic and ecological conditions. The tool bar and the improved ghatta have another interesting feature in common. Both represent improvement in old technologies in response to the introduction of changes, such as the use of iron implements, tractor-drawn implements and turbines. Significantly, both the tool bar and improved ghatta incorporate some elements of these changes. Innovations in these case studies also responded to the increasing and diversified needs of the people, i.e. the need for flexible tools for different operations in the case of the tool bar and the growing need for processing, irrigation and electricity in the case of the improved ghatta.

The symbiotic interaction with new technologies is also evident in the case of artificial reef and bait. The fishermen have been experimenting continuously with non-indigenous materials such as cement pipes, old tyres and synthetic fibre. The innovations from Nepal and India represent non-conservative situations where local people are continuously trying to improve local technologies.

Socio-economic benefits

Innovations have wide-ranging socio-economic benefits. The technologies are viable not only in purely economic terms, they are also ecologically sustainable. Moreover, they utilize locally available materials and skills. The innovations help upgrade local skills and thereby develop local technological capability. The development of local technological capability was most sharply brought out in the cases of the tool bar and the improved ghatta.

Policy issues

The Asia case studies underline the need to recognize peoples' technology on the same footing as research undertaken by formal R&D. The need is to strengthen indigenous technology systems by combining local experience with scientific knowledge through linkages with the formal R&D systems. It was recognized, however, that developing, nurturing and strengthening these linkages is an extremely complex and difficult task. Among other things, it requires a reorientation of the values of the scientific community, policy makers and development workers.

The case studies suggest a variety of ways in which a beginning can be made. The implementation of subsidy schemes provided the platform for interaction between local producers/fabricators and formal R&D personnel. A similar interaction was facilitated by a bank (ADB) and two voluntary agencies (ITDG, GATE) in the case of the improved ghatta. These agencies also helped development of the improved ghatta in a variety of other ways such as arranging credit and organizing training programmes. The initiative to develop such linkages in the case of artificial reefs came from a local NGO which helps to organize fishing communities into co-operatives and village groups. This NGO has been working with the community for a long time and has participated in various struggles of the fishermen. Therefore, the link between the NGO and the fishing community is not only technical but has also other dimensions which make the NGO part of the community.

The Bangladesh study envisages developing linkages and interaction through a training programme where more popular and better skilled blacksmiths will transfer their knowledge to other blacksmiths. The formal R&D and the scientific community will facilitate this process and make efforts to upgrade the skills of the artisans through involvement in these programmes.

Obviously, there is not simply one way of developing linkages between the formal and the informal technology systems. Linkages have to evolve on the basis of the conditions prevailing in a specific region. For example, the role of credit and subsidy systems may be quite important in some regions, as in the cases of the improved ghatta, tool bar and blacksmithy. The need to organize producers/users in the form of a co-operative village group or union may be a more important prerequisite in other situations, such as artificial fishing reef. Once the relevance of indigenous innovation is recognized, the institutional support needed to nurture indigenous innovation processes will evolve over time.

Farmers, fabricators and formal R&D — the pipe frame multipurpose tool bar in Gujarat, India

RAKESH BASANT

Introduction

Many of the earliest improvements in farm tools are made by users themselves or by local artisans in response to user needs. The interaction between farmers and local fabricators/repairers of agricultural implements results in a flow of information from the former to the latter. Users' experience is continuously transmitted to the fabricators. At times, this information takes the form of specific problems with particular implements but it can relate to problems of farming in general. Specific problems need to be solved immediately and the local fabricators usually find short-term solutions. Some long-term solutions also emerge over time. The farmer-fabricator interaction is often the major source of adaptive improvements in agro-mechanical technology.

The nature of agriculture and agro-climatic conditions differ considerably across regions. Therefore, the innovation and adaptation activities carried out by local fabricators gain added significance as they can contribute significantly to the diffusion process. Unfortunately, formal R&D normally works in isolation, within the confines of laboratories and test stations. Its interaction with local fabricators and users is insignificant.

Most studies on technological change in agriculture emphasize the 'transfer' of technology and de-emphasize or exclude the informal research within agricultural production systems. This focus on 'centre-periphery' information and technology flows undermines an equally or even more important process of horizontal transfers of knowledge.

This paper examines the development and adaptation in the pipe-frame multipurpose tool bar during 1960–88 in the Saurashtra region of Gujarat state of India. The paper seeks to highlight the contribution of local suppliers (fabricators) and users (farmers) and the restricted role of formal R&D in upgrading agro-mechanical technology.

Attempts at developing appropriate animal-drawn multipurpose wheeled tool carriers have been largely unsuccessful in the Third World. The Saurashtra tool bar probably provides the only case of popular animal-drawn multipurpose equipment.

DR R. BASANT (India) works at the Gujarat Institute of Area Planning. Areas of research: agricultural technology, agricultural labour markets and the rural non-farm sector.

Evolution of the tool bar

The Saurashtra region is located in the western part of Gujarat state and consists of Junagadh, Amreli, Bhavnagar, Surendranagar, Rajkot and Jamnagar districts. These districts occupy an area of 64,000 sq km which includes about 33 per cent of the geographical area of Gujarat state. According to the 1981 census, more than two million people (male and female) were cultivating in the Saurashtra region, either as self-employed farmers or as hired agricultural labourers. These people use four basic kinds of bullock-drawn agricultural implements:

1 A local plough is used for primary tillage;
2 Single straight-blade harrows are used for primary/secondary tillage, interculturing of widely spaced crops such as pearl millet, cotton and castor, harvesting of groundnuts and covering of seeds immediately after sowing. Harrows used for different operations/crops differ in size and weight.
3 Twin straight-blade hoe/harrows are used only for interculturing of crops such as groundnuts, cotton, wheat, millet and castor. Two rows can be intercultured simultaneously with this implement.
4 Seed-drills with two, three, four or five coulters are used depending on the row-to-row spacing for different crops.

One of the major drawbacks of traditional bullock-drawn implements is that each has its own body and beam in addition to its working parts. The farmer has to buy two pieces of hardware in order to perform one new task. Within a region like Saurashtra, the inter-row distance varies according to the crop. Farmers keep seed-drills with different distances between coulters for different crops. Different blade hoes and harrows are maintained also.

The number of implements possessed by a farmer depends upon his capacity to invest. This is determined mainly by the size of his farm, cropping patterns and the extent of irrigation. The number of implements owned may be one in the case of a plough, one to three in the case of single straight-blade harrows and seed-drills and one to five in the case of twin straight-blade harrows. Not all farmers can afford to maintain a large number of seed-drills, blade hoes and harrows.

Over time, with the introduction of the new seed varieties, irrigation and the use of chemical fertilizers, the distance between crop rows has changed. Changes in agro-climatic conditions have also necessitated changes in the distance between rows. In addition, as plants grow, blade hoes/harrows of smaller sizes are required to interculture the crop. If large blade hoes are used, the crop may become damaged. In commercialized agriculture such damage is serious and oil seeds are an important crop in Saurashtra. Maintenance of many implements of different sizes has become increasingly difficult, due to the rise in the cost of wood.

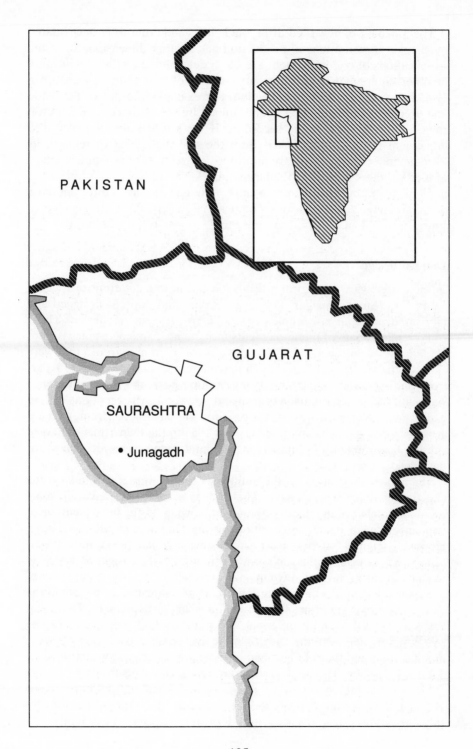

The purchase of new seed-drills, blade hoes and other tools necessitated by changes in conditions of production has another dimension. Since the specifications of one implement are often determined by the specification of other equipment in use, the introduction of new tools can disrupt a farmer's overall implement collection. For example, the size of the blade hoe used for intercultivation is determined by the distance between crop rows, i.e. by the size of the seed-drill. If the size specification of a new implement is radically different from the one it is going to replace, its introduction can upset the relationship between various implements a farmer is using. In this case, the farmer may have to change the whole set of implements, rather than adding a single one. Fabricators in different parts of Gujarat have devised various modifications in agricultural implements to solve this problem. The multipurpose tool bar also offers a solution.

Tool bar design

In the early 1960s, four rural artisans located in four different districts of Saurashtra (Surendranagar, Jamnagar, Rajkot and Amreli) designed and fabricated multipurpose implements of a roughly similar design. These could replace some of the implements farmers need, mainly some types of blade harrows and seed-drills. The designs for the multipurpose tool were close to the traditional designs of implements they would replace. Apart from the improved implements being multipurpose, the major difference was that headpieces are made of iron and not wood. All except one artisan had used a galvanized iron (G.I.) pipe for the headpiece (frame). These artisans applied almost simultaneously in 1965 to the Department of Agriculture, Government of Gujarat for their implements to be recognized for the subsidy schemes.

The implement designs for the multipurpose tool were found to be crude and the headpieces very heavy. The designs also did not have adequate provision to change the depth of ploughing/sowing. In the first round, these implements were denied recognition by the Department of Agriculture. However, scientists at the Research, Testing and Training Centre (Agricultural Engineering), Junagadh, saw possibilities in the designs and decided to guide the artisans to modify and improve their multipurpose implements.

Meanwhile, an artisan from another part of Saurashtra approached the Department of Agriculture for subsidy on a similar implement. The scientists suggested the use of three-inch G.I. pipe for the headpiece and some other minor modifications. By 1968, all five artisans had adopted these modifications and their designs had become popular in various parts of the Saurashtra region. The implements were recognized for subsidy.

Many other fabricators in the region were fabricating tool bars as well although they had not approached the Department of Agriculture for subsidy. Six out of 32 artisans interviewed for this study have been fabricating a tool bar since the mid-1960s. By 1969, the number of artisans fabricating this implement had increased from 4 to 40 and some 1,000 farmers had purchased one.

The Junagadh Centre gave wide publicity to the new implement through the media and public demonstrations. Tool bars were sent to all the agricultural research centres of the Gujarat Agricultural University in different agro-climatic zones of Gujarat. The District Agricultural Officers and Taluka Development Officers were also informed. All these efforts generated a lot of discussion and provided feedback for further modifications and improvements.

Quite independently of the Junagadh Centre and in response to local farmers' needs, fabricators made a variety of modifications in the tool bar during the 1970s. These modifications aimed at reducing the tool bar's weight, required draft, friction and vibration and at improving the flexibility of the implement to suit bullocks of various sizes, soil conditions and cropping patterns. Significantly, similar adjustments were made in all parts of Saurashtra. Recently, many artisans in the Saurashtra region have designed new coulters which can be fitted in the tool bar to use it as a seed-fertilizer drill. Coulters have also been designed for top dressing, i.e. to apply chemical fertilizers along crop rows.

In the late 1970s additional funds were made available for the subsidy schemes from the Oilseeds Development Programme. A large share of these additional funds were allocated to Saurashtra, as it is an important oilseed region. A committee formed by the Department of Agriculture discovered that the tool bar was one of the most popular improved agricultural implements.

The tool bar has five main parts:

1   the frame or headpiece;
2   the beam;
3   the coulters used for sowing;
4   the iron prong or stem which is fixed in the frame and in which the blade is fixed; and
5   the blade.

Fabricators in the Saurashtra region have modified all of the five parts.

The headpiece frame
A variety of changes have been made in the headpiece. According to some fabricators, the first version of the tool bar was actually an iron version of the traditional (wooden) seed-drill. While some used iron channels, others used four-inch galvanized iron (G.I.) pipe to make the frame of the seed-drill. The farmers found the iron seed-drill heavy and difficult to manoeuvre. The subsequent changes in the headpiece were introduced mainly to reduce the weight of the implement without adversely affecting its sturdiness and durability and to make the implement multipurpose.

107

The size of pipe used to fabricate the headpiece has undergone a series of changes. Channels are not used any more to fabricate the frame. The size of the pipe has been gradually reduced from four inches to two-and-a-half inches. While some fabricators still prefer a G.I. pipe of three inches diameter, some others have adopted a two-inch pipe for light soils. At the moment, a pipe of two-and-a-half inches is most popular.

The number of holes in the pipe has been increased from about 13 to 27. This makes the tool bar more multipurpose because the farmer can sow and interculture a larger number of crops with different inter-row distances. He can also introduce more changes in the distance between crop rows without changing the tool bar. In most cases, the number of holes is no more than twenty. The fabricators and farmers are normally not in favour of increasing the number of holes beyond 20 because of the fear that the structure of the implement will weaken.

Initially, the holes made in the headpiece to fix coulters and blades were round. Almost all fabricators now make rectangular holes. This change has been made mainly to reduce friction and vibration in the implement.

The headpiece is now made in three to nine parts. This modification has been introduced to incorporate additional implements in the tool bar such as the large harrow (Dhundia). The other reason for making this change was to reduce the weight of the tool bar, at least for those operations where the headpiece of full length is not required. In certain operations such as interculture, the long frame used to cause damage to crops. A frame or headpiece in three to five pieces is most popular. The farmers and fabricators prefer fewer joints because it reduces vibration and friction and is easier to handle.

The beam

Two main changes have been made in the beam. In the beginning, a wooden beam was used in the tool bar. Subsequently a G.I. pipe of one-and-a-half inches diameter was used as the beam. The farmers found it heavy. The beam is now made in three parts using pipes of three sizes. The most commonly used sizes are one-and-a-half inches, one inch and three-quarters of an inch. On average, the length of the beam is about 10 feet but is adjusted according to the size of the bullocks so that the feet of the bullocks do not get hurt.

In earlier versions of the tool bar, the beam was welded to the frame (headpiece). Consequently, the farmers could not adjust the depth of work. The beam is now fixed with the help of clamps, nuts and bolts. The depth of harrowing or sowing can be adjusted easily now.

The coulters

The coulters are fitted to the frame for sowing purposes. Initially the coulters were fitted on to the headpiece with the help of iron pieces (*phachar*).

This was as in traditional wooden implements where the wooden pieces were used to fit the coulters on the wooden frame. Now the coulters are fitted with nuts and bolts. The coulters fitted in this fashion are more stable and reduce friction and vibration.

The fabricators have designed special coulters to apply basal doses of chemical fertilizers. In one version, sowing and application of fertilizers is done simultaneously (a coulter with two holes) as two seeding funnels are tied to the frame. The other version is used to apply chemical fertilizers before sowing seeds. This coulter is also used sometimes for top-dressing where the fertilizer is applied along crop rows. The use of the tool bar to apply chemical fertilizers is relatively recent and not very popular as yet.

Stem/prong

As with coulters, stems are also fitted to the frame with the help of nuts and bolts. A special type of stem is designed to keep the headpiece above the ground. This design reduces the required draft and is useful in harvesting groundnuts.

Blades

A T-shaped blade has been designed to be fitted to the frame. This blade can be used very close to the crop rows without causing any damage. This design is similar to the design of the blade made in the Kheda region of Gujarat.

In addition, the fabricators have designed a variety of new implements which can be attached to the tool bar. Some fabricators have also made tines to convert the tool bar into a cultivator. An attachment has been designed also for bunding and ridging.

Standardization

Tool bars made in different regions and by different artisans were not of uniform quality and a wide range of designs and specifications were prevalent. Field tests in different parts of Saurashtra were organized in consultation with fabricators and farmers. An attempt was made to standardize the design and specifications of the tool bar for the Saurashtra region. Subsidy was (and is) provided only to those artisans who use this standardized design. The price for this design was fixed at 750 rupees.

Opinions are divided on the validity of this standardization procedure. Officials of the Department of Agriculture claim that the design and specifications are flexible enough to take care of variations in the quality of soil (especially its moisture content) and the cropping patterns. Some artisans and farmers argue for more flexibility due to wide inter-regional variations in the agro-climatic conditions in the Saurashtra region. At the district level, where the subsidy claims are processed, the officials are not particularly strict about the standardized design. As a result, slightly modified

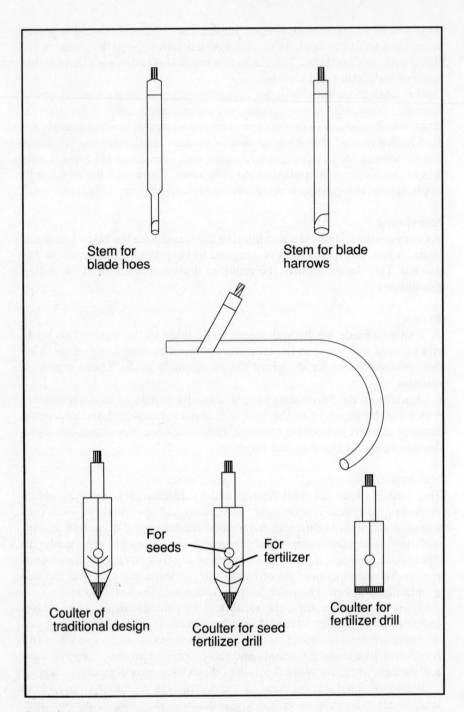

Stem for
blade hoes

Stem for blade
harrows

For
seeds

For
fertilizer

Coulter of
traditional design

Coulter for seed
fertilizer drill

Coulter for
fertilizer drill

Changes in the stem, and coulter of the tool bar

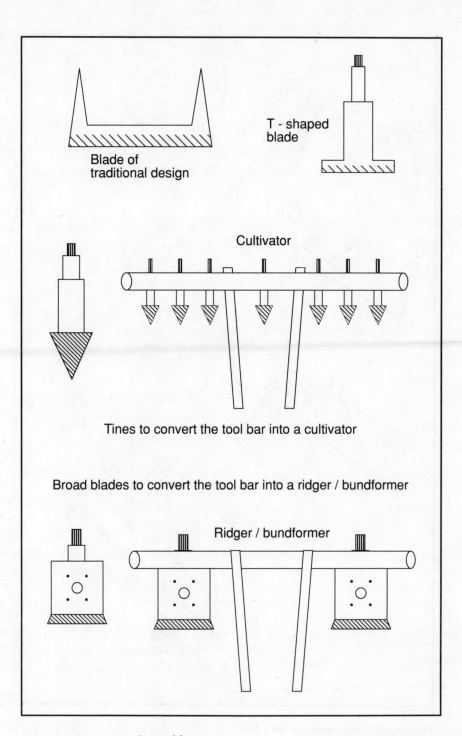

Blade of
traditional design

T - shaped
blade

Cultivator

Tines to convert the tool bar into a cultivator

Broad blades to convert the tool bar into a ridger / bundformer

Ridger / bundformer

New attachments to the tool bar

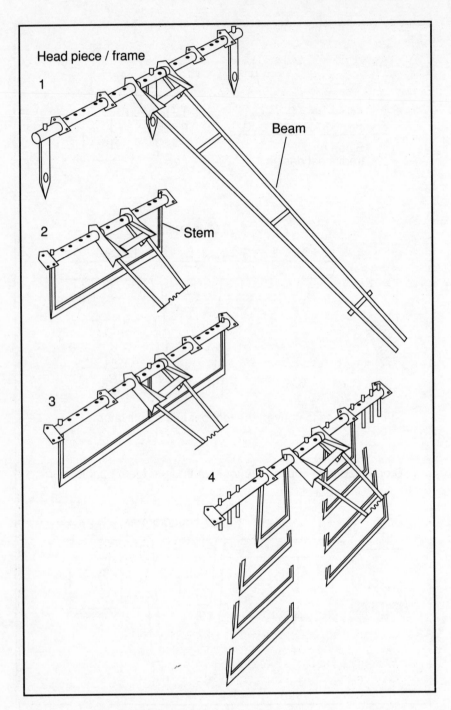

Pipe framed multipurpose tool bar

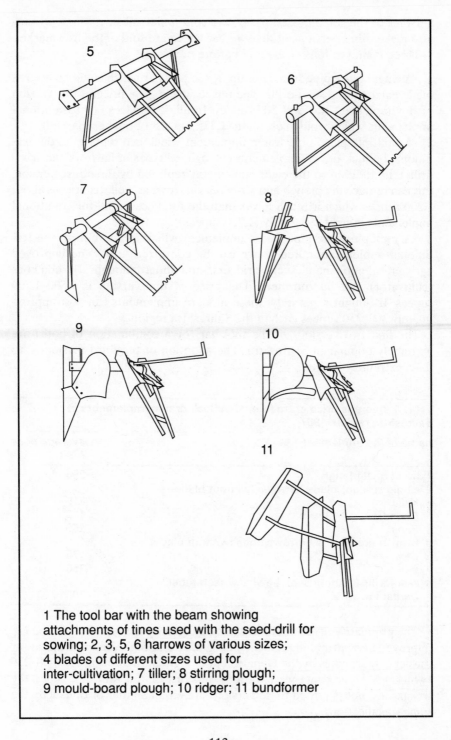

1 The tool bar with the beam showing
attachments of tines used with the seed-drill for
sowing; 2, 3, 5, 6 harrows of various sizes;
4 blades of different sizes used for
inter-cultivation; 7 tiller; 8 stirring plough;
9 mould-board plough; 10 ridger; 11 bundformer

versions of the standardized design are sold under subsidy. Many artisans also make other versions of the tool bar which are sold in the free market.

Three main versions of the tool bar are now used:

1 A single-piece pipe frame multipurpose tool bar which could be used as blade harrows and seed-drills. The unsubsidized 1988 price of this version of the implement was 750–800 rupees. In all, it replaces eight traditional implements which would cost about 1,375 rupees if bought separately.

2 A multiple-piece pipe frame implement which can replace all the traditional bullock-drawn implements (plough, all types of harrows and seed-drills). In addition to the eight implements replaced by the above version, this can replace the plough and *Dhundia* (harrow) as well. Its price is about 1,200 rupees which is much lower than the total cost of all the traditional implements bought separately (1,750 rupees).

3 A multiple-piece pipe frame implement which in addition to the traditional implements noted above can be converted into some improved agricultural implements such as ridgers, mouldboard ploughs, Baroda hoes (cultivator) and bundformers. The price of this version is 1,500–1,700 rupees. If bought separately, these modern implements can cost approximately 300–350 rupees each in the Saurashtra region.

The first two versions of the tool bar (or a combination of both) are extremely popular in Saurashtra. The adoption of the third version is, to date, extremely limited.

Table 1 Average price of traditional bullock-drawn implements in Saurashtra region, 1987

name of the implement	average price (Rs.)
1 traditional plough	250
2 single straight-blade harrows (without blade):	
Kalia	175
Dhundia	125
Rapat	150
3 twin straight-blade harrows/hoes (without blade)	
Bela	175
Beli	150
4 seed-drills (without seed bowl and seed tubes)	
Dantal/Vavania	200

The popularity of the tool bar can be gauged by the fact that, out of 735 improved agricultural implements recognized and registered in Gujarat for the subsidy schemes by the Department of Agriculture during 1965–88, 236 (which is 32 per cent) were various versions of the tool bar. Since the designs are not patented these versions are either similar or of exactly the same specifications.

The tool bar is fabricated in all parts of the Saurashtra region and seems to be most popular in the Rajkot, Amreli and Bhavnagar districts. Many of the fabricators contacted by us reported that farmers from other districts also purchase their tool bars.

Table 2 Distribution of recognized fabricators by districts: March 1989

district	no. of fabricators	per cent	no. per 1 000 farmers
Rajkot	62	26.3	0.31
Surendranagar	21	8.9	0.20
Junagadh	31	13.1	0.13
Amreli	53	22.5	0.38
Jamnagar	17	7.2	0.11
Bhavnagar	52	22	0.28
Saurashtra	236	100	0.23

Source: Gujarat Agro-Industries Corporation Ltd. Ahmedabad

The spread of the tool bar has been limited to the Saurashtra region and has not been adopted in the rest of Gujarat. The reasons probably lie in the agro-climatic conditions and the cropping pattern of the Saurashtra region which are significantly different. There is some evidence to suggest that the tool bar was not found to be suitable in irrigated areas of Kutch and central Gujarat and in the heavy black soils of South Gujarat. Some efforts were made to adapt the tool bar to the agro-climatic conditions of other parts of Gujarat but these versions have not become popular.

While reasons for the non-adoption of the tool bar in other parts of Gujarat need to be probed further, the fact remains that the bar is one of the most popular pieces of bullock-drawn equipment in Gujarat state. The tool bar can be fabricated and repaired by local artisans, with locally available materials. However, some mechanized fabrication facilities are required.

All the fabricators contacted by us owned grinding, drilling and welding machines. A large number of them also owned a lathe, hack saw, power press and cutters. Such facilities are not normally available to village artisans. Fabricators having access to these facilities are usually located in large villages or towns. It is possible that some fabricators have not approached the Department of Agriculture for subsidy because they do not have adequate fabrication facilities to meet standards prescribed by the department. Some fabricators invest in equipment as a response to the introduction of such schemes.

Field tests indicate that, compared to its traditional substitutes, the tool bar is lighter, requires less draft and is more efficient and superior to terms of seed-rate, plant spacing, and quality of work. Not all farmers and artisans, however, are convinced about the higher efficiency of the tool bar, though most of them agree that it requires less effort. The major factor contributing to the popularity of the tool bar is its cost advantage. All respondents interviewed by us agreed that it is less costly both in terms of the initial investment, and repair and maintenance costs. The equipment is multipurpose, and, if adopted fully, can replace 10 traditional and three improved implements. The cost advantages become even more significant when the farmer is eligible for subsidy. Under the present scheme all scheduled caste and scheduled tribe farmers (socially backward farmers) are entitled to a 90 per cent subsidy on the tool bar. (The total amount should not exceed 500 rupees.) Small and marginal farmers, with land holdings of less than three hectares, are entitled to a 50 per cent subsidy also subject to the limit of 500 rupees.

While the subsidy adds to the price advantage of the tool bar over traditional implements, it is almost impossible to isolate the impact of the government subsidy on the diffusion/adaptation process. However, it is certain that the subsidy scheme has contributed significantly to this process.

Almost all the fabricators contacted by us had introduced the tool bar in the market before they were recognized for subsidy. However, five out of 32 said that they had started the fabrication of the tool bar in anticipation of being recognized for subsidy. More than 80 per cent of the 236 registered units were registered with the Department of Agriculture in the early 1980s, after the subsidy schemes was revived. While the cost advantage and the durability of the implement were quite attractive even without the subsidy, smaller farmers have been able to acquire the equipment far more easily under the subsidy scheme.

The tool bar's detachability/attachability feature permits farmers to adopt attachments in stages. Once a farmer buys the pipe frame (head-piece), the choice of accessories/attachments is left to him and he can stagger his investment. This feature provides a lot of flexibility to the farmer in terms of time-phased investment decisions.

Overall, the tool bar has a decisive price advantage over the traditional implements it substitutes due to its relatively low initial cost, longer life, low maintenance costs, multipurpose nature and higher efficiency. The subsidy has added to this cost advantage. However, over the years, the sales of the tool bar have not been stable. The number of pieces sold per year by artisans contacted varies a great deal. While some reported that they sell 30-35 pieces per year, others claimed annual sales of 800 to 1,200. The availability of subsidies may raise or stabilize sales, but a bad monsoon has adverse effects.

Impact of the tool bar

It is difficult to assess the full impact of the introduction and widespread use of the tool bar. A few observations may be made:

1 Changes in occupational pattern: Large-scale use of the tool bar is likely to reduce the need for wooden bullock-drawn implements. Under these circumstances, some carpenters primarily engaged in the fabrication of agricultural implements may diversify to other carpentry-related work such as construction. Some other carpenter households may shift to blacksmithy and other occupations. Eight of the 32 fabricators interviewed by us reported that either they or their forefathers had been engaged in carpentry work.

The fabrication of the tool bar requires the availability of some mechanized fabrication facilities. Not all artisans, however, are able to acquire these facilities. Those who cannot may need to shift to other occupations. Changing market conditions also affect the artisans' production versus repair activities. The relative importance of the latter is likely to increase for those artisans who are not able to acquire mechanized fabrication facilities.

2 Local technological capability: Widespread use of the tool bar has encouraged some artisans to acquire mechanized fabrication facilities. The introduction of the government subsidy on the tool bar also encouraged some fabricators to invest in such facilities. Others who already had such facilities have diversified into the production of the tool bar. The diffusion of the tool bar has contributed both to upgrading production technology and to intra-enterprise diffusion of fabrication facilities. The diffusion of the tool bar has therefore contributed to the wider availability of fabrication equipment. Diffusion has improved the technological capacity of local workshops with respect to the new technologies. Many of the fabricators interviewed by us have diversified into the production and repair of tractor-drawn and other mechanical equipment.

3 The pace of mechanization in agriculture: The emergence of improved bullock-drawn implements (mainly for harrowing, sowing and applying chemical fertilizers) has retarded the adoption of tractor-drawn equipment. The use of the multipurpose tool bar does not affect the magnitude and nature of labour utilization in agriculture. Diffusion of the tool bar has not resulted in any change in the composition of farm labour. However, insofar as the widespread use of the tool bar has slowed down the process of mechanization, displacement of labour is likely to be less.

4 Agricultural productivity: Agro-mechanical technology does not affect yields directly. Yields associated with different techniques are variable and depend on factors such as the use of other agricultural inputs, agro-climatic conditions and the timing of agricultural operations. The widespread use of the tool bar can contribute to improvements in agricultural productivity in two ways. Since the purchase of the tool bar involves less capital investment and maintenance and repair costs, its adoption can release funds for other yield-raising agricultural inputs such as HYV seeds and chemical fertilizers. Also, as the tool bar is now used increasingly as a seed-fertilizer drill, the spacing and the depth of fertilizer application is better controlled. Consequently, the efficiency of fertilizer use and its yield response is likely to increase.

117

The process of tool bar innovation and its widespread adoption has given rise to a variety of external linkages. The most important among these are communications between farmers, fabricators and formal R&D personnel.

Participants and the learning process

Apart from farmers and fabricators, some formal R&D personnel were actively involved in the design and development of the tool bar. The farmers' interest was mainly to reduce the investment they need to incur on the purchase of agricultural implements and their maintenance. Most of the fabricators became involved in the process of production and adaptation of the tool bar because of farmer demand.

Engineers at the Junagadh Research Centre were mainly involved in this work because of their own research interests and the conviction that the tool bar is an extremely useful implement. The government-sponsored subsidy schemes provided a forum where technically trained personnel were required to undertake a technical assessment of the agricultural implements and interact with the fabricators.

Local fabricators not only made the original design but also contributed to further adaptations and diffusion of the tool bar. Modifications to the tool bar were the result of a continuous interaction among local fabricators, farmers and technical personnel. This interaction also provided useful feedback and encouraged use of the local technological capability of local farmers and fabricators. It needs to be emphasized that this interaction was a consequence of the individual initiatives of the R&D personnel at the Junagadh Centre and not of any institutionalized arrangements.

An analysis of the adaptations and modifications which the tool bar has gone through over the years suggests that the changes embody solutions to various problems encountered by the users. The original design of the tool bar was meant to solve some of the problems faced by the farmers. Subsequent modifications are incremental in nature, intended to make the tool bar more multipurpose and flexible by adding adjustments for spacing, depth and other operations. Although modifications are conditioned by local technological capability, the changes are demand-induced.

Some R&D professionals have been in continuous contact with local farmers and artisans to get repeated feedback on the implement. Quite often the R&D people worked on ideas provided by local artisans. Contact was not institutionalized but took place because a few enthusiastic professionals wanted to develop the linkages.

The imitation of popular designs by local artisans is cost-effective insofar as the transfer of technology does not entail any costs. The issue of patents becomes important in this context. Agricultural implements are not adequately covered by the patents act. Consequently, an artisan can approach the Department of Agriculture for a subsidy with a slightly modified version of an implement which has been recognized already. In fact, many artisans in Saurashtra have been granted subsidy for essentially the same version of the multipurpose tool bar. The absence of any registration of the implement designs under the patent act has facilitated the adaptation and diffusion of the tool bar and consequently the transfer of knowledge.

Diffusion is good but the quality of the implement may suffer in the process, as the quality of knowledge acquired by the imitator may not be as good as that of the innovator. All fabricators insisted, though, that modifications effected by them have to be approved by the farmers. Some of the fabricators also have land and can test the implement on their own farms. Other fabricators have farmer friends who use the modified or new implements on their farms and provide feedback. The tool bar was subjected to similar informal field testing before it was sent for its field testing by the Department of Agriculture.

The interface between learning-by-doing (at the level of fabricators) and learning-by-using (at the level of farmers) has contributed significantly to the design, adaptation and diffusion of the tool bar. Such a process of learning has two broad dimensions: knowing how something works and knowing why it works the way it does. These two stages signify two distinct stages in the process of learning.

Farmer-fabricator interaction generates information flows not only about technical problems relating to the innovations, but also about the problems of the farmers. In this way the artisan's knowledge of 'users' is enhanced. In the case of the tool bar, concerned non-artisans have made conscious efforts to understand problems and bridge the gap. The success of their efforts illustrates the potential of professional involvement in the innovation-adaptation-diffusion process.

The policy implications

The story of the tool bar brings into sharper focus the issue of centralized and decentralized innovation-diffusion systems. The centralized (classical) diffusion model has dominated the thinking of scholars and policy makers. Classical diffusion theory fails to capture the complexity of relatively decentralized diffusion systems in which innovations originate from numerous sources and evolve as they diffuse.

This case study substantiates the argument that the diffusion process does not consist primarily of centrally managed information dissemination. The study points to an alternative model of diffusion, based on the concept of decentralized horizontal diffusion of innovations among adopting units. Decentralized, horizontal diffusion systems depend mainly on peer networks for transferring technical innovations amongst local level units.

Given the large inter-regional variations in agro-climatic and other conditions of production, the process of adaptation in agricultural implements has to take place at a decentralized level. There is a need to strengthen artisan-based fabrication networks and combine local experience and scientific knowledge through linkages with the formal R&D systems. A useful starting point for developing these linkages may be an assessment and analysis by R&D personnel of the adaptations and modifications being made at the local level. The absence of such linkages probably explains the non-adoption of multi-purpose tool carriers developed elsewhere.

The technical assessment of various improved agricultural implements in the government subsidy schemes provides a forum for such an interaction. However, such sporadic interaction may not be adequate to understand the underlying reasons behind the tinkering undertaken by farmers and fabricators. More continuous interaction, such as the Junagadh Centre was able to develop, is essential to reap the full benefit of the interface between farmers, fabricators and formal R&D. These linkages should be institutionalized. The initiative for this can come from the state, non-governmental organizations, formal R&D networks or donor agencies.

The state subsidy schemes have contributed in a variety of ways to the development and diffusion of the tool bar. There is a strong case for subsidizing such implements, at least in the short run until sales stabilize. However, present subsidy schemes are not utilized to develop linkages between 'formal' and 'informal' R&D schemes. It may be useful for the Department of Agriculture to monitor and assess the changes which are introduced in the subsidized implements across regions and over time, instead of acting only as a subsidy giving agency.

NGOs and donor agencies can contribute to this process by undertaking funding projects with in-built requirements for developing such linkages. In the long run, the most effective solution lies in the right kind of training for R&D professionals. A curriculum which emphasizes the role of local knowledge in defining the 'context' of the so-called 'scientific' knowledge will go a long way in developing these linkages. Once the beneficial effects of such interaction are understood by R&D professionals, such linkages will grow automatically.

Such interaction will be useful in several ways. It will help to identify the essential technological elements of changes which can be generalized (such as fabrication of the headpiece in three to five pieces). Such interaction will provide insights into the kind of know-how/know-why required to raise local technological capability to meet the local needs. Such an assessment can ascertain whether know-how can suffice to provide the required technological capacity. If so, do fabricators need to follow a sequence of technological upgrading? Assessment can also identify types of training that contribute to the process of innovation, adaptation, and diffusion. Farmer-fabricator-R&D interaction will help to frame policies to enhance local technological capability. This is the important factor influencing the process of technology development and diffusion.

Blacksmithy in Bangladesh

M. MAINUL HAQUE, M. NURUL ISLAM and
M. NAZRUL ISLAM

Introduction

In Bangladesh, blacksmithy is one of the traditional trades, with about 10,000 units. Some 91 per cent of these are located in rural areas, of which 20 per cent are in rural trade centres. Blacksmith units in Bangladesh account for 4.8 per cent of gross output, 8.7 per cent of value added, 22.7 per cent of employment and only 1.4 per cent of fixed assets in the total metalworking industries in the country. Among cottage-type metalworking industries, blacksmiths play a very significant role, representing 41 per cent of all units, 39 per cent of employment and 22 per cent of sales value. Blacksmithy as a profession has an important bearing on the economy of Bangladesh. Small-scale manufacturing as a whole contributes 50 per cent of the manufacturing share of GDP.

Blacksmith units are spread widely but unevenly all over the country. They make a wide variety of products, which can be classified according to various uses:

1 land preparation (plough tip, spade etc.)
2 interculture (hand hoe, rake etc.)
3 harvesting (sickle, curved knife)
4 household (knife, kitchen knife, dao, haisha etc.)
5 housing (carpentry tools, iron pin, angle frame etc.)
6 non-household (rickshaw body parts, trowel, hullar clamp etc.)

Blacksmithy has a very important role in rural Bangladesh in view of its linkages with a variety of other economic activities such as agriculture, and housing.

The main objective of this study is to identify indigenous innovations in blacksmithy in Bangladesh. The study examines not only what influences blacksmiths to work in blacksmithy, but also what inspires them to remain within that profession. The report also looks at factors that help and hinder the development and spread of blacksmithy products in Bangladesh.

The study was carried out in various geographical locations of the country on the basis of concentration of blacksmith units and on reputation for good

DR M. HAQUE, DR N. ISLAM and DR N. ISLAM (Bangladesh) work for the Institute of Appropriate Technology, BUET, Dhaka..

Table 1 Distribution of blacksmith units in Bangladesh

district	no. of units	population	area (sq km)	no. of units per ten thousand population	no. of units per ten sq km
Dhaka	1 038	10 013 731	7 469	1.0	1.39 III
Mymensingh	432	6 568 474	9 668	0.7	0.46
Faridpur	692	4 763 737	6 881	1.5 III	1.00 IV
Tangail	237	2 443 992	3 403	1.0	0.69 VI
Jamalpur	209	2 451 719	3 349	0.9	0.62
Chittagong	598	5 491 330	7 456	1.1	0.81 V
Noakhali	230	3 816 020	5 459	0.6	0.42
Sylhet	5 593	5 655 543	12 719	1.0	0.46
Comilaa	457	6 881 003	6 602	0.7	0.69 VI
Chittagong Hill Tract	104	751 692	13 180	1.4 IV	0.08
Rajshahi	235	5 270 141	9 456	0.4	0.23
Bogra	191	2 727 973	3 887	0.7	0.50
Rangpur	951	6 510 050	9 595	1.5 III	1.00 IV
Dinajpur	266	3 199 965	6 565	0.8	0.38
Pabna	387	3 423 704	4 732	1.1	0.81 V
Khulna	569	4 329 320	12 167	1.3	0.46
Jessore	1 038	4 019 993	6 573	2.6 I	1.58 II
Barisal	520	4 666 734	7 298	1.1	0.69 VI
Kushtia	584	2 291 997	3 439	2.5 II	1.70 I
Patuakhali	257	1 843 001	4 095	1.4 IV	0.62
Total in Bangladesh	9 588	87 120 119	143 993	1.1	0.656

* The old districts have been divided under the present administrative reorganization and presently the number of districts is 64.

Source: Statistical Yearbook, BBS, 1986 and BSCIC Survey, 1983

quality blacksmithy products. The study covers 11 out of 64 newly created administrative districts: Bogra, Brahmanbaria, Chittagong, Comilla, Dhaka, Jessore, Kushtia, Lalmanirhat, Mymensingh, Rangpur and Thakurgaon. Out of these districts six were chosen for intensive investigation and samples from these six were collected for testing. The selection of blacksmith artisans for detailed investigation from each district was made on a random sampling basis. This was after due consultation with a wider audience of people from the locality in order to have a mix of well-known and ordinary artisans from each location. The technical analysis of products has been restricted to only two products which are in wide use in Bangladesh: the plough tip (used in land preparation) and the kitchen knife.

122

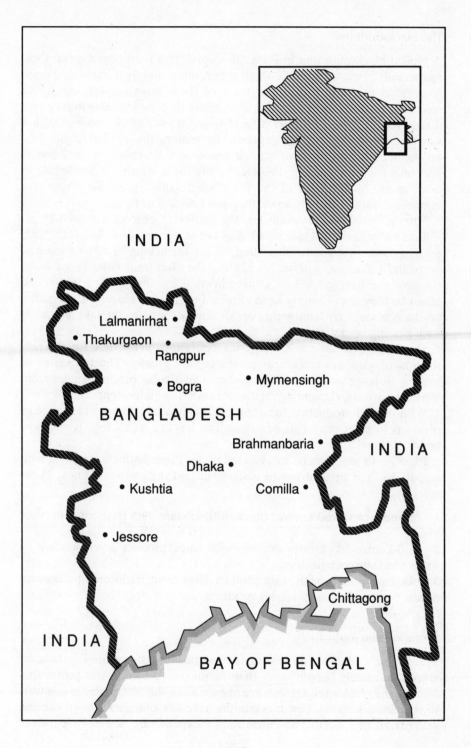

The blacksmith unit

A typical blacksmith unit in Bangladesh produces hard-edged metal tools and usually operates within a small space, often merely a four-sided open room with thatched roof. Since most of these units are located at the roadside, in open places or under trees, there is scope for using more space if required. A blower (*hapor*) is fixed at one corner of the room in such a way that the shallow bed in the ground for making fire and the forging bed are nearer and within hand-stretch reach of the artisan. A tool box is generally used for holding the blacksmithy tools, which are handmade in most cases. At the right of the place where the artisan sits, there is a quenching bath — usually an earthen pot full of water.

Forging and heat treatment are the two main processes known to artisans in Bangladesh. Plain water and salt water are used for quenching. Some artisans use spent lubricating oil for quenching of some products, particularly machinery parts. For heating, the blacksmiths mostly use wood charcoal and bamboo as fuel. During heating, the flow of air is controlled either by blower or rotating hand blower. Forging and shaping blacksmithy products is done by hammering on an anvil or a heavy metal piece after each heating operation.

The forging, heating and tempering operations performed for the fabrication of various blacksmithy products vary greatly. The frequency of heating, forging and cooling cycles for a particular product varies from artisan to artisan, depending on the artisan's own judgement.

With limited production facilities, blacksmiths fabricate a wide range of products to meet consumer demands. The level of technology is very low and traditional.

Blacksmith units can be categorized under three distinct categories with respect to their present use of equipment and their product lines. These are:

1 ordinary (not well known) blacksmith artisans with traditional product lines;
2 well-known blacksmith artisans with some product diversification or some product specialization;
3 blacksmith units with wide product lines from traditional blacksmith products to modern engineering products.

Evolution and motivation

Traditionally, blacksmiths belong to a particular caste of the Hindu community but lately people other than Hindus have chosen this profession. Usually the blacksmith artisans are known as *karmaker* (master in fabricating blacksmith tools). Few blacksmiths have any other sources of earning apart from this work. The entire family expenditure is met by earnings from blacksmithy, which varies between Tk1,000 and Tk3,500 per month depending on the number of workers engaged in the business.

Family members (usually males) associate themselves with black-smithing activities from their early childhood. Children come to the work-place as helping hands and gain substantial skill and experience during their apprentice years. They then start their own separate business or continue with their elders as working partners. As a result, family earnings are not so badly affected after the death of the head of the family. Family earning security is a prime motive in various family members being involved with the business.

Innovation

Innovations in blacksmithy have taken place either for incremental tech-nological change or to match particular requirements of users.

Traditionally, the blacksmith artisans produced agricultural and household tools. Demand from customers for new products, particularly non-household items, has motivated the artisans towards newer skills. Non-traditional black-smith products (such as carpentry tools, angle frames, machine parts and rural housing hardware) have a good demand throughout the year. Tra-ditional products (such as plough tips, spades, kitchen knives, sickles and hand hoes) have a more seasonal demand (and longer replacement period).

Urban demands for non-traditional blacksmithy products have stimu-lated product innovation from blacksmiths, as is evident from the follow-ing example. In Mymensingh district, one artisan reported that he is now producing certain products (such as the steering fork of a rickshaw, power tiller blades, and trowels) which were not in his product list three years ago. When asked why he changed his product line, the reply was very simple: 'I produce according to customers' demand'. He added that he feels proud in producing these products because no other artisan from his locality can do so. Another question was asked about the incentive behind the new effort. The artisan reacted sharply and said that the profit margin in these products is much higher (40 to 100 per cent) than in traditional products. Hence it appears that diversification in product de-mand ensures better profit for the artisans and that motivates the artisans towards newer skills.

In most cases, blacksmiths inherit the business from their ancestors and continue to work with the knowledge and skill they acquire from their forebears. So, at the start-up of their business they usually do not think about skill development. However, they bear the responsibility of meeting the demand for agricultural implements, household tools and various im-plements used in all farm activities. Blacksmiths must produce quality products with their limited installations and equipment in order to stay in business.

The interaction between blacksmiths and their customers contributes towards product development innovations.

For example, in Comilla and Brahmanbaria districts it was observed that blacksmith artisans are quite effectively producing blade hoes and rotavator blades which are used in farm implements like power tillers and tractors. Traditionally, after showing wear-and-tear these blades would have been replaced with new ones which were not of local origin. Over time, encouraged by farmers, blacksmiths have managed to start producing these blades.

In Brahmanbaria, the artisan who was making rotavator blades when the researchers visited him was asked how he started making blades. The artisan nodded towards the farmer who came in with the order and explained that they had discussed the blades about a year ago and he produced a sample set for the rotavator. These worked well and from then on orders started coming in. Blacksmiths can produce these blades at half the cost of imported ones. Farmers are satisfied with the durability of blades produced by the artisans.

The blacksmith units situated in various regions/districts of the country cater mainly to local (regional) needs but some have a market outside the regions, spreading over other parts of the country. Traditional marketing practices of these units can be classified under the following heads:

1 catering to small individual orders;
2 direct sales at the market place;
3 sales through showings at the place of work;
4 advance supply to the hardware shops for future marketing.

Blacksmiths usually service individual orders placed directly by the customer and they usually depend on the local markets. Occasionally they receive orders from customers far away. Customers may travel 40 km to more famous artisans whose products are more durable and of better quality.

The marketing pattern has changed greatly in recent years. Along with the traditional channels, new marketing practices are in place. These include whole order supply (usually to middlemen or to hardware shops) and sub-contracting. In those areas where light engineering workshops exist or are being established, many artisans receive wholesale orders from these workshops. This change in marketing patterns is a stimulating factor for the artisans because they find that their skills are in great demand.

Blacksmith units producing non-traditional items are usually more involved in supplying wholesale orders and occasionally sub-contracting (though artisans do not happen to know that they are working as sub-contractors). Their work includes the production of components and sub-assembly.

Innovations in blacksmithy: technical findings

In order to identify the innovations in blacksmithy, samples of plough tips

126

and kitchen knives were collected from among the surveyed units. Necessary laboratory tests were performed to form an opinion about the fabrication techniques used, heat treatment performed (if any) and possible results to be expected during use. The tests were performed basically to establish why the products of some artisans are considered superior and are sold at higher prices.

The major raw material for kitchen knives and plough tips is mild steel. This is procured by blacksmith units both from wholesalers and retailers situated in and around the place of operation. Sometimes blacksmith units purchase raw materials from 'hawkers', rural floating traders. Quite often the necessary raw materials are provided by customers. Raw materials are identified by artisans from their intuitive judgement and experience. Artisans apply their intricate knowledge either by hearing the sound, by scratching or by seeing thickness.

Forging

Blacksmithy products are invariably hot-forged. If forging is performed at temperatures about the recrystallization temperature of the metal, then one gets well-developed metal grains with no deformation. On the other hand, if forging continues below the recrystallization temperature then the metal grains are distorted and the metal grains somewhat harder. This indicates residual stress on the piece of metal. Therefore, knowledge about recrystallization temperature and temperature measuring is crucial for hot-forging.

Since blacksmithy artisans do not have any formal knowledge about the recrystallization temperature, they usually apply their intuitive judgement by seeing the colour of the hot metal. No temperature measuring devices are being used at present by the artisans and they rely solely on their experience. Technical findings suggest wide variations in forging operations performed by various artisans leading to differences in product quality. Determining appropriate forging temperatures for different products requires ingenuity and a level of skill.

Heat treatment

Heat treatment is a very important part of blacksmithy. Small differences in heat treatments may cause noticeable variations in the properties of the product. The major aspects in heat treatment are the temperature to which the metal is to be heated along with the duration of heating and the cooling rate. The cooling rate is one of the important factors which controls the hardening of the product.

The correct heat treatment procedures varies with the composition of the metal used. Heat treatment temperatures and cycles are different for different types of metal. Most artisans are now aware of this. Different quenching baths (water, brine, oil etc.) give different cooling rates. Most of the artisans invariably use water as a quenching media. Correct perception about the heat treatment procedure leads to better quality products.

Table 2 shows a summary of the technical findings along with innovations identified. Metallographic examination for hardness is the best of the sample. It may be noted from the investigation that the market value of the kitchen knife of the third artisan and plough tip of the last artisan is higher than the market value of the same products of other artisans. Customers are knowledgeable about the availability of superior quality products of specific artisans. If these better products are available, customers prefer them even at a higher price. Profit margins vary from 10 to 92 per cent which indicates people's perceptions of quality. When the customers notice the durability of a particular product they note its maker. This confidence remains for ever and whenever they buy blacksmithy products they look for products by the same artisan.

The learning process in blacksmithy is not a one-shot affair. It is continuous in nature. During the learning process artisans apply their own intuitive judgement about each of the production processes. This leads to product quality development as well as product diversification. In blacksmithy, learning takes place in various forms, and all these forms have their distinct contribution towards innovations that are taking place.

Learning by doing

Learning by doing is fundamental for the skill development of blacksmithy artisans. Any blacksmithy activity or fabrication of a particular product is a simultaneous integration of a large number of discrete past experiences gained through learning by doing. The main feature of artisans' skill is their intricate knowledge about the product under question and the metal to be used, along with the production operations to be performed.

Traditional kitchen knives have two parts: a blade and a wooden flat bar with hooks. The blade has to be fixed to the wooden bar. The knife is fabricated by the blacksmithy artisan and the wooden flat bar is procured separately by the client/user. One artisan from Brahmanbaria who has popularity throughout the region for his quality kitchen knives developed a knife with two metal stands which need not be fixed with the wooden flat bar. The design was accepted by the customers and quickly became diffused throughout the market. This change in design which the artisan brought ensured him an additional profit margin of 80 per cent over the production cost. Now the same design is being duplicated by other artisans.

Responding to these developments, the artisan from Brahmanbaria has evolved a new strategy of putting an identification mark (the artisan's first name) on his products. Due to customers' confidence, this kitchen knife product is sold in the same region at a higher price.

Learning by seeing

The blacksmithy artisans do not use technical drawings. They usually rely on their own intuitive judgement and sometimes on verbal instruction from clients. Replication or imitation is widespread in blacksmithy. By seeing prototypes, particularly for non-traditional products, the artisans learn enough to fabricate the same. Rotavator blades, power tiller blades and huller clamps are some of the products which the artisans have learned to produce by seeing prototypes. However, not all the artisans replicate or imitate equally, due to differences in judgement and ability.

Learning through informal exchange of ideas

Interaction between artisans and users through exchange of experiences and/or ideas about a particular product is an important form of learning. This contributes greatly to the process of innovation in blacksmithy.

Many new product lines come from interaction between artisans and user/client groups. It may be noted that this exchange of ideas between the artisans and users is virtually costless, while it provides important benefits to the learning process of the artisans as well as to the felt need of the users.

For example, in surveyed areas (particularly in Comilla and Brahman-baria) it was observed that farmers are using different sizes of plough tips in their bullock-driven ploughs. The size and shape of the wooden frames of the plough also differ to some extent, requiring different sizes of plough tips. The farmers inspired this change through noting problems caused by variations in draft power of their bullocks, and variations in soil types. Fabrication of different sizes of plough tips was not considered to be a problem by the blacksmiths and they responded to the innovative change.

Learning through training

Apart from the interaction between artisans and users, the exchange of ideas among the artisans themselves is crucial for the dissemination of knowledge and skill development. The potential of learning through training has not been reaped fully and is still family-based due to the absence of an organized drive to create training facilities for artisans. Informal interaction between the artisans takes place regionally but such interactions are inadequate for effective learning. Skill development in blacksmithy is mostly linked to on-the-job training.

Diffusion of process innovation takes place at a slower rate compared to the diffusion of product innovation which takes place at a faster rate, keeping pace with market/user demand. This is because, in blacksmithy, the skill is individual specific. The skill of a good artisan cannot be

Table 2 Summary of technical findings for the products of different artisans

product	raw material used for fabrication	hardness	forging	heat treatment	observation	areas of innovativeness
boti	mild steel containing <0.2% carbon	– somewhat higher hardness than normal with such steel – some residual stress remains	– grains slightly distorted indicating forging continued until temperature dropped below recrystallization temperature	no heat treatment performed	– choice of material improper – forging should have stopped at higher temp. – no hardening, so not likely to give good result	nil
boti	mild steel <0.2% carbon	– gradual increase in hardness from bottom to the top of cutting edge	– structure different at the bottom and top end of cutting edge – small but well-developed grains at the bottom indicating a fast cooling rate – top edge quenched – forging temperature correctly chosen	no heat treatment performed	– not possible to retain sharpness at the bottom – can be rectified by reheating to above transformation temperature and quenching in water and tempering	○ forging ○ quenching
boti	mild steel containing about 0.2% carbon	– only the cutting edge hardened – hardness is maximum that can be obtained from the steel of this composition	– original fabrication structure lost because of heat treatment	heat treatment done successfully	– fabrication technique and heat treatment cycle chosen correctly and applied intelligently	○ fabrication technique ○ forging ○ heat treatment ○ a little in raw material selection

Table 2 Summary of technical findings for the products of different artisans

product	raw material used for fabrication	hardness	forging	heat treatment	observation	areas of innovativeness
boti	mild steel containing <0.2% carbon	– no hardening performed – hardness of cutting edge and blunt edge different	– grains well developed, forging performed at temperature above the recrystallization temperature – variation in structure between cutting edge and blunt edge	no heat treatment performed	– two pieces of metals welded by hot-forging or after forging – cutting edge was carborized by prolonged heating in charcoal – likely to develop a very high hardness at cutting edge by quenching	o forging
boti	very low carbon steel containing <0.12% carbon	– not likely to develop hardness by heat treatment	– forging temperature was adequate	no heat treatment performed	– material selected not suitable	o forging
fala	mild steel containing <0.2% carbon	– uniform hardness on all the points	– no deformed grains, forging performed above recrystallization temperature	no heat treatment performed		o forging
fala	low carbon steel containing <0.15% carbon	– higher hardness than normal – some residual stress remains	– distortion in grains, forging continued at lower temperature	no heat treatment performed	– likely to corrode at faster rate	nil
fala	mild steel containing <0.2% carbon	– hardness uniform all over – no residual stress	– grain well-developed forging temperature correctly chosen	no heat treatment performed	– likely to corrode less severely, but wear out at faster rate	o forging

1. mild steel; carbon content 0.15%–0.45%
2. suitable raw material for knives and other sharp items is medium carbon steel: carbon content 0.4%–0.6%
3. recrystallization temperature: temperature at which the crystals are formed afresh (re-birth of crystals)

transferred verbally unless one follows his production operations very carefully for a long period of time. That is possible only by working with him in a learning-by-doing process.

Blacksmiths commented that other forms of learning, such as organized institutional training and exchange of experience and demonstration, are not helpful to newcomers at the initial stage. A new entrant must first of all become used to the nature of the job and must develop an open mind to become a good artisan. However, demonstration is carried out as a medium of instruction for learning by doing.

Many come for training from master artisans, but due to the tough nature of the job very few are retained and get fully trained. Normally, those who come for training work as assistants to the artisans. The artisans interviewed trained, on average, two people each, in addition to family members.

Among various production and marketing constraints, the study shows that lack of sufficient working capital is the most significant factor putting blacksmith units at a disadvantage. Lack of investment capital and non-availability of raw materials are two other significant factors aggravating the problems. Asked to comment on the order of priority, blacksmiths spoke of the non-availability of raw materials as the second most serious problem after the need for working capital. Investment capital problems were placed in the third position.

All the artisans expressed zeal and enthusiasm for better utilization of their skills. One artisan from Lalmonirhat said 'We know the art of survival and whatever comes our way we try to fabricate'. He continued, 'skill is not given, it has to be acquired and for that we rely most on learning by doing. Whatever we have achieved is by our own efforts and we have never received any formal support.' Such observations of the artisans are quite revealing and demonstrate their latent potential. Their need is to consolidate socially, economically and technologically in order to promote their innovations for the benefit of the economy. They are confident enough to meet future skill requirements in blacksmithy if due attention is given to their problems. They do not want help out of sympathy because skill is their strength. They want support in upgrading their skills, because better application of skills leads to higher productivity.

When questioned, artisans said that currently they do not borrow money from any institutional source. Among non-institutional sources, only friends and relatives were mentioned as possible sources. But such borrowing does not constitute any significant amount and is for a very short period of time.

Formal R&D support is needed in the production process, not only to introduce innovations but also to promote the existing innovations of the artisans. This contributes towards skill development and an increase in productivity. The formal R&D support should concentrate on the following three areas of innovation as identified through laboratory investigations.

1   A 'spark test' is a simple visual technique to identify the carbon content of the metal. One can hold the metal on a grinder and watch the sparks from it. Long and continuous sparks indicate low carbon content while short and scattered sparks indicate high carbon content. Such tests help the artisans to identify raw materials. For the test, the artisans need access to a grinder at the time of raw material purchase. Whether keeping a grinder in retail shops is feasible and how effectively the artisans would benefit are some of the issues for research. Again, how to impart knowledge about the appropriate properties of metals suitable for different product types has to be looked at along with the form of knowledge dissemination.

2   Could artisans be made aware of the re-crystallization temperatures of different metals through training programmes or could suitable and easy-to-handle temperature-indicating devices be made available to them at reasonable cost? Is it possible to standardize the knowledge of the skilled artisan about forging for the benefit of others? Resolving these questions would benefit the artisans in their development of skills.

3   R&D organizations should try to disseminate information among artisans about the correct heat treatment procedures for different metals. Whether formal training is enough for the purpose should be explored.

Good communication between formal R&D organizations and black-smithy artisans is required. Unless R&D people try to understand problems of the artisans, no effective results will emerge. Formal R&D support needs an informal method of dissemination. This is possible through informal contacts and through the drive to understand others.

Principal training needs are for selection of raw materials, forging and heat treatment. Artisans with different skill levels cannot be trained in one batch. Some of the skilled artisans (master craftsmen) may be used to train the people at lower levels. There is a need to train new people to take blacksmithy as a profession. Those in the trade should be selected for training programmes. Newcomers may receive training from artisans in the trade.

Bangladesh Small and Cottage Industries Corporation (BSCIC), with the assistance from UNDP/ILO, has undertaken to provide 'on the job' training on carpentry products to groups of artisans from a selected six districts of the country. As part of the incentive, trained artisans are assured of bank loans. Artisans not participating in the training course do not receive easy credit from the bank. Similar product-specific (kitchen knife, plough tip, etc.) modular training should be organized in groups for the blacksmiths with different skill levels throughout the country. Bank loans on easy terms should be ensured for them.

Recommendations

At the national level there is a need to mobilize policy support in favour of blacksmiths so they can find required raw materials in the market at a reasonable cost. The products under study are not substitutable with machine-made products and hence they enjoy a monopoly. But their quality largely depends upon the quality of raw materials used and upon the skill of the artisans. These products are not imported and hence the whole domestic demand is met from local production. Domestic protection of these products should be directed towards innovation promotion to achieve productivity gains and ensure better quality.

Blacksmith artisans need help to meet their fuel needs. They use charcoal from wood and bamboo, which has low heating value. Previously the artisans used to use coal/coke, but now this is not readily available.

Since artisans have limited knowledge about the size of the market, they need reliable market information about raw materials and products. Blacksmith artisans should have their own forum. As they are not organized in a group like private investors from the formal sectors, they cannot lobby to mobilize policy support in their favour. The artisans need to be organized in a group, like a trade association, so they can raise their voice and bargain for their demands.

Blacksmithy is one of the most important non-farm activities in Bangladesh. It has an important bearing on agriculture, housing, household and non-household sectors of the national economy. Blacksmiths should be recognized as an important social group and as important agents for rural economic development. They have much knowledge and skill to contribute to the generation and development of innovations. Wide product diversification that has taken place in blacksmithy indicates their capability to meet changing demands over time.

Technological innovations in blacksmithy need to be assessed for their potential for large-scale diffusion. The basic approach towards technology assessment in blacksmithy should include:

1 synthesis of experiences due to artisan-user interaction;
2 identification of formal R&D support needs for informal R&D system;
3 skill development through appropriate training;
4 assessment of marketing support needs;
5 credit needs.

In order to undertake these tasks, an appropriate stance relating to innovation promotion in blacksmithy has to be formulated. An appropriate institutional framework for development of innovation needs to be developed. The following suggestions are made for the promotion of innovations in blacksmithy:

1 Existing innovations in blacksmithy deserve appreciation. Formal R&D support needs should be assessed, keeping in mind the informal R&D

processes that are taking place in blacksmithy. R&D efforts should be directed mainly towards skill upgrading.

2 Training programmes should be organized in modular form for different categories of blacksmiths as well as in different areas of innovation. Considering the huge and widespread training requirement, both government and non-governmental organizations should come forward to undertake the task.

3 Various alternative credit facilities should be explored for providing both working and investment capital on easy terms to potential artisans.

4 Necessary marketing support (supply of raw materials, information on price etc.) needs to be ensured on a sustainable basis.

5 To upgrade the manufacturing base of existing blacksmith units for future innovations, the Bangladesh Small and Cottage Industries Corporation (BSCIC), which is responsible for the development of small and cottage industries, may help in selecting appropriate tools, instruments and machineries required by different categories of blacksmith artisans. BSCIC may also make recommendations for loans from financing agencies.

6 Products produced by different blacksmiths should be catalogued along with test results. This should be available to prospective buyers. In addition, these products may be displayed at different BSCIC offices along with the identities of the artisans.

7 For effective use of resources, it is necessary that assistance to the blacksmiths is provided in packaged form, linked to their training programme. The package may include skill-development, supply of hardware, supply of credit and marketing assistance. To facilitate the delivery of the package assistance, the formation of blacksmith organizations should be encouraged.

Indigenous innovations in blacksmithy play an important role in the context of rural Bangladesh. Most of these innovations remain untapped and/or under-utilized. Therefore, a strong political and administrative commitment is needed to promote innovations in blacksmithy as part of non-farm technology development.

Improved ghattas (water mills) in Nepal

GANESH RAM SHRESTHA and KIRAN MAN SINGH

Background

Nepal is a small landlocked country which borders on China to the north and India to the south, east and west. Agriculture is the mainstay of Nepal's economy, accounting for more than 68 per cent of GDP and 75 per cent of exports. Farming provides a livelihood for 94 per cent of the population. According to the 1981 census, Nepal has a population of about 15 million with a growth rate of 2.66 per cent annually. The per capita income was estimated at only US $160.

Of the total land area of 141,000sq km, 32 per cent is covered by forest, 52 per cent is under pasture, meadows, barren and perpetual snow and only 16 per cent considered to be arable. However, the country can be divided into three well-defined physio-geographical belts running east to west: the *mountain* region with altitudes ranging from 16,000–29,000 feet, the *hill* region with altitudes of 1,000–10,000 feet and the *terai* region with altitudes varying between 200–1,000 feet above sea level. The terai is narrow flat land, average width of 30km, along the southern border which is an extension of the Indian Gangetic plain. This terai region covers approximately 23 per cent of the land area and produces the bulk of the country's food grains. The hill region consists of high ridges and steep slopes, interspersed with many river valleys. It covers nearly 43 per cent of the land area. The majority of the population lives in this region. The snow-capped mountain region runs parallel to the border with Tibet on the north. The region covers around 34 per cent of the country. Livestock play an important role in the economy of this mountain region.

Nepal is drained by numerous rivers. Depending upon their source and discharge, they can be classified into three types:

1 *major* rivers: Karnali, Gandaki and Kosi. These rivers originate in the Himalayas and carry snow-fed flows. They are therefore perennial and offer promising water sources for irrigation and hydropower development.
2 *medium* rivers: Babai, West Rapti, Bagmati, Kamala, Kankai and Mechi. These rivers originate in the Mahabharat Range and are fed by

MR G.R. SHRESTHA (Nepal) was Section Chief of the Agricultural Development Bank in Nepal and is now Director of the Centre for Rural Technology, Kathmandu.

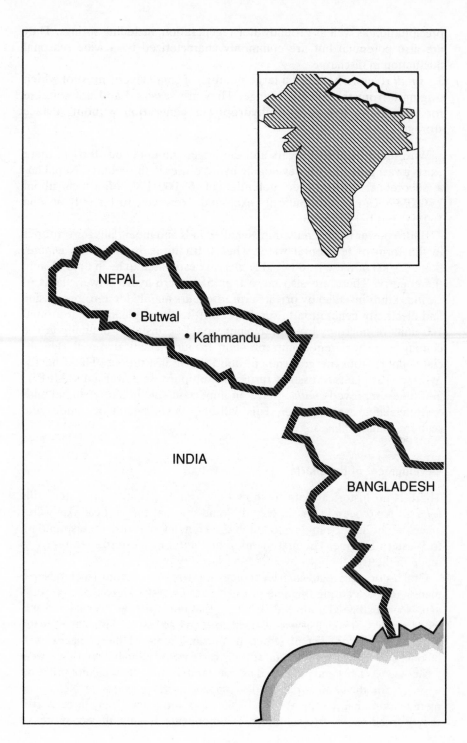

precipitation as well as groundwater regeneration, including springs. They are also perennial but are commonly characterized by a wide seasonal fluctuation in discharge.

3   *small* rivers: There are a large number of small rivers, most of which originate from the Siwalik Range. They are seasonal and not suitable for year-round irrigation or hydropower generation without surface storage.

With these numerous rivers and the largely mountainous terrain, there exists a vast potential for developing hydro power in the country. Nepal has a theoretical hydropower potential of 83,000MW, of which about 25,000MW can be economically exploited. However, so far only around 160MW has been tapped.

Hydro power has been used in Nepalese hills and mountains for centuries in the form of horizontal water wheels, traditionally known as *ghattas*. Some 25,000 of these traditional *ghattas* are estimated to be in operation in the country. There are also more than 550 micro-hydro power plants of various kinds installed by private entrepreneurs mainly for agro-processing and electricity generation in rural areas. It has been planned that around 100 units of micro-hydro power plant would be installed annually in the coming years by potential entrepreneurs through technical as well as financial support from the government and lending institutions. These micro-hydro power plants (crossflow turbines, multipurpose power units (MPPU) and other improved *ghattas*) have an important role in harnessing abundantly available water power. This will help development of remote and scattered small villages.

Development of the *ghatta*

There is no historical data to show how long the traditional water mills (*ghatta*) have been in use in Nepal. Some say that the vertical axis water wheel might have been developed in the Himalayas, its use then spreading to Western Europe. The first mention of *ghattas* in Western literature was made in the travel books by Kirkpatrick in 1793.

Oral history tells that *ghatta* technology was transferred from Tibet to Nepal many years ago during the time of the Newar Dynasty. More than 300 years ago, Nepal had good trade with Tibet. At that time Tibet was considered as a 'bowl of gold'. Though it was difficult to travel across the Himalayas, many Nepalese went to Tibet in search of fortune. Some of the Nepalese who belonged to the *Nakarmi* (metalworker) caste were fascinated with the *ghatta* technology in Tibet and pioneered its transfer to Nepal. But it did not prove an easy job for them. In order to develop one working *ghatta* in Nepal, the metalworkers had to travel over 10 times to and from Tibet. In each visit they learned one or two solutions or components. Finally, they could make

138

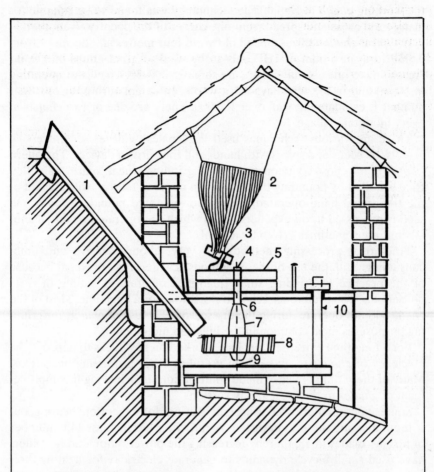

1 Chute, delivering the water to the side of the wheel behind the shaft
2 Hopper (basket)
3 Bird (vibrator) to keep the grain moving
4 Rynd (forged metal piece)
5 Grinding stones
6 Shaft, metal
7 Hub, wood (thick shaft)
8 Wheel or tirl, with obliquely set paddles on thick shaft
9 Metal pin and bottom piece
10 Lever, lifting device to adjust gap between grinding stones

Source: B.R.Saubelle and A.Bachmann

Traditional horizontal water mill

the working *ghatta* in Nepal. The technology was found to be suitable for many rural areas and spread from one corner of the country to another.

A typical *ghatta* utilizes a head of two to four metres and develops from 0.5HP to a maximum of 1HP only to be used to grind grains into flour. According to one estimate, there are some 25,000–30,000 *ghattas* operating in Nepal and in the Himalayas as a whole. In neighbouring regions their number is estimated at well over 100,000. There are one or two *ghattas* in every mountain village.

There are various techniques used in Nepalese villages for processing cereals, oil seeds and spices with hand- and foot-driven devices. The quern (*janto*) is the most common method of grinding wheat, maize or millet. Rice is hulled by pounding it in a wooden or stone mortar, with the aid of the traditional hand-operated and/or foot-operated pounder (*dhiki*). Oil seed is processed in oil expellers (*kols*) which are operated mainly manually but are sometimes driven by animals.

Traditional processing methods are very labour-intensive and time-consuming. Still, the use of these methods is widespread in Nepal because of the practice of grinding small quantities of grain at a time in rural households. The preference is not to store flour for a long time. Most of the *ghattas* do not operate during the dry season. The use of *ghattas* for grinding purposes is most common in the hills and mountains.

For a long time entrepreneurs have worked on new ideas to improve the efficiency of *ghattas* to make them useful in other processing operations. Many of these thinkers have made contributions in achieving the improvement of *ghattas* to the present-day version.

Some experimenters tried using ball bearings for the bottom bearing, but without a casing these soon rusted. A carpenter has increased the number of turbine blades to 18, thereby increasing the power output. Some millers have used small bicycle dynamos to generate electricity for lighting their mills. During the 1950s the establishment of rice and oil mills was promoted in the terai to respond to an increased market for processed foods. Powered by diesel engines or by electricity where available, the mills were owned mainly by wealthier farmers and businessmen due to higher capital costs. This provided further incentive for local *ghatta* innovation.

In the 1960s the Balaju Yantra Shala (BYS), a joint venture between the Swiss Development Corporation and the Nepalese Government, undertook to design, fabricate and install a small number of propeller turbines to drive grain-milling machines. These machines quickly became popular but owners/operators faced serious maintenance and repair problems. The design of the system allowed sediment to enter into the turbines, resulting in rapid wear and tear of moving parts. The interest of entrepreneurs in propeller turbines gradually decreased due to the high occurrence of repair and maintenance problems until the early 1970s. Then the massive increase in oil prices changed the situation in favour of small hydro power plants.

Operating costs in the diesel-powered mills rose considerably. Both donor agencies and Nepalese artisans and entrepreneurs initiated new investigations into micro-hydro power development for small rural mills. From previous experiences with propeller turbines, it became clear that the ideal turbine would have to be adaptable to the different conditions of various rural locations. One of the operational problems encountered in the original propeller turbine was that of controlling the inflow of water to allow an installation to be operational even with a reduced volume of water in the dry season. It soon became clear that turbines constructed on the Banki-Michell model (also known as a crossflow turbine) could be suitable to accommodate the above requirements. These turbines are characterized by a simple drum-shaped runner and a right-angled water inflow, which permit the turbine to be welded in simple engineering workshops.

The development of the new locally-made crossflow turbines solved many of the problems facing mill upgrading, but not all of them. These turbines required higher heads and larger flows than those available to many traditional mills. Even though the crossflow turbine mills could support a wide range of processing operations, their costs deterred poorer mill owners. More local innovation, inspired by local artisans, developed new possibilities for *ghatta* improvement.

Evolution of the improved *ghatta*

Even after the development and distribution of the crossflow turbine on a much wider scale, it was always felt there was a need to develop an appropriate technology for modifying the *ghatta* technology. The aim was to improve efficiency to make it suitable to run rice hullers and oil expellers in small mills in the rural areas. Rather than radically altering the design (as in the introduction of crossflow turbines), the new innovations sought small, simple improvements upon the basic *ghatta*. One local artisan, Akkal Man Nakarmi, a small workshop owner, has been a major creative participant in four modifications introduced during the 1980s. Both on his own and working with technology agencies, Nakarmi has enabled upgraded mill technology to be available and affordable to poorer mills and communities.

Improved ghatta 1 — *RECAST*
The first effort was made at the Research Centre for Applied Science and Technology (RECAST) following a suggestion in 1980 by Mr Jean Gimpel, a French scientist. Mr Gimpel furnished drawings of a Romanian horizontal water mill. The main modifications in this prototype consisted of the replacement of the wooden blades, and a new bottom bearing. Other improvements were a closed chute and a covered grinding chamber. The prototype was tested in a mill above Godavari. The power output was improved by around 80 per cent. However, the grinding performance was

improved by only 50 per cent as the grinding technology was not taken into consideration for improvement. Although RECAST planned to work for the improvement of the grinding device, these endeavours did not go beyond the pilot stage.

Improved ghatta 2 — GATE

In the meantime, GATE (the German Appropriate Technology Exchange) was involved in a project to improve the traditional Nepalese water mill within the scope of the programme 'Activating traditional indigenous techniques'. After a lot of studies and the recruitment of technical personnel, GATE organized a workshop on the improved water mill in Nepal in co-operation with RECAST in December 1984. GATE and RECAST joined together to improve the *ghatta* by introducing wooden runners as well as a wooden crossflow turbine developed by Mr G. Dotti of France. The major assumptions made for both the designs are the possibility of getting the wooden parts from millers or local craftsmen, and the ability of local black-smiths to manufacture certain metal parts in rural areas. However, the GATE wooden runner and the Dotti wooden crossflow turbine did not succeed under Nepalese conditions. Further R&D and promotional work on them was discontinued.

Nakarmi's own efforts — the MPPU

In 1981, Mr A.M. Nakarmi made a valuable contribution to the direct improvement of the *ghatta* by developing the multipurpose power unit (MPPU). Efforts made by Nakarmi helped in the further development of the *ghatta*. The MPPU is a water turbine based on the traditional *ghatta*, but made of metal instead of wood. The turbine is manufactured by the National Structure and Engineering Company (NSEC) with the design and collaboration of Mr Nakarmi. It is far cheaper and simpler to manufacture and install than a crossflow turbine. Because its design includes a power take-off feature, it can grind maize and other processing units such as rice hullers, oil expellers, and dynamos and generators.

The MPPU helped but did not solve the whole problem. The scale of investment required for MPPU installations (around 30,000 rupees for about 5HP output) was high for many small entrepreneurs. As certain workshop facilities are needed to manufacture the MPPU, many local craftsmen were excluded.

Considering these problems, and building upon his work experience with RECAST and GATE, Mr Nakarmi succeeded in producing a small-scale MPPU. This is made of local materials and can be produced by village craftsmen. It is simple in design, consisting of a runner, a metal axle and bearings supplied for rural millers to assemble themselves and install on-site. With the exception of the metal parts, mainly the runner, shaft/axle, and belt pulley, the rest of the *ghatta* (the chute, framework, stone grinder, canal and intake) can be maintained easily. The structural conversion of the traditional *ghatta* to the improved ghatta can be carried out by local labour. This machine is also suitable for poor millers with very limited means, and millers who do not need to run supplementary machines other than rice hullers and small electricity generators.

Building upon Nakarmi's work, GATE initiated a project in Nepal for the promotion and dissemination of improved *ghattas* in rural areas. The other important objective of this project was to train local craftsmen or millers in manufacturing the metal runner for the installation of improved *ghattas* (or the replacement of traditional *ghattas* by the improved *ghattas*). When the project was terminated in 1988, it had been successful in installing 80 improved *ghattas* and in training 10 craftsmen from different locations around the country to manufacture the improved kit and to undertake site installations, maintenance and repair work.

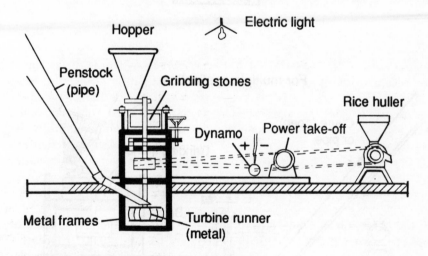

Source: A.Bachmann and A.M.Nakarmi

Multipurpose power unit (MPPU)

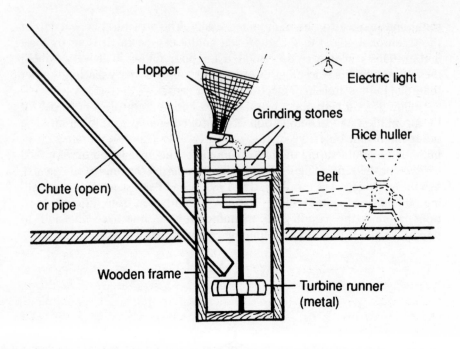

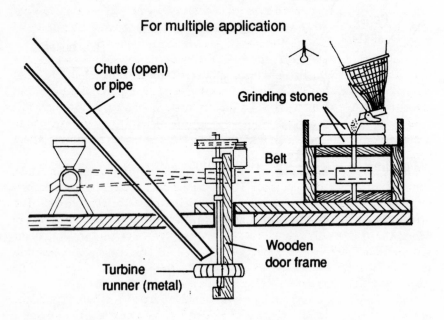

New Nepali water mills for improved grinding

Policy support — the ADBN

The Agricultural Development Bank of Nepal (ADBN) has taken a keen interest in the above development process and has provided credit assistance to both private sector manufacturers and entrepreneurs. This has encouraged them to try out the new innovations. Through its wider field networks, such as the Small Farmers Development Project (SFDP) and its field offices, the ADBN has assumed a supporting role in efforts to improve the traditional *ghatta*. The credit agency plays an intermediary role between farmers and local millers for the installation of turbines and improved *ghattas*.

Technological aspects — improved *ghatta*

The improved *ghatta* is a modified version of the traditional *ghatta*. The improvements have increased the power output of the *ghatta* from one horsepower to something like three horsepower or more, depending upon the head and water flow at the specific site. With the increased power output, the improved *ghatta* becomes a reliable and cheap source of power. This opens up further possibilities of driving a lot of small machines. Examples of this are operating a mill for sawing, polishing and turning of wood and timber, processing of agricultural products, and running of pumps for lifting irrigation water. The production of increased power output from the improved *ghatta* is made possible by the technical improvements. The principal improvements made in the improved *ghattas* are described below.

In the improved *ghatta*, hydraulic efficiency is improved by modifying the traditional wooden blades and making design changes in the chute. This has increased the efficiency of the traditional *ghatta* from around 20 per cent owing to the use of flat wooden blades, to the level of 50 per cent or more.

In order to utilize the hydraulic head more efficiently, the wooden chute is converted into a penstock with wedge inserts to achieve a nozzle effect (only a small amount of water flowing in).

The runner of the improved ghatta resembles a turgo runner, in which hemispherical forged buckets are welded to the hub. A metallic band circumscribing the runner and welded to each bucket reinforces the runner. The drive deflects the jet of water back, in contrast to the traditional *ghatta* in which the water only strikes the blades and 'splashes off' without being systematically deflected in a backward direction. This water deflection utilizes the residual energy, thereby improving the hydraulic efficiency. The improved *ghatta* therefore produces more power for the same flow.

Improvement of the grinding unit is achieved by correct selection of the millstones and correct working of the stones. It has been observed that the use of incorrect millstones has resulted in reduction of the flow of corn and the decline of the quality of flour.

145

Economic aspects

The capital cost of the improved *ghatta* varies according to water flow, distance from the water source, and local topography. Although initial expenditure on improved *ghattas* requires higher outlays than for traditional *ghattas*, the diversification of uses also brings higher returns. The return on total capital employed for the improved *ghatta* ranges from 46 per cent (small capacity utilization) to 92 per cent (medium capacity utilization) in comparison with 47 per cent in the case of the traditional *ghatta*. In absolute terms, the annual profit from the improved *ghatta* ranges from 11,000 to 27,000 rupees whereas it is only 5,600 rupees in the traditional *ghatta*.

Costs and benefits to farmers

Household processing devices driven by the direct application of human labour (*janto, kol, dhiki*) are all very labour-intensive and time-consuming. Processing times for one quintal of crops by different methods are presented in the following table:

Table 1 Processing times, one quintal of crops (time in hours)

crops	hand devices	traditional ghatta	improved s.c.u.[1]	ghatta m.c.u.[2]
paddy	30 to 100 in dhiki	–	2.0 to 3.5	1.0 to 2.0
wheat/maize	23 to 72 in janto	3 to 11	3.0 to 5.0	1.5 to 2.0
mustard	124 to 281 in kol	–	20.35	10–15

1 s.c.u. = small capacity utilization
2 m.c.u. = medium capacity utilization

Time-saving by the improved *ghatta* is considerably higher in all cases compared to both hand devices and traditional *ghatta*. Time-saving is greatest in the case of oil seeds.

Processing prices

In rural areas, the prices charged to villagers by the millers are paid in kind or in cash. The rate of processing for one muri of grain by different methods is presented in Table 2. (One muri equals 50 to 60kg depending on the type of grains.)

146

Table 2 Rates for processing one muri (amount in Rs.)

particulars	hand devices	traditional	improved ghatta
wheat	180	250	250
maize	180	240	240
millet	180	200	240
paddy	240	–	280
oil seed	750	–	500

Calculated on the basis of time (hours) and labour charge of one person only at the rate of Rs. 30 per person per day

The processing costs for paddy, wheat, maize and millet are lower for hand devices than for the traditional *ghatta* and improved *ghatta*. However, while working out processing costs for the hand devices, the wages are considered for only one labourer. With the hand devices, more than one person is needed for processing tasks (at least two for *dhiki* and *janto*, and five for *kol*). In the case of the traditional *ghatta* and improved *ghatta*, only one person carries the grains to the mill site and gets the processing done. It is cheaper to have the grains processed with the improved *ghatta* than by other means. Processing costs to customers for mustard is much cheaper with the improved *ghatta*.

Processing yields
There is not much difference in the yield of grains (maize, millet and wheat) ground in *janto*, traditional *ghatta* and improved *ghatta*. But the huller yields a slightly lower percentage of rice and broken rice than that of the *dhiki*. The lower yield, however, is compensated by the increased quantity of finer and better quality rice husk produced, which can be used as good livestock feed in the rural areas. The mechanical oil expeller yields a higher percentage of oil to the villagers from mustard than does the *kol*. The increase in oil yield from mustard ranges from 7 to 30 per cent depending upon the make and efficiency of the expeller.

Social and environmental aspects

Besides generating a good return on investment for the miller, saving of processing time, and providing a higher processing yield for some products, the improved *ghatta* has a favourable impact on society, at community and national levels:

1 saving of time The introduction of improved *ghatta* saves time and effort in processing food grains, compared with the traditional means. The time and effort saved is used for agricultural and non-agricultural productive activities, and for better child care. This improves the income and quality of life for the rural population.

147

2 welfare of rural women The creation of processing facilities from the improved *ghattas* has relieved rural women from the physically arduous task of grain processing using traditional means.

3 improvement of rural setting According to the villagers, the improved *ghatta* provides better meeting places for women where they can exchange news and other information. While waiting their turn, they talk about many ideas ranging from individual problems to new agricultural methods and practices. This makes them more responsive and positive towards appropriate technologies and innovations.

4 forward and backward linkages Provision of better processing facilities develops forward and backward linkages between improved farming practices, harvesting, processing, transporting and marketing, resulting in more opportunities for employment and increased income for the rural population. The introduction of improved *ghattas* has a positive effect on local workshops and craftsmen. They have more jobs for making spare parts and more work on repairs.

5 rural electrification Some improved *ghattas* are used also for electricity generation. During the day, *ghattas* run agro-processing units. In the night, generators are operated to produce electricity. Available data on hydropower development in Nepal indicates the desirability of these private electrification schemes for remote and scattered small villages of the country. They are cost-effective — around 20,000 rupees per kW of installed capacity as compared to about 73,000 rupees per installed kW for small and medium micro-hydro power plants. Other advantages besides cost are that these *ghattas* are easy to operate and maintain.

6 saving of petroleum products and improved balance of payments The generation of power by improved *ghatta* saves diesel fuel which is otherwise needed to run agro-processing units in rural areas. Similarly, the generation of electricity from the improved *ghatta* saves considerably on kerosene required for rural household lighting. The saving of diesel and kerosene has a positive effect on the spending of valuable foreign currencies. This improves the country's balance of payments.

7 environmental impact Private electrification schemes provide environmental benefits. The use of electric cookers can help to reduce the consumption of fuelwood for cooking.

Recommendations

One factor responsible for the slow pace of improvement of traditional *ghattas* is the lack of knowledge about the availability and performances of improved *ghattas*. Programmes should be launched to establish demonstration units in order to educate and motivate rural people for the adaptation of improved *ghattas*.

In every village there are blacksmiths who work with metals for making tools and utensils. These people are competent to do the metalwork required for the installation and after-sale services of improved *ghattas*, provided the blacksmiths are given necessary skills. Training programmes should be staffed to upgrade the skills and knowledge of village black-smiths to make them capable of undertaking *ghatta* improvement work.

The establishment of the improved *ghatta* requires investment which is still beyond the capacity of many village millers. Arrangements should be made to include the improved *ghatta* as a priority on lending for financing institutions of the country. Greater commitment of all financing agencies is an essential requirement for the widespread dissemination of improved *ghattas*.

To encourage rural millers to replace traditional *ghattas* with improved *ghattas*, millers should be provided with technical assistance in the form of training to improve their technical skills and management competence. Programmes should be formulated to organize observation tours and ex-change visits to successfully improved *ghattas*. Publicity material on the benefits of the improved *ghattas* would help as well.

The creation of a micro-hydro power development centre would help to co-ordinate research and provide technical support to private sector manu-facturers. The centre could conduct skill and development training for entrepreneurs and staff of various agencies connected with micro-hydro development. Besides providing technical support, this centre could also look into socio-economic and environmental aspects of micro-hydro de-velopment. The centre should function in close collaboration with research agencies, private manufacturers, lending agencies and relevant government departments.

Artificial fishing reef and bait technologies by artisanal fishermen of south-west India

JOHN KADAPPURAM

Introduction

It has been recognized in India that artisanal fishermen are still the masters in traditional gear technology. It is the traditional artisanal fishermen who pioneered original designs of most traditional fishing crafts and gears operating in Indian waters. Artisanal fishermen are continuously involved in innovating new fishing technologies and adapting them to their local marine environment. Technical capability of artisanal fishermen has been kept in low profile and was known mostly in regions of origin.

Through continuous interaction with the ocean and fish, artisanal fishermen accumulated over generations a treasure of scientific knowledge on diverse marine ecosystems and fish behaviour. The technical capability of artisanal fishermen is based on this knowledge and has endured for thousands of years, like *Ayurveda*, an indigenous form of medicine. Rejecting this traditional knowledge as 'primitive', modern fishing technologies developed in temperate waters, like trawling, purse-seining and mechanized fishing boats, were introduced in the mid-1960s. The end result of these are overfishing, destruction of marine ecosystems and a fall in fish production.

Formal R&D institutions and personnel neglected the traditional sector almost totally. Commercial interests, profit and government support motivated the formal sector to concentrate on the newly imported modern technologies, especially for shrimps.

Early 1980 witnessed explosive social unrest amongst fishing communities. It was a turning point for both traditional fishermen and the state government. The state was forced to rethink its earlier policy on fisheries technology and traditional fishworkers turned to alternative small-scale technologies. From 1980 onwards, fishermen took an active interest in constructing artificial reefs as a way of regenerating the natural marine habitat greatly damaged by bottom trawling and overfishing.

MR J. KADAPPURAM (India) is co-ordinator of the Programme for Community Organization in Trivandrum, Kerala. This is an organization working with artisanal fishworkers by way of fisheries research, training and village level development activities. He holds a masters degree in social work and worked in Nigeria, teaching community organization and community development. He is presently involved in fisheries research.

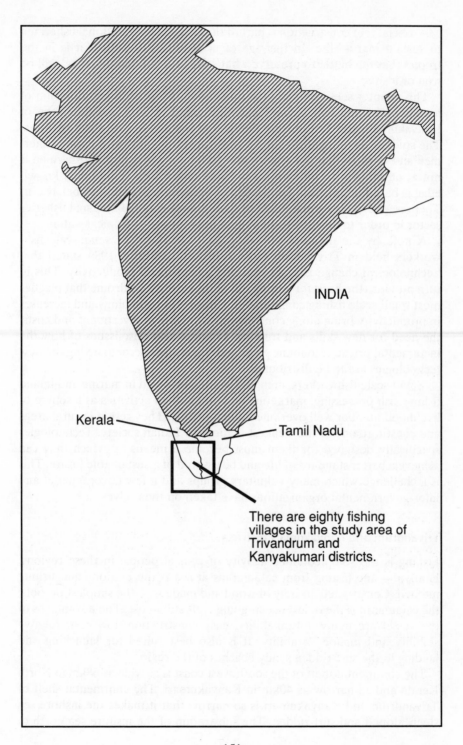

INDIA

Kerala

Tamil Nadu

There are eighty fishing
villages in the study area of
Trivandrum and
Kanyakumari districts.

Artificial reef construction is part of the struggle by traditional fishermen to sustain marine life. In this age of ecological destruction, it is in the tropics that the battle to preserve what scientists call 'bio-diversity' will be won or lost.

This chapter seeks to study the innovation, adaptation and diffusion of artificial reef and bait technologies developed by artisanal fishermen of Kanyakumari and Trivandrum districts of the south-west coast of India. The study aims to highlight the technological capability of artisanal fishermen and to show that the science and technology of artisanal fishermen is not at all inferior to modern science and technology. Traditional knowledge is based on intricate knowledge of oceanography and fish behaviour. There is a need for formal R&D to study thoroughly the artisanal fisheries sector in order to develop technologies appropriate to tropical waters.

A note by the national workshop on technology for small-scale fishworkers held in Trivandrum from February to March 1989 stated that 'technological change is a pre-requisite to enhanced productivity. This in turn provides the basis for getting out of the poverty syndrome that plagues most small-scale fishing communities. Changes in technology and increases in productivity bring along concomitant increases in investment and costs, the need for new skills and training. Changes also raise issues of how the incremental private economic gains and social costs accompanying the new technologies are to be distributed.

'Small-scale fishworkers, men and women involved in marine and inland fishing, fish processing, marketing and other allied activities as a source of livelihood number well over one million people. They reside in rural areas and constitute one of the weakest sections of Indian society. Technologies specifically designed for them must become a means by which they can achieve a better standard of life and be assured of a sustainable future. This is a challenge which many voluntary groups and a few governmental and inter-governmental organizations have taken on themselves.'

Trivandrum and Kanyakumari districts

Fishing is the sole economic activity of coastal people in these regions. Hook-and-line fishing from catamarans at sea is the predominant fishing method. Constructed entirely of wood and made with the simplest of tools, the catamaran is the oldest ocean-going craft still in use. The advantages of the vessel are many: unsinkability, easy construction, low cost, relative stability and manoeuverability. It is also best suited for launching and landing in the surf-ridden sandy beaches of the region.

The continental shelf of the south-west coast is as wide as 68km in North Kerala and as narrow as 40km in Kanyakumari. The continental shelf of Trivandrum and Kanyakumari is so narrow that it makes the inshore sea steep, sloped and surf-ridden. The substratum of the inshore sea north of

152

Quilon is mostly slushy or muddy due to around 35 rivers emptying into the sea. Trivandrum and Kanyakumari have sandy substratum due to the lack of muddy inflow into the sea. The coastline of Trivandrum is a regular sandy beach except in Kovalam (the international tourist beach resort) and Vizhinjam. There is rocky outgrowth in the inshore sea in the depth range of 18–40 fathoms. In Kanyakumari, the coastline is largely irregular with patches of rocky outgrowth extending from the shore to deep sea.

Prompted by these oceanographic features, fishermen of Kanyakumari and Trivandrum developed highly skilful hook-and-line fishing and catamaran sailing and rowing.

Artificial fishing reefs

Natural reefs are the result of biogical or geological processes taking place in the sea bottom. An artificial reef is any external object or stable structure placed in the sea bottom to attract and aggregate pelagic migratory fish and residential reef fish.

As an age-old practice, traditional fishermen of Trivandrum operating shore seines used to dump rocks fastened with coconut fronds into the sea bottom to attract fish closer to the shore. Fish which were aggregated over the bottom structures were caught by shore seines locally named *karamadi* (*kara* = land, *madi* = seine), a gear pulled from the beach from two sides by about 10 fishermen on each side. This practice was based on knowledge that fish tend to congregate over bottom structures. Alien objects of virtually any kind placed in the water can cause some form of fish congregation.

During the Second World War, a ship was sunk off Anjengo fishing village 45km north of Trivandrum at a depth of 24.5fm. Efforts made by authorities to locate the wreck became futile. After nine years, in 1949, a man called Sukkurappan discovered the wreck while engaged in hook-and-line fishing. The wreck measured 50m long and 45m wide and 7fm deep from the top of the ship. The wreck turned into a rich fishing reef which attracted line fishermen from the southern villages. The southern fishermen fished from the reef without bait or using artificial bait. Artificial bait hooked more fish than natural bait used by local fishermen. Infuriated by this, locals chased the eight southern fishermen out of the wreck. They justified their action on the basis of their belief that it was morally unjust to catch fish without giving food. Artificial bait would chase the fish away from the wreck. But the southerners achieved a fishing right by marrying women of Anjengo and settling down there. This was possible because of the systems prevalent in the fishing communities of Trivandrum and Kanyakumari districts.

Almost simultaneously, two anchors were lost and sunk at 12fm from the ships berthed at the Valiathura Pier, 5km west of Trivandrum City. One

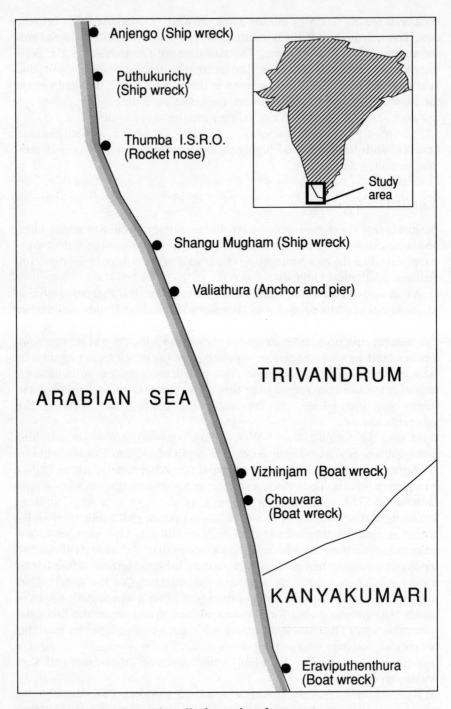

Fishing villages with accidentally formed reefs

anchor was taken from the sea bottom by a diver, the late Mr John. He was not able to find the second one. About 10 years later, line fishermen located the anchor which by that time had become a rich fishing spot. There were the earliest known examples of external bodies attracting fish and maturing into good locations for fishing. Recently, there were many such wrecks in the inshore waters of the south-west coast.

Creating reefs for fishing

Attempts to create artificial reefs were made originally in Puthiathura of Trivandrum in 1953–55 and in Eraviputhenthura village of Kanyakumari in 1957. Line fishing is the predominant fishing method still followed in Puthiathura, where fishermen have been fishing in natural reefs. One rocky reef is at 12fm and 2.5km off the coast. Since they found the nearby rocky reef in Karimkulam was higher than theirs and more productive, the men decided to enhance the productivity of their own reef by adding height. Two full lorry-loads of rocks packed in bags were dumped on the top of the reef, making it 0.5m taller than before. Productivity substantially increased six months later. This was the first known attempt to enhance productivity through artificial means, though it was done on an already existing reef.

In 1957 the *Panchayat* (local government) authorities built a community well in Eraviputhenthura with concrete rings. One ring of 3m diameter and 0.5m height was left over after the completion of the well. The ring was taken by some fishermen and dumped at 11fm depth and 1.5km off the coast on a clay substratum, which was already being used as a fishing ground. This was the first time an external structure was dropped on the sea bottom. This soon became an artificial reef known as *Vattuparu* (*Vattu* = ring, *paru* = reef). These were the two original attempts to create artificial reefs in the 1950s.

The beginning phase was followed by 25 years of dormancy in artificial reef construction. Between 1957 and 1980 no effort was made by fishermen either to create new reefs or to service the existing ones. This may be due to the introduction of synthetic gear materials like nylon nets (polyester), synthetic lines (polyamide) and ropes (polyethylene). In the second half of the 1950s, these materials revolutionized fishing gear technology. The change from cotton to synthetic gear materials increased productivity per unit many times. Resources were not fished to the optimum, leaving room for steady increases in production.

With the start of 1980, efforts were made by fishermen of many villages to re-activate existing reefs and construct new reefs, especially in Trivandrum district. Fishermen started feeling the pinch of resource depletion which started in the middle of the 1970s. Mr T.R. Thankappan

155

Achari said that since the middle of the seventies, Kerala has been passing through a fisheries crisis. The characteristics of the crisis are broadly indicated below:

1   The demersal fishery wealth of the inshore sea of Kerala started diminishing from indiscriminate fishing leading to over exploitation. As a result, several bottom species are on the wane. A main example is prawns.

2   Production has been lagging behind since the middle of the seventies, in spite of the fact that high and intermediate technology inputs have been fast increasing.

3   The monsoon upwellings in the inshore sea (*chakara*), a manifestation of rich fishery of Kerala, have become a rare occurrence in recent years. This indicates certain changes in the environmental and ecological condition.

4   While offshore resources remain virtually unexploited, the inshore water is over-capitalized with more and more investment on production inputs.

The impact of the introduction of bottom trawling in the 1960s began to be felt severely towards the end of the 1970s. By ploughing the sea floor with fine-meshed trawling nets, the bottom trawlers caused heavy damage to the benthic vegetation, the food chain, young fish and inshore natural habitats, the most productive zone of the oceans.

As a measure of rehabilitation, fishermen have built 19 reefs since 1980 in Trivandrum and Kanyakumari. During the same period, the two reefs created in the 1950s and dormant for nearly 25 years were revived, serviced and enlarged.

Since 1988, two research institutions, The Central Marine Fisheries Research Institute (CMFRI), Cochin and Department of Aquatic Biology and Fisheries, University of Kerala have been co-operating in studying the biological aspects of reef development. The fishermen of Valiathura created the reef in 1988 with the financial assistance of the Intermediate Technology Development Group, London, through the South Indian Federation of Fishermen Societies, Trivandrum. This is the first reef construction where fishermen and an outside agency collaborated in financing, planning and construction. The CMFRI researchers placed 12 specimen materials on the newly created reef to understand the most suitable materials for reef building. The results are not yet released. The total cost of the reef was 10,000 rupees. This reef, measuring 30m long, 15m wide and 0.75m high, was supposed to be larger than the previous one built by the same fishermen. A structure was built, for the first time using worn-out tyres fastened with concrete rings. While transporting these structures on catamarans from the shore to the reef site, the rings ripped apart. Attempts to place them underwater failed initially.

156

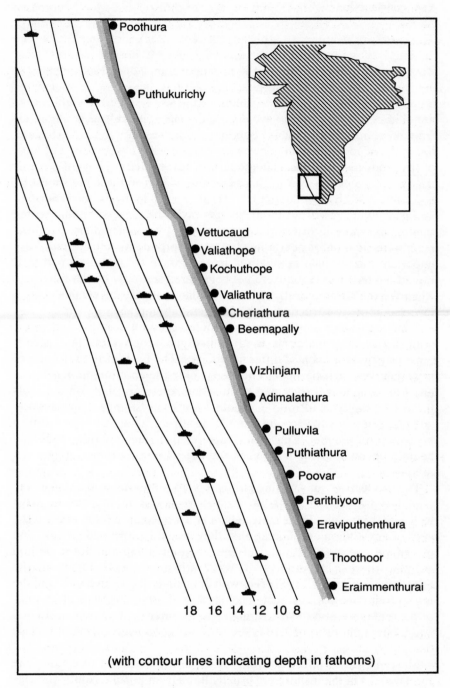

Poothura

Puthukurichy

Vettucaud
Valiathope
Kochuthope

Valiathura
Cheriathura
Beemapally

Vizhinjam

Adimalathura

Pulluvila

Puthiathura

Poovar

Parithiyoor

Eraviputhenthura

Thoothoor

Eraimmenthurai

18 16 14 12 10 8

(with contour lines indicating depth in fathoms)

Distribution of artificial reefs in Trivandrum and Kanyatumari

157

Reef construction

The success or failure of an artificial reef depends primarily on the site. The parameters used by fishermen in selecting sites off most of the reefs were wave damage, shore seine operating range, gillnet operating range, easy accessibility, live-bottom and poaching. All but one of the 22 reefs were built in the depth range of 9 to 16fm. As the sea is surf-ridden, the waves are quite strong. In order to avoid wave damage, the reefs were placed far from the shore. Shore seiners operate from the beach to nine to 11fm, and hence the need to keep these away from shore seine obstruction. For most of the productive seasons, gillnet operates beyond 18fm. Users of the artificial reefs are mainly older fishermen and children so these reefs must be accessible easily by hand oaring. Reefs constructed in the locations north of Beemapally are restricted to 'members only'. The reefs were built within sight of the shore in order to avoid poaching by non-members. All these reefs were sited on or near a live bottom or productive substratum. Very important factors such as siltation, internal wave strength, fish path and rate of biomass formation were not considered seriously by the fishermen when the reefs were constructed. No marine biologists or engineers were involved in the construction of the first-generation reefs.

Concrete rings, stones, coconut fronds, coconut stumps, and screw pine plants were materials used in first-generation reefs built simultaneously by fishermen of different villages. The basis of the selection of materials was the fishermen's knowledge of the sea bottom, its vegetation and fish behaviour. Fishermen know from experience that fish use reefs for shade, shelter and food. Coconut fronds and stumps help plankton and other biomass to grow on them. This attracts small fish which in turn become food for reef fish. High structures like rings provide shade and heaps of stones provide the niches and holes for shelter and refuge from predators.

The productivity of a fishing reef is related to the size and shape of the reef. The average size of first-generation reefs was about 20m long, 10m wide and 0.5m high. Initial materials were dropped at random without the help of any equipment, hoping that they would be dropped straight and placed on the sea bottom. But this random dump-and-hope method didn't work well. The productivity was low in these reefs compared to the Sangumughom reef, the only reef with 3m height and 18fm depth, still the most productive artificial reef. The number of fish increases with the size of the reef. The ratio of structural height to water depth has been studied and a minimum ratio of 1:10 is required for good aggregation of pelagic fish.

Most (14 out of 22) reefs were placed in the east-west direction. The local current in the inshore sea usually flows from north to south and vice versa. In order to line-fish in the reef, the catamarans have to stay just above the reef so that lines with hooks and lead weight go straight down to the reef. By constructing the reefs in the east-west direction across the northerly and southerly current, the catamarans could anchor either south or north of the reef as the current may be. In this manner each catamaran will have sufficient space over the reef and collisions of catamarans can be avoided.

Fish behaviour and reefs

Shade, shelter and food are the main attractions of a reef for fish. All the 49 fishermen interviewed agreed with this point. 'One of the fundamental reasons for fish to be attracted to a reef may be related to instinct. Some species may be seeking a dwelling in the fish reef. This probably explains the strong tendency of bottom dwellers to flock to a fishing reef. The mid- and upper-layer swimmers may be using the reef as a resting and or feeding station. Other fish use a reef as a shelter or refuge from predators.' (Grove and Sonu, 1983).

The behavioural response of fish to reefs changes with light conditions. The Puthiyathura fishermen are of the opinion that the hooking rate which is highest early in the morning gradually reduces to almost nil at noon. The hooking rate then increases gradually to almost half that of the morning.

Reef fishing happens from December to March, the fair season in the south-west coast of India. As the marine water is non-turbid, the clear sunlight goes deep down. To escape from the heat and for food, fish are more aggregated during this season. For the rest of the year, inshore water is turbid and rich with planktonic organisms due to 'monsoon upwelling'. This also produces a cooling effect in the sea.

Whether or not spawning takes place in a reef is the most debated point among fisheries scientists. However, Puthiyathura fishermen confirmed that cuttlefish (*Sepia pharonis*) spawned in their reefs. Agreeing with this, Thoothoor fishermen said that cuttlefish not found before in the inshore water of the region were aggregated in their artificial reef. With clear water, fishermen were able to see young cuttlefish in their reefs. As Sheehy has said, 'Perhaps the most likely application for designed reefs for commerical fishing would be related to their use to create or expand nurseries or spawning grounds. Most American reef researchers debate whether artificial reefs actually increase productivity or merely attract and concentrate organisms from surrounding areas. Japanese scientists generally have little doubt that artificial reefs, when properly designed, sited and placed, can be used to increase the productivity of desired species.'

Sanjeeva Raj has been experimenting with artificial fish habitat and fish aggregating devices in Madras. He says that in the east coast the most encouraging feature was that about five species were collected amidst the coconut fronds. It is suspected that these species might be breeding at these artificial fish habitats. This point is now being investigated.

Fishing methods in reefs

The only fishing method used in these reefs is hand-lining from catamarans. The most popular baits used in the reefs are artificial. Natural baits are also used occasionally, particularly to catch reef resident species.

Artificial reef materials

Initially, reef builders concentrated on recreating the complexities and surface of the natural ridges. Material selection was based mainly on knowledge of natural reefs. The builders looked for cheap materials that were easily and locally available.

From the experience gained from first-generation reefs the following modifications were made in reef materials:

1   stones packed inside coir or rope nets: The sandy bottom of the inshore sea is much subjected to the fury of monsoon waves and upwelling. The cumulative effect of this process exerts heavy siltation and gradual burial of reef materials placed in a scattered manner. In order to withstand the siltation and burial, the Puthiyathura Beemapally fishermen packed stones in large coir or rope nets. The nets had a mesh size big enough for fish to enter and small enough to retain the stones together. Similarly, parts of trees were packed and dumped to create vegetation in the reef site. The decay will enhance nutrients available.

2   painted stones: In Thoothoor, fishermen observed that a natural reef with red colour attracted certain resident reef fish. Motivated by this, fishermen created an artificial reef with stones painted a red colour. Japanese reef builders construct structures for target species. The fish workers in Thoothoor claim that stones painted with different colours will attract fish with different colours. Fishermen also claim that 'maturing' of an artificial reef can be reduced considerably if the materials used are painted with the desired colours.

3   tyres fastened with concrete rings to give 'shape' to reef materials: A recent development in reef construction in Valiathura is characterized by model-making. Discarded tyres were used with rings to give particular shapes to attract fish using the spaces as hideouts.

4   materials modified for protection of artificial reef: Drift nets are menaces to the artificial reefs. The 'sliding wall' effect of drift nets keep fish away from the reef. Nets may get entangled in the reef and this may act as a barrier to fish entering the reef. Reef builders make many modifications in reef construction to protect the reef from entangling and to avoid the sliding-wall effect of drift nets.

Artificial bait

Bait is a piece of meat, live or dead fish or similar material used to lure fish. Hooks have bait attached and these are offered to the fish. There are several incidents quoted by fishermen about *artificial* bait. Three of these incidents have a close relationship with the innovative thinking of fishermen.

Cat and feather
Once corrugated, lines used for fishing may not yield a good catch. Hooks with baits have to stay straight, suspended on a straight and untwisted line in order for fish to bite. To straighten used lines, fishermen used to stretch rolled lines on a sandy beach. When re-rolling, cats are attracted to fast-rotating feathers entangled in the lines. The cats mistake the feathers for a prey. This is 'bait' for a cat. This behaviour has been observed often by fishermen. The first clue to artificial bait was derived from the relationship between cats and feathers.

Conflict between shore-seiners and line fishermen
Before the discovery of artificial bait, natural bait was the only way line fishermen could catch fish by hooks. Fishermen collected bait fish from shore seiners. For some unknown reason, a conflict arose between line fishermen and shore seiners in Kadiapattanam and the line fishermen were stopped from collecting bait fish. In their search for alternatives, line fisher-men found that old coir fibre from the wing portion of a shore seine could be used as bait.

Indian underwear and tuna
Once a line fisherman found that his underwear, hanging out, was bitten by a tuna. These fish occasionally jump out of water. Immediately he took off the underwear and tore it into pieces to use as bait. Surprisingly, tunas were hooked.

Hook-and-line fishing methods

Line fishing is defined as the method of fishing in which fish are offered bait presented in such a manner that it is difficult for the fish to let go once the bait is taken. Hook-and-line units are generally used for fishing in deeper waters. The fish has to be baited by live or artificial bait attached to the hooks. The line is weighted-down either with iron weight or stones. It is the weights which will determine the position the line will take in the waters. It is the size of hooks and the depth of the line that determine the nature and size of fish caught. After the line is laid, the craft may either remain an-chored or drift with the current.

161

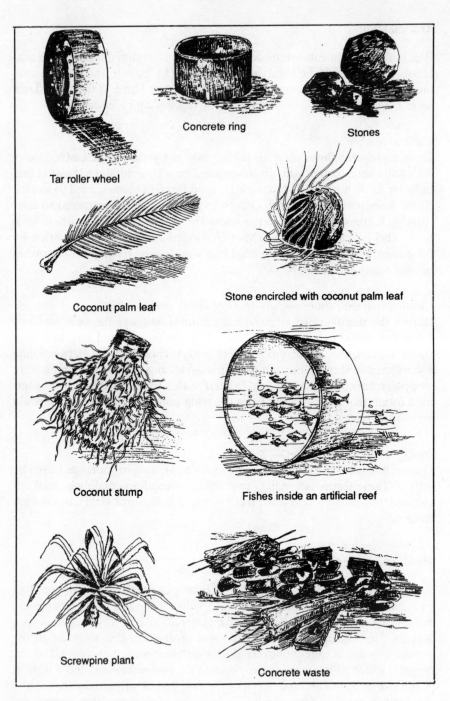

Concrete ring

Stones

Tar roller wheel

Coconut palm leaf

Stone encircled with coconut palm leaf

Coconut stump

Fishes inside an artificial reef

Screwpine plant

Concrete waste

Artificial reef materials

Ring with iron hooks

Tyres tied to concrete ring

Stones painted red

Reef protected with pillars

Stones kept inside a bag

Reef protected with anchors

Prawn, lobster, shark and cuttlefish are the four important groups of marine seafood earning foreign exchange for the country. Shark and cuttlefish are caught mainly by line fishing. The most common types of line fishing followed in Trivandrum and Kanyakumari are hand-lining, set-lining and troll-lining.

Hand-lining

This is the oldest type of line fishing. One end of the line is secured between the forefinger and thumb and the other end is weighted and baited to attract fish. Once bitten by fish, the line is hauled in, fish removed and the process repeated.

Troll-lining

Ottathumbu is the modified version of *Thumbu*, traditional surface hand-lining. Instead of being jerked by hand, the line is pulled through the water by means of a sail or engine. Hand-lining, set-lining and troll-lining have helped artisanal fishermen to catch all varieties of fish belonging to all columns of water and reef.

Types of bait

For a passive and selective gear like hook-and-line, it is essential to have materials which can excite fish so they may be attracted to a bait. Different fishing methods and types of baits were developed on the basis of fish behaviour observed over the years.

Live bait

A live bait is any small fish used live to catch big fish. Big fish subsist on small fish, a basic process of the food chain. Live baits were developed for each target fish from the observation and experience of artisanal fishermen regarding predatory relationships of diferent species. Bait fish are kept alive in a palm bag partially submerged in water. The mouth of the bag is tied to the rear end of the catamarans. Big-sized, pelagic migratory fish are attracted by live bait. For example, to catch tuna, seerfish and sailfish, live bait such as mackerel and rainbow sardines are used. Generally, a single hook is operated with live bait.

Natural bait

Natural baits are pieces of meat offered on hooks generally to catch bottom-dwelling fish. With pieces of meat, more hooks can be baited and productivity increased. The size of meat bait depends on the size of the target fish. Fish caught by natural baits are catfish, scianids, sharks, rays, skate and reef fish. Whole dead fish are used as bait to catch residential reef fish. Dead whole bait swim in the water like live bait in response to current and waves. Squid is often chosen as dead whole bait.

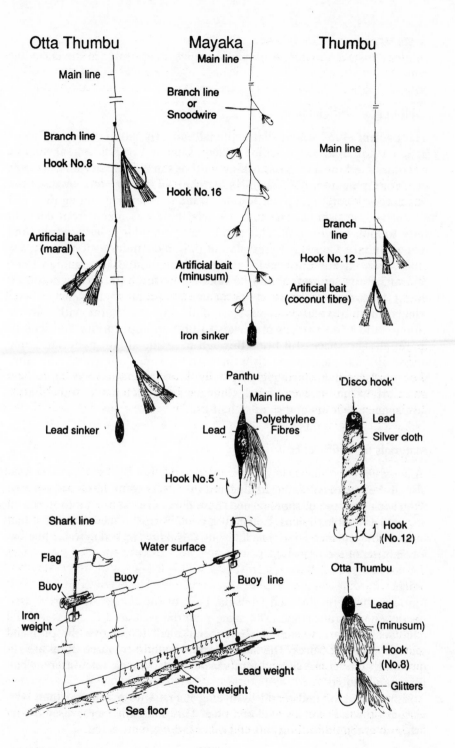

Otta Thumbu

Main line

Branch line

Hook No.8

Artificial bait (maral)

Lead sinker

Mayaka

Main line

Branch line or Snoodwire

Hook No.16

Artificial bait (minusum)

Iron sinker

Thumbu

Main line

Branch line

Hook No.12

Artificial bait (coconut fibre)

Panthu

Main line

Polyethylene Fibres

Lead

Hook No.5

'Disco hook'

Lead

Silver cloth

Hook (No.12)

Otta Thumbu

Lead

(minusum)

Hook (No.8)

Glitters

Shark line

Flag

Water surface

Buoy

Buoy

Buoy line

Iron weight

Lead weight

Stone weight

Sea floor

Artificial baits

165

Artificial bait

Artificial baits are materials prepared to give an appearance similar to live bait.

Evolution of artificial baits

The present study found that artificial bait originated about 300 years ago in a Kadiapattanam fishing village. Line and trap fishing have been the oldest and most popular fishing methods in Kadiapattanam. Specific oceanographic features, such as patches of rocky outgrowths from beach to offshore, make the Kadiapattanam fishermen among the most skilful in line fishing. The first artificial bait was made from coconut fibre to look like prawns. This bait became popular in Trivandrum and Kanyakumari. Coconut fibre was the only bait material for nearly 200 years, without any noticeable change. Then about 100 years ago came 'maral', fibres separated from 'Erukkalam' tree bark. White-coloured maral continued to be used for nearly 50 years. In the early 1940s, fishermen in various villages started dyeing the maral with various colours and tried various materials to find an appropriate multicolour material. The successful breakthrough in artificial bait materials came about 30 years ago when fishermen tried using 'minusum', the fibre separated from glittering clothes. Evolution continues as more and more bright materials are tried. Changes have been made in the materials, shapes, colours and sizes of bait used.

Materials for artificial bait

Coconut fibre

Usually yellow in colour, aged, fine and shining, coconut fibres are selected from wing portions of shore seine. These fibres are cut to a uniform size in a way to resemble prawns. Red cotton twine is tied in the head of the bait to resemble a prawn's eye. The line with this bait is jerked in water like the locomotion of the prawn.

Maral

Maral is the fibre obtained from the bark of the 'Erukkalam' tree, used previously as branch line. The same material was used later as artificial bait. Soaked bark is combed by coconut shell to remove the pith and segregate the fine fibres. The fine and shining white-coloured fibres are cut uniformly. These are shaped into various sizes to look like different bait fish, mainly squid.

Fishermen modified maral by dyeing it first with green and then with various other colours like red and blue. This made the maral resemble fin fish with green dorsal portions and other fish were attracted.

Other local materials

In the search for durable and multicolour brighter materials, fishermen in different villages of Trivandrum and Kanyakumari tried with many materials. Efforts included cotton twines, jute fibres, woollen fibres, black human hair, mantle of petromax, cotton clothes, nylon twine, rope (polyethylene), minusum (nilex), polypropylene tape, silver chinese hook, silver clothes, thankam (glitters) and OBM plugs. Among these, jute fibres, human hair and mantle are no more in use. Cotton twine, nylon twine, woollen fibres, cotton clothes, OBM plug and silver chinese hooks are only occasionally used. The most popular and widespread materials are maral, minusum, rope, silver clothes and glitters.

Minusum (nylex cloth)

Minusum, the nylex cloth, is used mainly by muslim women for blouses. Women observed that certain pieces cut from clothes and stored in heaps in the corner of tailor shops have shining fibres. Puthiathura fishermen separated the fibres and used these as bait.

Latest developments in artificial baits

Silver clothes shining similarly to squid tubes in the night are used with squid jig to catch cuttlefish. Invented in 1984 by fishermen of Valiathura/ Puthiathura, this has become popular with hook-and-line fishermen. Glitters were used previously with minusum to resemble stripes on the body of fish. About three years ago glitters themselves became bait.

These are now manufactured and marketed by textile industries and available in local shops. The hook-and-line and artificial bait materials are manufactured mainly in Madras and Bombay and distributed to local shops through main shops in Manavalakurichy. The market and distribution network played a significant part in making these materials available and popular.

Another latest development in artificial bait is the use of discarded spark plugs of outboard motors (OBMs). The bakelite portion of the plug resembles a squid tube. This has been used by Enayamputhenthura fishermen only since 1987.

Trends in the evolution of artificial bait

The evolution of artificial bait reveals certain trends in the modifications made. Most important of among these are:

1 from single colour to multicolour: The basic consideration taken for coconut fibre bait was its resemblance to prawn. With maral, Kadiapattanam and Enayam fishermen began to make bait in accordance with the appearance of fin fish and seasonal changes in marine water colour. White maral was dyed with green, blue and red and used in single colour. With minusum and glitters of various colours, fishermen were able to make bait more or less exactly like fin fish with complex features such as multicolour skin and stripes.

2 from natural to synthetic materials: In the innovations, natural materials such as coconut fibres, maral, jute fibres, cotton twines and cotton clothes were increasingly being replaced by synthetic materials. Rope (polyethylene), nylon twine, minusum and glitters are now standard and popular in Trivandrum and Kanyakumari.

natural	→	synthetic
coconut fibre	→	rope (polyethylene)
cotton twine	→	nylon twine
cotton clothes	→	minusum and glitters

3 from single materials to multi-materials: Artificial baits made from single materials are still undergoing change to become bait made of a combination of materials. This gives the bait a complex appearance, similar to real bait fish.

4 from tedious to easy preparation: Preparation of bait from materials like coconut husk and tree bark is a tedious and time-consuming process. With minusum, rope and glitters, bait-making has become comparatively easier and faster.

5 from less shining to more shining materials: Line fishermen learned from fish behaviour that light is most important among the parameters which cause fish in the water to become excited. The brighter the bait the higher the hooking rate. Fishermen have always been in search of brighter materials. Each successive bait innovation is brighter than preceding ones.

Problems related to natural bait

Prawns and subsequently squid were the baits most preferred by hook-and-line fishermen. Before the discovery of artificial bait, fishing possibilities for line fishermen were dependent completely on the availability of natural baits. If no bait was available no line fishing was possible. Line fishermen were at the mercy of shore seiners who provided prawn and squid. In times of fish scarcity, line fishermen were charged heavily for the bait. The fight between line fishermen and shore seiners in Kadiapattanam and the consequent refusal of bait triggered a frantic search for an alternative. After the second half of 1950, the situation worsened as prawn, which was once cheaper than mackerel, suddenly became highly-priced. The same happened to squid. These two are now generally scarce. Line fishermen have always looked for cheap baits. During lean years, when prawn would be extremely scarce, most line fishermen would be unemployed.

Natural bait (meat of prawn and squid) must be used before becoming spoiled. As soon as they get bait, fishermen rush to the reef and often do the cutting, cleaning and baiting on the drifting and shaking catamarans. This results in a loss of baits and improper baiting. If there is no hooking on a particular day due to changes in current and light, the entire lot of bait will have to be thrown to sea. Fresh bait must be found for the next day's fishing.

Overfishing and bottom trawling

The accumulated effect of trawling introduced in the mid-1960s resulted in the degradation of the marine environment. The effect was felt especially on natural marine habitats and on fragile coral reef systems in south-west coastal waters. In a 1987 study on the status of natural reefs, the author was told by the late Mr Arogyam, then aged over 90, that in his younger days he used to fish from at least 150 small natural fish habitats on reefs. All of these habitats have been destroyed now or rendered unproductive by 'Norway ships' — the local name for trawlers introduced with the help of Norway. The impact on resources began to be felt severely by 1980. Line fishermen whose main source of fish is reef sites began to build artificial reefs as a rehabilitation or enhancement of areas impacted by trawling.

All except one reef were built in the depth range of 9–16fm. This was to bring fish as close as possible to save fuel and labour. The reefs can be reached by oars without the help of outboard machines introduced since 1980. Although fishing in the outer reefs is done individually, a crew of six fishermen go in a plywood canoe powered by a motor to reach the reef. Maintenance of engine and fuel cost become unbearable for them. An artificial reef in close waters solves these problems.

The role of formal R&D

Until recently, formal scientific R&D institutions and personnel maintained a 'don't care' attitude towards the artisanal fisheries sector. This was because of the fisheries policy followed by state and central governments since planned development began in 1950s. Neglecting the fishing knowledge and methods of artisanal fishermen as 'primitive and unscientific', governments with the support of formal R&D went all out for modern technologies like trawling and purse-seining. The complete attention of formal R&D was concentrated on the modern mechanized sector for prawn export and profit.

Technology development based on the traditional sector was ignored. Hence, the initiative for developing traditional technologies fell on the shoulders of the fishermen themselves and non-governmental organizations supporting the artisanal sector. The popular motorization of country craft in Kerala today had its early experiments at Muttom of Kanyakumari district of Tamil Nadu in 1970. This was under the Indo-Belgian Fisheries Project, a non-governmental organization and through Marianad Fishermen Co-operative in Trivandrum District in 1974.

169

The formal scientist community in Kerala came to know of the construction of reefs by artisanal fishermen in 1980 when the author described this in an all-Kerala Fisheries Conference held in Trivandrum in 1987. Initially, the scientists did not believe it. On the same day, the Director of CMFRI and a team visited Valiyathura and confirmed what the author said about reef construction. Formal R&D has not played any role in the development of artificial reef technology. The Central Marine Fisheries Research Institute, Vizhinjam and Department of Aquatic Biology and Fisheries University of Kerala started collaborating with fishermen of Valiyathura since 1988. They are studying the biological process of the reef about which fishermen do not know much. But in designing, applying and spreading reef construction, formal R&D had not played any role at all.

Apart from the 1988 South India Federation of Fishermen Societies (SIFFS) reef, all the 21 reefs constructed were by the fishermen. The only outside help received was a donation of 700 rupees from the village church for the construction of one of the reefs.

The study reveals that artificial reef construction is an area where artisanal fishermen (with their intricate knowledge of oceanography and fish behaviour), marine biologists (with their knowledge of reef biology) and marine engineers (with their knowledge of structural engineering) could co-operate improve productivity. The productivity of all but one reef is very low because many biological and engineering parameters were not considered well in the reef construction. The rate of siltation, time of reef maturity, reef materials and structuring of the reef were not properly assessed before the construction. This is where formal R&D could help.

Artificial bait was entirely innovated, designed, adapted and spread to their peers by fishermen themselves. The most popular artificial bait, known as 'minusum', evolved on the basis of knowledge acquired through constant interaction between fishermen and fish and observation of fish behaviour in relation to bait.

Economic impact

The parameters used to gauge the techno-economic impact of artificial reefs and bait at the micro-level are cost and earnings. Resource management and energy conservation are considered at the macro-level.

Artificial reefs constructed with massive support and left open, like one in the village of Eraviputhenthura, cost nothing. Materials used such as concrete rings, coconut fronds and stones were easily available. Transportation and labour were contributed freely by prospective reef fishermen. However, reefs constructed by and restricted to specific groups and individuals cost from 900 rupees in 1983 for Valiathura reef to 10,000 rupees in 1988 for the SIFFS reef. Reefs varied from no cost to low cost depending on the types of materials used and the size of the reef. In 1984 the Kochuthope reef was built at the cost of 6,000 rupees. Initially 100 fishermen used to fish from this reef and membership subsequently rose to 300. About 94 per cent of the reef fishermen were able to earn a daily income of 18 to 50 rupees. Around four per cent of them had up to 200 rupees per day per fisherman during high catches. An average of 39 rupees was earned by fishermen per fishing day. According to a rough estimate of the society, fish worth 10,000 rupees were caught from the reef built at the cost of 6,000 rupees in the first year of operation.

The cost of available artificial fish habitat complex is around 2,000 rupees upwards. The average income per day has been 600 rupees but some of the higher incomes have been 2,000 to 3,500 rupees and a single record catch was 10,040kg of round scad sold for 3,500 rupees.

Reef fish landed fresh and in time for marketing fetch higher prices. The addition of the amount over and above the normal market price is a bonus for bringing in the fish fresh. Artificial reefs built in the close coastal waters enable fishermen to make more than one trip to a reef within a day.

Artificial reefs earn more than their cost. It is truly a low-cost technology. There is tremendous scope for increasing the productivity of artificial reefs if these are constructed with the help of marine biologists and engineers. Because of the random dump-and-hope method followed in the construction of all but one reef, the materials were placed in unoriented piles or mounds. Maintenance and reinforcement of the reefs become necessary every year soon after the monsoon. Though the initial coast is very low, recurrent costs to maintain them would be high.

Innovation of artificial bait began with bait made from coconut fibre freely available in Kerala (*Kera* = coconut tree, *Kerala* = land of coconut trees). For many years artificial bait didn't cost anything. With the introduction of 'maral' made from the bark of a tree, artificial baits began to be economic goods. These still cost very little compared to natural bait, especially prawn and squid.

The cost factor lowers further with the fact that artificial bait can be used repeatedly. With the innovation of minusum, the number of hooks on a line increased tremendously. Fishermen who were using two hooks with natural bait are now using 25 to 50 hooks, thereby increasing the hooking rate per operation. The availability of artificial reef materials in plenty assures all-year line fishing. Fishermen are able to set the lines with hooks and baits on the previous day, making the next day's line fishing operation certain. There is no seasonal variation in the price of artificial bait, as in the case of natural bait. Sometimes natural bait cannot be bought even if available because of its exhorbitant price at lean season.

Ecological and social sustainability

A technological innovation should be not only economically sustainable

171

but also socially and ecologically sustainable. While the formal R&D in fisheries concentrates on harvesting and post-harvesting technologies, artificial reef by artisanal fishermen is essentially a pre-harvesting technology. It is regenerating the vegetation much devastated by commercial bottom trawling. This is a way of nourishing the sea or, as Nalini Nayak fondly calls it, 'nurturing nature'. By creating the marine habitat, artificial reefs preserve what the scientists call 'bio-diversity'. If knowledge is the mother of all resources, the physical, chemical and biological process of resources is the father. It is only by blending both the mother and father aspects judiciously that we can utilize resources in a sustained manner and leave them without permanent damage.

Traditional fishermen innovate and develop technologies in response to both these aspects. For example, the only method used to catch fish from reefs is hook-and-line fishing which does not disturb the reef environment and catches only the targeted fish, leaving the young and other species. Selective and passive line fishing keep the 'ecological succession' or food chain undisturbed. Materials used for reef constructions are non-polluting and mostly biodegradable to enhance growth of marine organisms. The reefs provide ecological niches for fish to feed and breed. It is essentially an eco-technology.

Effect on employment

Artificial reefs makes line fishing possible year-round except during the monsoon season (June–August) when the sea becomes turbid and turbulent. In the past, line fishermen of Trivandrum and Kanyakumari went from beyond 50fm up to 150fm for deep water and reef fish. It took two to three days to complete the fishing operation, including journeys both ways. Using sails powered by wind, fishermen often get stuck in the sea for lack of appropriate wind. Only daring and adventurous fishermen used to take such risks. Deep-water line fishing was undertaken during the fair weather season (December–March). Most line fishermen depended on reefs within the 16–24fm range. As these reefs were all destroyed or rendered unproductive, these fishermen were affected badly — particularly the old and the young. After a certain age, sight often becomes too poor to see landmarks in the detail necessary to locate fishing spots. Younger fishermen learning the fundamentals need to be closer inshore to be safe. Artificial reefs constructed in close waters not only provided employment for both these sections of fishermen throughout the year, but also for other fishermen during the peak fishing season.

Non-availability of natural bait very often kept line fishermen out of employment for days. They were forced to restrict their fishing time according to the amount of bait. Natural bait gripped by the fish would get lost while removing the fish. Artificial bait removed the premium placed on

172

fishing time and the number of fishing days. Fishermen willing and climate favourable, line fishing can be done throughout the year with artificial bait as some bait can be used repeatedly. As there is no shortage of artificial bait materials, hook can be baited one day and kept ready for use another day.

Resource management and energy conservation

At the macro-level, artificial reefs may be a resolution of the conflict between the artisanal fishermen and commercial fishermen. Reefs are built to regenerate natural fish habitats. The reefs are also protection grounds for marine-living resources by effectively obstructing bottom trawling in inshore waters.

Reefs built in close coastal waters save fuel which otherwise would be spent reaching far fishing grounds. All catamarans fishing in the artificial reefs use oars as most of the reefs take only 45 minutes to reach.

The learning process

Learning generally takes place through three domains: the cognitive, psychomotor and affective. Reading and writing are prerequisites for learning through the cognitive domain. As the fishermen in Trivandrum and Kanyakumari are generally (80 per cent) illiterate, their learning of fish and the environment takes place through the psychomotor domain, requiring very skilful movement of hands and legs. Fishermen also use the affective domain, requiring acute human senses. All work simultaneously to give a 'feel' of fish and the ocean.

The sum and substance of artisanal fishermen's science is their intricate knowledge of fish and their environment. Line fishing is an individual operation. Therefore, fishermen in Trivandrum and Kanyakumari are always learning to be independent producers. The art of lining up a specific fishing spot or reef is required if a fisherman is to become an independent producer on his own catamaran.

Fishermen must have knowledge of visual triangulation by lining up geographical marks and fishing spots. The men must know about fish and their behaviour and local wind and currents to judge the drift of a catamaran. All this and more is learned, accumulated and passed from generation to generation. Although knowledge is passed from father to son, a fisherman has to acquire more and more skills and practise fishing regularly to master the art.

Trivandrum and Kanyakumari fishermen have extensive and detailed knowledge of reef ecology and fish behaviour. This is based on their fishing experience in a limited number of natural reefs. With the plumb line they learn about the length, width and height of a reef with reasonable accuracy.

173

From the pieces of materials entangled in the hooks (such as plants, corals, and other organisms) they learn the biota of the reef. These give them the clues to artificial reef construction.

Though line fishing is an individual operation, fishermen do it as a crowd over and around reefs. While fishing, they talk in order to avoid the monotony and drudgery of waiting for the bait to take effect. The behaviour of fish is so interesting a subject for fishermen that it takes most of their conversational time. If one fisherman is seen to catch more fish, his materials are used at once by others. Artificial baits are shared by fishermen. Though there is secrecy sometimes in regard to a certain fishing spot, sooner or later others will find it. Formal R&D scientists use marine ecology and biology theories to explain observation of fish behaviour. It took 25 years for the best scientists to accept what fishermen said about the damage of bottom trawling. While fishing in the reef, fishermen observe fish behaviour, form theories and test these by further observation. Changes in artificial bait are made in response to changes in fish behaviour. The interaction between fishermen and fish is a continuous process by which new bait materials were innovated. One fisherman stated that 'fish teach us, we teach fish'.

Spread of innovations

Knowledge of the marine environment and fish behaviour has accumulated through generations. This knowledge leads to innovations that are spread horizontally. In the case of artificial reefs, what one fishing village does on reef construction is observed by neighbouring villages. The south-west coast is a long stretch of villages situated very closely. Collection of materials, transportation and dumping are done so openly that it is easy for anyone to follow. Fishermen talk openly about reef construction. Within a span of eight years, reef construction has spread to 17 villages from one end of Kanyakumari to the other end of Trivandrum. Artificial baits became common and popular with all hook-and-line fishermen throughout the south-west coast of India. Recently, Valiathura fishermen who visited an east coast village in Madras to learn about reef materials dumping were surprised that fishermen of that region are ignorant about artificial bait.

Social occasions such as festivals can help spread the artificial reef and bait innovations. Ideas spread also by inter-village links — for example, there is one system whereby a man becomes godfather to children of friends in other villages.

Peoples' technology

Peoples' technology is the answer for overfishing. The international market controlled by multinational companies dictates technology options to fulfil the requirements of multinationals at the cost of artisanal fishermen. Trawling for prawns as an export commodity has contributed to a large extent to the destruction of natural fish habitat and overfishing. The politics of overfishing is to extract maximum resources in minimum time to maximize profit. People's technology is based on 'give-and-take'. Fishing considered as taking or capturing or hunting only has desertified the sea. Artificial reef, which reforests the sea bottom, and artificial baits do not disturb the ecosystem.

Suggestions

1 Artificial reefs could be propagated throughout the coast of India, particularly on the south-west coast from Cape Comerin up to Alleppey. The largest concentration of hook-and-line fishermen is in this area. In the immediate future, extension of artificial reef construction in other villages of Trivandrum and Kanyakumari must be tackled.

2 The state and/or central government should appoint a task force to study the problems and prospects of artificial reefs. Construction of artificial reefs should be subsidized as these are an effective tool for conservation of marine living resource.

3 As this is pro-people technology and good for ecological regeneration, small-scale technology development agencies like ITDG through SIFFS may take responsibility for having consultancies on marine engineering and the marine biology of reef building before big size reefs are constructed in the region.

4 An immediate study must be undertaken to find out the siltation rate and the maturing time of artificial reefs of various materials to find out what is best-suited to the marine environment. The Central Marine Fisheries Research Institute may be requested to take up this study as it is the best equipped agency in India to do such a study.

5 Future artificial reefs should have reef materials important for desired target species, especially cuttlefish. The experience of Thoothoor and Puthiathura artificial reefs confirm that cuttlefish, otherwise not found in the inshore water, were attracted to and spawned in the artificial reefs. As cuttlefish do not have any permanent ground, they settle as a colony locally known as *mada* in different places in different seasons and years. Artificial reefs structured to suit sheltering, feeding and breeding cuttlefish may be the future direction that artificial reef construction must take.

6 An information centre on reefs must be started to pool the experience and information from artificial reefs built, and to disseminate this information to artisanal fishermen. In the case of artificial bait information, experiences of fishermen in various villages were spread horizontally by fishermen themselves, mostly while engaged in fishing as groups around a reef. But very little was shared about reefs among them.

175

7 Food, shade and shelter are the main attractions of a reef to fish. The size of the school of fish depends on the size and height of a reef. Studies in other countries reveal that the height of the reef should be 10 per cent of the water depth. The majority of the 22 reefs didn't maintain this ratio. Future reefs must be taller structures.

8 In the selection of reef site, fishermen were guided chiefly by two factors: nearness to shore and the already-known productive muddy ground. But these factors are not very important as far as the life and productivity of a reef is concerned. Reefs created on an already live bottom would disturb the natural fish habitat there and sink very fast as the bottom is soft and muddy. Artificial reefs must be sited on a firm sandy bottom in the fish path.

9 There are not many suggestions to put forward in the case of artificial bait as the fishermen themselves with their deep knowledge of fish behaviour have developed various kinds of artificial bait which work extremely well. One aspect in which fishermen can be helped is on bait-making. Segregating fibres from clothes, cutting them into uniform sizes and tying these securely to hooks are very cumbersome processes consuming much time on land. This can be saved if specific artificial baits to catch specific species are standardized, prepared and made readily available.

Conclusion

It is necessary to find out the indicators of tradition in order to go to the post-modern era with a clear perception. Kerala is a state which keeps traditions in high esteem. For example, Kerala is trying to preserve traditional arts like *kathakali* and indigenous medical systems like *Ayurveda*.

This generation is looking to the post-modern era. We can reach the post-modern era only by looking at the indicators of tradition in the light of modern science and technology.

Even today there are people in Japan who construct tall buildings without drawing any plan but using traditional knowledge. But their science is not taught in the engineering colleges. We have to integrate the essence of tradition with time. There is no meaning in keeping the indicators of tradition in museums. They must be subjected to analysis and reinterpretation.

PART III

Latin America

Latin America — regional overview

GUILLERMO ROCHABRUN

To many observers from the developed world, Third World countries' areas are essentially similar. In one way or another, they lack what is most important: development. However this is an external statement that says little about a region's own nature and process.

For example, Latin America (LA) is not only an underdeveloped region, it is also part of the western world. We should say that from a comparative perspective, its most characteristic feature is to be the underdeveloped area of the west. The history of this link is crucial to understanding the current situation and to comprehending some peculiarities of technological transference.

To begin with, we have the people. The official face of LA, as it appears not in posters for tourism but in the faces of élites, is a white or a near-white face. LA is a *mestizo* continent and there is no doubt about it, but the most prestigious ethnic mixtures are those in which the white element neatly predominates. In countries where the native population still exists, be it a large segment of the whole country or a very tiny minority, this is confined to a subordinated and marginalized role. In contrast with South Africa, the native population is ruled by groups that are not really white but pretend to be so. Their 'whiteness' is seen as a sign of 'civilization' and 'modernity'.

An important way in which this condition manifests itself is language. In contrast with African or Asian élites, LA ruling and intellectual classes do not speak native languages. With the exception of Paraguay, there is no country in which a native language is recognized as an official one. This marginalization creates huge cultural barriers within each society.

This situation originated nearly five centuries ago, including three centuries of colonial European rule — especially from Spain and Portugal — plus more or less 170 year of independent political life. In brief, the colonial era meant the complete destruction of the social, political, technological and cultural structures of native societies. At the same time, in contrast with the United States, important segments of native groups have survived and still have important economic roles, especially in the Andean countries

MR G. ROCHABRUN (Peru) is a sociologist at the Faculty of Social Sciences, Pontifical Catholic University of Peru. His areas of special concern are history of social ideas and the present state of sociological theory.

179

of South America and Mexico. But, in direct contrast with British rule in many Asian countries, the Iberians did not use to their own benefit either native political forms or local élites. Colonials neglected and even rejected native agrarian technologies.

The native technological world combines original knowledge and principles with Western techniques that were brought by Spanish and Portuguese colonials. In many cases the latter have been transmitted with almost no changes until present times. This complex mix varies from region to region, from community to community, depending mainly on ecological and economic conditions. This variability ensures that the problems, resources and solutions are very different from case to case. But as a whole, this native knowledge is disregarded by society at large.

A lot of knowledge was lost along the way. In countries such as Peru and Bolivia which have an important native population, many efforts to 're-cover' pre-hispanic technology have been carried out. However, this path has its constraints. In many cases present-day indigenous people ignore native techniques and do not recognize them as their own. These techniques can require large amounts of labour and time.

The people organize their lives with a routine established through a painstaking process of trial-and-error. They are not ready to change for just any claimed 'improvement'. The pre-colonial technological realm had a social and political organization that powerfully enhanced individual and familial productive forces, at the level of communities, valleys and even whole regions. With this organization now lacking, any large-scale technological innovation that cannot replace it in one way or another would be damned to failure.

How then can the assimilation of intermediate or alternative technologies be assessed? Many attempts to diffuse different kinds of technologies have met obstacles because important factors have not been taken into account. For instance, the distribution and meaning of time, the extra-technological dimension of technological knowledge and practices, and the system of needs of the concerned populations. The innovator faces an even more complex situation as a result of the cultural and social gap that exists between the people and the innovator. He, like the state, is an alien. He comes in most cases from the 'external' world, so it is not easy to trust him.

Cultural differences and distances result in the existence of different *technological languages*. The differences are clear. Western technological language pretends to constitute an absolute technological realm, defined by a pure instrumental logic. Distinctly, 'native' technological language is at the same time society, art, culture, belief, and myth. From a strictly abstract point of view, the former is easy to teach the latter. But in order to be absorbed and assimilated, this purely technological knowledge must become impregnated with the indigenous culture. Some kind of 'translation' is necessary to let the dialogue flow. As difficult as this is, it must be multi-dimensional. But who should the translator be? In LA there is a great distance between universities and people's organizations. At their best, Latin American universities have been involved very little in native knowledge and technology.

Perhaps the most immediate obstacle cutting across the cases we have examined is how to know the strongly felt needs of a population. Projects to introduce electricity have failed because 'God created the night with no light'. We knew about reforestation projects that could help children and old men avoid walking long distances to obtain wood. But people may have plenty of time to spend walking in the Chilean desert, and they may enjoy it. Even more, what would they do with the 'free' time? In their cultural horizon and historical memory there may be no relationship between wood and water. So why should they plant and care for trees?

Lack of trust is also pervasive. After reforestation has raised its value, the community land could be expropriated and then planted by the state. The state generally appears as the most mysterious, distant and over-powerful external agent. NGOs are more likely to be accepted. Generally, NGO staff are more devoted to people and the 'working-day' can have 24 hours. NGO staff can afford to be more adaptable to unexpected circumstances. Relations with them are face-to-face and they are removed from the power of the state.

But NGO staff have important limits. NGOs operate generally through very small-scale projects. Each one of them constitutes a wealth of experience. The challenge is how to systematize those experiences and transform them into general propositions that transcend the local level.

The cases we examined in the Latin American group show the difficulties of being successful in technological innovation. We need to work out ways to overcome the difficulties. For example, does the specific innovation pertain to the same *technological family* — as we call it — of that we pretend to improve? In other words, does the innovation use materials the people use, in the ways they know? Does it respect the population's beliefs and values? For example, in some parts of Venezuela a new model of stove was easily adopted because people mastered the materials, although they changed the model in order to cook *arepa*, the most important food-staple in the region.

The innovator must give people enough room to innovate. This has happened, paradoxically, in some cases where the innovator did not know very much about the new device. The technical gaps *had* to be filled by the ingenuity of the people.

The most important lesson we have reached through the discussion of the LA experience is the central and crucial importance of people's self-organization.

Peoples' innovations in housing construction in Huancayo, Peru

FLOR DE MARIA MONZON

Introduction

Most projects which aim to support and improve the living and working conditions of popular sectors view the latter's participation only in terms of implementing programmes suggested by specialized institutions. Thus, attention is directed at explaining the technical aspects of programmes to people. Much time is expended upon the creation of popular organizations which will stimulate and channel the activities needed to make the programmes work.

However, this method has failed so often that it may be necessary to change its basic assumptions. Only successes tend to be reported and this strengthens the belief that innovation and technological change can be achieved only by the intervention of experts and scientific personnel. This approach ignores the fact that ordinary people confront very difficult conditions in their daily lives and that their survival depends upon their responses to these problems.

The processes of change experienced by people are complex and affect economic, social and political relations and the culture of various social groups.

In the technological sphere, people have to integrate, reject or re-shape elements of both traditional and modern methods. The result is a distinctive, practically-tested technology which has achieved a balance between the two. However, the nature of this process has received little attention.

This study considers this phenomenon from the perspective of the use of building techniques and materials in the housing construction process. We have chosen the *barriadas* (squatter settlements) of Huancayo in the Peruvian *sierra* because of the intense process of social change which the area is experiencing. A new city is emerging as a result of the dislocations and innovations brought about by rural-urban migration. There is pressure for modernization and increasing adoption of urban behaviour and consumption patterns. This process is taking place in close social and physical proximity to

MS F. DE M. MONZON (Peru) is an anthropologist. She has done applied research on problems of technological innovation in construction and has supported women's organizations on health issues through an NGO in suburbs of Lima. She is currently in charge of the newly-formed ITDG Mineral Industries and Shelter programme in Peru.

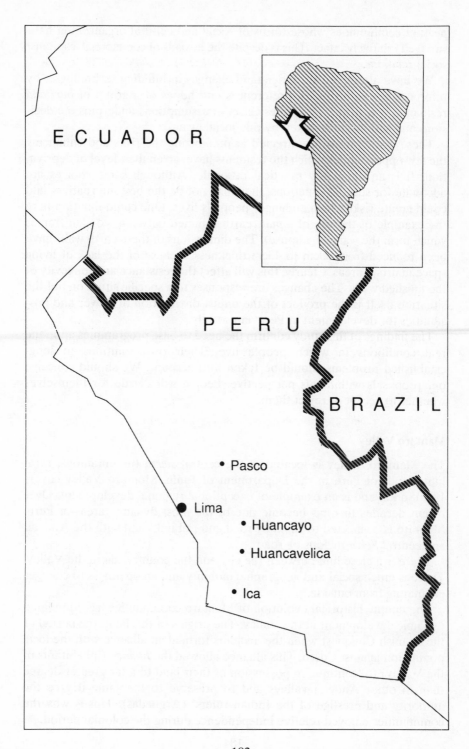

peasant communities whose forms of social and cultural organization have survived relatively intact. This is despite the inroads of commercial, capitalist social relations.

We have attempted to understand changes in building technologies by reference to the attitudes, preferences and hopes of a group of *barriada* residents. It is clear that a cohesive set of assumptions underpins the decisions and actions undertaken by this social group.

These assumptions are directed at minimizing the risks and enhancing the few opportunities which the residents have, given their level of deprivation. It is an eminently practical rationale. Although some choices are adequate for specific situations, they may not be the best alternatives and could create risks which endanger people's lives. One could mention here the example of the use of *tapial* (earth rammed between wooden frames which form the walls of a house). The dimensions of these earth walls have been reduced from 60cm to 40cm thickness because of the lack of living space in urban areas. Clearly, this will affect the resistance and longevity of the finished walls. The changes are responses to a specific situation but the situation itself is the product of the unjust distribution of power and possibilities for development in Peruvian society.

The findings of this study confirm the need to base programmes upon the real conditions in which people live. Their own solutions to long-established problems should be taken into account. We should conceive our proposals within this perspective. People will decide for themselves whether to accept or reject them.

Mantaro Valley

The Mantaro Valley is located in the central *sierra* (mountainous, rural hinterland) of Peru in the Department of Junín. Montaro Valley covers 1,000 sq km and is an example of exceptional regional development. Over recent decades this has become one of the most dynamic areas in Peru. Mantaro is connected to Lima by road and rail links and with the Andean and central *Selva* regions by road.

There is a close link between the city and the countryside in the Valley. There is much social and geographic mobility and an openness to changes emanating from outside.

The unique historical evolution of Mantaro communities has stimulated dynamic development in the Valley. The origins of this lie in the period of the Spanish Conquest when the invaders formed an alliance with the local population against Cusco. This alliance allowed the *huanca* (inhabitants of the Valley) to 'continue in possession of their land to a far greater degree than in other Andean valleys and to preserve to the same degree the authority and prestige of the Indian rulers' (Arguedas). This is why the communities enjoyed relative independence during the colonial period.

184

From the beginning of the twentieth century, modern communications networks linked the Valley to the coast, commerce flourished and mining production began. All of these developments were to the advantage of the agricultural communities.

Urban growth was rapid. The city of Jauja was the most important centre until 1861 when the Province of Huancayo was created. The creation of the Province of Huancayo resulted in the separation of the central-southern area of the Mantaro Valley. Huancayo occupied a strategic position during the Wars of Independence. The weekly market was established to cater to the needs of the armies. Later, it became the most important Sunday market in the region. However, its importance as an urban centre was limited until the present day.

Following its designation as provincial capital, the city's political and administrative control over the southern part of the Valley began and its importance as a commercial centre increased. By the 1930s its hegemony was consolidated and in 1931 it was acknowledged as capital of the Department of Junín.

During this period of consolidation, the migration of peasants to either the mining centres or the towns in search of work became a constant feature. Huancayo is one of the main recipients of migrants from the Valley, the neighbouring Department of Huancavelica, the *sierra* around Lima and from Cerro de Pasco.

Growth of Huancayo

Huancayo is a city of approximately 200,000 inhabitants. The constant arrival of migrants, the lack of planning for city growth combined with the rising cost of urban land have resulted in the *tugurización* of the oldest city areas. (This is the process of established neighbourhoods becoming slums.) Entire families live in one cramped room, lacking basic services and at the mercy of landlords who are constantly raising rents. At the same time, on the outskirts of the city there are empty plots of land which would be suitable for housing. However, this is agricultural land and is difficult to expropriate in order to facilitate the growth of the city.

One can detect three patterns in the growth of Huancayo:

1 a 'natural' increase through the consolidation of new urban zones — such as Chilca and El Tambo — which eventually become districts. This growth is not always accompanied by the provision of adequate services such as drinking water and street lighting.

2 the development of *urbanizaciones* (planned housing estates) which provide public facilities and are occupied by the middle and upper classes.

3 the formation of *barriadas* as a consequence of invasions of State and

185

privately-owned land. As with the first type, inhabitants lack all services and demand these from the State. Their problems are compounded by the legal and social conflict associated with the seizure of land by force.

This study is concerned with this third pattern of housing development.

There were many land invasions in Huancayo during the 1980s. They were particularly frequent before the 1983 Municipal and 1985 Presidential elections when the authorities were loath to use force. As a result, there have been no significant evictions and the residents' organizations are now immersed in 'a war of documents' with the owners of the land. Some invasions were promoted by municipal authorities controlled by different political groups with the aim of creating clientalist relationships with residents.

There are neither documents nor studies which describe this process in detail. The information presented here is based upon statements by individuals indirectly involved in these events. Their testimony demonstrates that not all the invaders came from the poorest groups. There were a significant number of state employees who were unable to buy their own plots as a result of the economic crisis and also individuals who saw this as an opportunity to make a profit through land speculation. There were also many poor peasant migrants, many of them escaping from the war zones of Ayacucho and Huancavelica. As a result, it is difficult to ascertain who actually *needs* land in these new settlements.

The Federation of Human Settlements and Pueblos Jovenes of Huancayo was formed in 1983 and represents the majority of settlements. It has played an active role and achieved much. However, the neighbourhood organizations suffer from internal divisions and poor participation.

Migrants from peasant communities are an important social force in the new settlements. They continue to maintain links with their villages but also experience the rapid changes and trauma of life in a modern city.

The urban settlements

The new settlements experience intense social change. This process contributes to the problem of popular housing and has a decisive influence upon the selection of building techniques.

The three settlements selected for the study were:

1   **Santa Rosa de Lima** This was the first invasion during this period. It is a small settlement in the centre of Huancayo.
2   **Juan Parra del Riego** This is a medium-sized settlement on the periphery of the city.
3   **Justicia, Paz y Vida** This is one of the most recent and the largest settlements. It is interesting because of the dynamism of its neighbourhood organization and its self-managed development programme.

Formation

The settlements were the products of spontaneous invasions. The first, on 2 September 1983, occupied a disused brewery on the banks of the River Shulcas in the centre of the city, on the boundary of the Huancayo and El Tambo districts. The abandoned land was the property of a public charity, which has expressed no interest in the land since the invasion. This became the Santa Rosa de Lima settlement.

Other invasions followed during the same month including one on 17 September in the north-east suburbs on abandoned land belonging to CENTROMIN (the State Mining Corporation). This invasion was by a group of homeless skilled and unskilled labour, according to a leader. This was the Juan Parra del Riego settlement.

In 1985, another wave of invasions occurred. Justicia, Paz y Vida is one of the settlements sponsored by the Provincial Municipal authorities. Privately-owned land was occupied on 26 July 1985. This constitutes the largest invasion and is on the western periphery of the city, beside one of the railways which connects Huancayo to the rest of the Mantaro Valley.

General features

The term 'temporary', with reference to the quality of housing being built, has different meanings in each settlement. In Santa Rosa, all houses built during the last five years are temporary because many may have to be pulled down and re-built according to the ground plan, once the final distribution of plots is made. For some Parra del Riego residents, the fear of eviction forces them to erect temporary buildings. For the poorest among them, 'temporary' may be understood as a desire to improve their homes in the future.

The neighbourhood organization in Justicia, Paz y Vida proposed the construction of temporary housing while residents decided upon the design of permanent accommodation. With the assistance of the provincial council, and as part of their Development Plan, they are now designing model houses.

Background of residents

The following is a socio-economic profile of residents interviewed in the three settlements:

1   Twenty-three residents, all heads of household, were interviewed (nine in Justicia, Paz y Vida, nine in Santa Rosa and five in Juan Parra del Riego);
2   Their average age was 38 years;
3   Three were women and the rest men;
4   Sixty per cent were from the Department of Junín, 22 per cent from the Department of Huancavelica and the rest from other places;
5   More than half of respondents had secondary education (either

187

complete or incomplete). The rest were divided equally between having only primary and having the addition of higher education.

6 The majority (34.8 per cent) were artisans (working in wood, tailoring, the manufacture of fireworks, textiles, etc.). The next largest group (30.4 per cent) were employed in small and medium commerce. Then came the self-employed, such as car mechanics, and lastly employees such as bricklayers;

7 In the majority of cases (60 per cent), all the family contributed to the maintenance of the household;

8 Sixteen preferred to use *tapial* in building houses, three preferred *adobe* (sundried brick), three preferred *ladrillo* (burnt brick) and one preferred a temporary material like canvas (*lona*);

9 Ten houses had living rooms and of these six were occupied by families with seven or more members;

10 Nine people had lived in Huancayo for between five and 10 years, and nine for a longer period.

Construction of popular housing

The majority of respondents came from the Department of Junín where the peasant *comunidad* is the main form of social and territorial organization. Mention has been made of various historical studies which show how the Mantaro Valley communities were able to maintain the strength of their organizations. These were based upon contributions of labour, determined by norms of reciprocity and mutual support. The dynamism of these practices positively influenced production and other aspects of the *comuneros'* life. (A *comunero* is a resident member of *comunidad*.)

More recent studies suggest that organizations in the *comunidades* are experiencing changes. Other forms of social relations, of a commercial, capitalist nature, are growing in importance. Despite this, it is still possible to distinguish characteristic features of the house-building process in the peasant community.

The building process

In the communities, detailed knowledge of building materials is possessed by *maestros* (master craftsmen), although all *comuneros* know something of building techniques. The *maestros* direct the activities of the other members of the community and take on the most difficult jobs themselves.

Sometimes, according to a resident of Justicia, Paz y Vida, it is necessary to employ labour: 'For the roof, you need a master carpenter, someone who knows timber. You also need a tiling expert, able to use *teja de barro* (clay tile) or *calamina* (roofing sheet), otherwise the roof will be no good.' (Interview No. 8)

The *comunidad* responds to the housing needs of its members by establishing a system of mutual support, a pattern of social relations which contributes to the strengthening of the community as a whole. According to one person: 'Here we practise *uyay* (mutual aid). In other words, we help each other. Thus, whatever activity is carried out, some job or building a house, we do it through *uyay*' (Interview no. 32, Santa Rosa)

Payment

Previously, work was 'paid for' by 'loans' of mutual labour. To the degree that a community has been integrated into the capitalist system, this custom has changed. Disposable income, coming from wages earned by family members has made contracted labour more common. However, the presence of money does not in itself represent a change in traditional relations. Rather, it plays a role within a system of collective reciprocity and exchange which is still structured by traditional attitudes.

Building materials

These are manufactured by the family which makes them from substances which are easily accessible. The materials include *tierra arcillosa* (clay), *ichu* (Andean grass), *paja de cereales* (straw) and eucalyptus wood. These materials do not usually involve a cash outlay. Roofing tiles, doors and window frames can be bought in the larger towns.

Customs linked to house-building

Collective labour takes on a festive character. The householders show their appreciation for their neighbours' help with *coca*, food and drink and sometimes music. One migrant describes such an occasion: 'We use *adobe* and *tapial*. The people undertake *minka* (collective labour). They eat and drink, and work. This is *minka*. All come to eat and drink. In this way, the house is finished within two or three days.' (Interview no. 8, Justicia, Paz y Vida)

The barriada

This section is based upon observations made in three Huancayo *barriadas* where migrant peasants have a dominant presence.

The building process

Mutual aid is an exception in the *barriada*. Building work is done by the nuclear family on its own. One resident remarked: 'We are all from different places but agreed to form a Housing Association in order to work together in *faenas* (co-operative labour). However, this has not worked out in practice. Many people do not have the time to work because of their jobs, others leave early, others stay away. There is no continuity.

189

Payment

Those who are on a fixed monthly or weekly income and cannot be responsible for building work because of the nature of their jobs employ wage labour. Methods of payment vary. Some labour is paid by contract, some by the day, some by the number of mud walls completed.

The payment of *maestros* is determined by communal traditions. They expect to receive their *descanso* (break) with a dose of coca and a glass of spirit at mid-morning. The cost of their labour depends upon whether or not they take lunch. Often, quite an intimate relationship is formed between the craftsman and the family. One female householder in Justicia, Paz y Vida relates: 'We pay him the basic wage but on top of this, he gets a bed, breakfast, lunch, supper and drinks . . . This has lasted for fifteen days already.' (Interview no. 10)

Building materials

In the city, everything is either bought or sold. This puts limitations on the options open to the poorest families.

Customs linked to house-building

Few families give parties and if they do it is only for a much smaller group of close relations and neighbours.

Changes in traditional building technology

Many aspects of building know-how derive from traditional knowledge built up over generations of experience. Our intention is to understand why this has survived and also to show the existence of these popular skills. To this end, we asked residents certain questions:

1 How do you know what kind of soil is suitable for the manufacture of *adobe* and *tapial*? Every resident knows that a certain kind and quality of soil is needed for these materials. There is a known gradation of soil. Thus, one person said: '. . . in order to make *adobe*, one needs yellow earth, which is neither too wet nor too dry.' (Interview no. 21, Santa Rosa)
2 How do you know if the soil is suitable for making *tapial*? Answer: 'When it's strong.' (The person makes a gesture with his hand as if pressing something). (Interview Constructor One)
3 What do additives, such as straw, contribute to the making of *adobe* and *tapial*? Answer: '. . . They give them a longer life. If you make them with pure soil, with nothing added, when they're wet they will break up.' (Interview no. 41, Parra del Riego)

We are dealing with specific, definite knowledge which does not contradict the explanations of scientific engineering. There are many examples of popular knowledge with respect to the building of foundations or the compacting of

Table 1 Changes in traditional building methods

	number	per cent
1 reduction in the size of the block	3	13
2 no adding of straw or grass	10	43.5
3 bad building work	3	13
4 neglect of structural supports and bad building	1	4.3
5 reduction in size of block and neglect of structural supports	3	13
6 no answer	3	13
total	23	100

tapial blocks. Popular knowledge has incorporated elements of modern technology. Not surprisingly, many migrants work in the civil construction sector in the cities. Thus, we are talking here of a dynamic process of which not enough is known.

It has been necessary to adapt traditional materials and techniques to new living conditions and changes in social relations. This is a conscious process. One can cite the example of the *adobe*. In the past, its dimensions were 90 × 45cm and it was combined with rope in order to give more resistant walls.This is impossible in the city because of limited space and higher labour costs and the restraints of commercial relations.

Respondents were asked what types of innovation had taken place in traditional building methods. Table 1 summarizes their answers.

Respondents were clearly aware of the importance of straw in the making of *tapial* but they were still not using it. The same can be said of other traditional methods. Although accepting the value of such methods, they used only those within their reach. One of the major reasons is the urgent need a family may have for a house. To this one must add the difficulty of obtaining materials or additives of rural origin (such as *ichu* and *paja de cereales*) in the city.

The reduction in the size of blocks is attributed to the lack of space in the city and particularly in the *barriada*. This is an intense problem in Santa Rosa where the plots are so small.

One group of residents believed that the mason introduced alterations because he wanted to finish his work quickly, to avoid putting any real effort into it: '. . . now everything is done for profit. In the past (the blocks) were well-made and well-formed . . . now . . . everything is done to get on quicker, to make more money.' (Interview no. 35, Parra del Riego)

When soil-based building techniques are transferred from their original context within the peasant *comunidad* to the urban environment they undergo dramatic changes. Commercial considerations prompt reduction of dimensions and simplification of methods.

Table 2 Views on home improvement

	number	per cent
1 yes, you can improve . . . with soil materials	3	13
2 yes – you can add more rooms	3	13
3 yes – superficial changes	2	8.7
4 yes, you can improve . . . with *material noble*	9	39.1
5 no, it's impossible	3	13
6 yes, but without specifying	1	4.3
7 yes, improving the *adobe*	1	4.3
8 no response	1	4.3
total	23	100

These innovations create risks in the event of a large-scale earthquake or flood. Many respondents described how *tapial* walls had collapsed owing to floods and water-logged earth. The previous practice was to incorporate changes into the traditional manufacture of building materials. This should be continued in order to prevent problems for residents in the future.

Migrants' expectations on housing

We will approach this subject from both long- and short-term perspectives.

Short-term housing improvements
39 per cent of respondents believed it would be possible to improve their houses by using *material noble* — building materials such as cement or concrete which are considered more durable. One resident said: 'Yes, it is temporary. When we're given the land title, then we must start working from scratch. Then we'll have the chance to work with *material noble*.' (Interview no. 14, Justicia, Paz y Vida)

Meanwhile, 26 per cent of those interviewed believed they could improve their houses using traditional materials and methods. Table 2 summarizes these views.

There is a gradation of demand. Those whose houses are made of temporary materials aspire to *tapial* or *adobe*, while those that have soil-built houses want *material noble*. There is, however, a generally held opinion that if soil-built houses are made well, they need little improving.

Some residents consider it will be difficult to improve their houses. Some make superficial changes (whitewashing the walls, for example) while others lack the capacity to do even that. The fact that the majority of houses do not have windows and the doors are made of *calamina* shows the extent of the problem.

Table 3 Features of the ideal house

	number	per cent
1 made of *material noble*	7	30.4
2 in pleasant surroundings	1	4.3
3 with creature comforts (nothing on type of material)	2	8.7
4 described in detail (rooms, 2 floors, flat roof, etc)	7	30.4
5 did not want to dream	4	17.4
6 no response	2	8.7
total	23	100

Families with limited economic resources can get building loans from state agencies such as the Housing Bank, the National Housing Fund (FONAVI), the Materials' Bank and mutual insurance associations. However, not a lot is known about these loans and they are not feasible for people who do not have fixed monthly incomes.

The gradual nature of house improvement and the observations made and opinions heard during the course of this study suggest that housing improvement occupies a secondary place on the scale of priorities of *barriada* residents. Once a family has a basic roof over its head, it is likely to be more interested in investing in a small business or the children's education.

Long-term perspectives — the 'ideal house'
Residents were asked what would be their ideal house, the house of their dreams?

The majority of residents opted for an urban type of house using *material noble*. This is seen in the following statement: '. . . we live in the city . . . it's not appropriate to build houses using rural materials. I believe it is better to build with more durable materials.' (Interview no. 32, Santa Rosa)

Closer attention to individual cases suggests another aspect. The majority, 13 out of 14, had received either secondary or higher education, nine had previous experience of urban life or had travelled a lot, and 10 had contact with Lima. The urban context was present in their socialization process.

Despite the fact that the majority came from places where building with soil predominates and their present housing is made of *tapial*, their aspirations are for 'more urban' building materials.

In contrast, the four individuals who refused to speculate about an 'ideal house' gave reasons like the following: 'It would be an illusion to believe that you could ever live in a beautiful house. With what resources? . . . I don't believe it's possible to imagine having a house better than the one I have now.' (Interview no. 28, Santa Rosa)

193

These residents have characteristics in common. Three had only primary school education. Three came directly from their villages to Huancayo and had not lived in other places. Two had never visited Lima. Their experience of life has been restricted to the place where they were born with relatively little contact with the outside, modern world. They live in a state of even greater deprivation than other respondents and thus their negative approach to house improvement is understandable.

These examples show what is happening to the sector most affected by the economic crisis, a group which survives through a combination of pragmatism and hopelessness.

Building houses in the barriada

In this section, we show how decisions about housing are based upon a logical rationale which operates in an environment which is constantly changing. Decisions relating to the choice of technique or the use of new materials are determined by a series of considerations which influence the resident while he is building his house.

Tapial is the most commonly used method in the new settlements in Huancayo. Until about six years ago, it was dominant mainly in high Andean areas where water is scarce, space is plentiful and there is much poverty. It is a method well-suited to a temporary situation such as residents in the *barriada* experience and it is the technique they prefer. The following comment supports this: 'The advantage of *tapial* is that it is quick to construct whilst *adobe* is double the cost and *ladrillo* the same. You can put up *tapial* walls rapidly, in one day between twelve and fourteen well-made moulds.' (Interview no. 8, Justicia, Paz y Vida)

People agree on the speed and labour-saving qualities of *tapial*. *Adobe* entails more work and expense and so is unsuitable for those with little to spend on building. The speed of the method is just right to meet the urgent need of residents who fear eviction from a site. No matter how limited its scope, building gives a sense of security and a guarantee of permanence to an invaded site. One resident of Justicia, Paz y Vida gave his reasons for using *tapial*: '. . . because we do not have any other building material, because we need a house so badly . . . and because *tapial* can be made using the soil around here.' (Interview no. 11)

This is another advantage, frequently not mentioned because others are considered more important. The possibility of using a material which is close-at-hand reduces building costs significantly. Other reasons for using *tapial* included lack of space, frequent floods and lack of water to make *adobe* bricks. Many would prefer to use *adobe* but economic circumstances affect their choice.

Another group considered that *adobe* produces better results than *tapial*. Comments included: '. . . *adobe* is stronger and . . . more resilient . . . As

194

tapials are large moulds, if the mould breaks then the house will fall down. *Adobe*, when it is mixed with clay, will not collapse.' (Interview no. 28, Santa Rosa)

The role of mortar as the cementing agent for *adobe* is seen as important. Again, popular knowledge runs parallel to modern science, although using its own language and reasoning.

One basic assumption underlying most popular housing projects is that people are resistant to change and to using new materials and technologies. This assumption totally ignores changes which have occurred in the past.

Many archaeological studies and various pre-hispanic remains show that stone was the main building material used in the *sierra*. Bernabe Cobo, the historian of the seventeenth century, relates: 'In the *sierra*, houses are made of stone and clay and then covered with straw. The stone is rough and unpolished and is arranged in a haphazard manner rather than being fitted smoothly together. Some houses are round and others have sloping roofs. The round houses are used commonly in cold regions because they are well sheltered.'

Although *adobe* was commonly used on the coast, it spread to the *sierra* after the Spanish conquest, along with new styles of houses. Inhabitants used *ichu* to roof their small stone houses. Even today, houses are built in this way in certain areas. The Spanish introduced the burnt clay tile and these were soon used widely as roof cover.

The widespread present use of the cement tile (and its variants, the 'Spanish' and the 'Dutch') in Huancayo and other towns in the Mantaro Valley is another example of the adoption of appropriate, alternative building materials and techniques.

Forty-three per cent of those interviewed had used cement tiles although a majority of these criticized their resistance to hail and heavy rain: 'The ordinary tiles are much better because they don't let in the rain . . . although hail does come through the small spaces.' (Interview no. 15, Justicia, Paz y Vida)

However, preference for the cement over the clay tile was also expressed: 'Cement tiles handle easier and you don't need a drying shed for cement. Also, clay is more labour-consuming and attracts insects. Thus, the cement tile is cleaner and easier.' (Interview no. 28, Santa Rosa)

It is difficult to make large quantities of clay tiles during the rainy season because of a shortage of roofed drying sheds and firing kilns. In the communal context of earlier periods, August and September were set aside for building work. The harvest was over, it did not rain in these months and the peasant had time to devote to building. The demands of city life destroy these customs and the rhythm they gave to peasant life. The growing demand for building materials in expanding urban areas is insatiable and should be satisfied by mass-produced materials.

Roofing with clay tiles requires more materials and some of these are not found easily in the city. The process is more complicated. You first put up a *tendido* (framework of a roof from ridge to eaves) of wheat straw, then a layer of clay mixed with straw and then the tiles. The cement tiles need only a wooden framework, a *gancho* (hook) and battens.

A roof is built quickly and without major problems with cement tiles and the urban resident knows this. The clean, presentable appearance fits in with his vision of urban life. The recent rise in the cost of cement will prevent its use by popular sectors and so lower demand. Despite the cost, cement tiles require fewer materials and can be made in a shorter time. The total cost is probably still less than clay tiles.

One can describe residents' attitudes as cautious in that they must assess the usefulness of new ideas such as the cement tile. People are not resistant to change as such. More needs to be known about the assumptions which influence their building practices.

Conclusions

As with other aspects of life in a traditional society, the building process is integrated into a framework of reciprocity and collective organization. This approach is lost in the city and replaced by capitalist social relations. It is not possible to understand the innovations occurring in building technology without taking this into account.

This study does not accept the argument that traditional techniques have disappeared because of the passage of time and the introduction of capitalism into the Andean region. Knowledge is preserved in the minds of migrants but cannot be implemented because of their poor circumstances. One can say that there is an awareness of changes in the use of *tapial* and *adobe*. Many *barriada* residents are influenced by traditional knowledge when they build their homes. The conditions affecting the building process include the urgent need to provide a roof to guard against the possibility of eviction and also practical factors such as economic resources, labour and access to materials.

Much has been said about the peasants' resistance to change. This study indicates that rather than opposition to change *per se*, the residents adopt a cautious approach based upon an assessment of the practicality of new ideas.

There is a consistent set of assumptions which shapes the decision-making process and directs the activities undertaken by residents. The transfer of *tapial* as a building method from the countryside to the *barriada* is an example of how this process works. *Tapial* adapts well to the urban context. It is cheap, does not involve complicated processes and is quicker than other methods. It also fits in with the resident's belief that his house is a temporary structure.

The idea of the 'permanent temporary house' enables one to understand that the completion of a house is seen neither as urgent nor as a vital

196

problem by the resident. Once you have a roof over your head, the completion of the house comes later. Other things are more important. The resident is far more preoccupied with working to support his family and the difficulty of finding sources of income. Building can be left to a better time. This should be taken into account by those introducing housing improvement plans. These should be geared to execution 'by stages' as this reflects the reality of the *barriada*.

Talk of the 'ideal house' and plans for future house improvement suggests that the migrant resident has a need to justify his decision to move to the city. His dreams are of a house made of bricks, iron and cement with living room, dining room, bedrooms, a second floor and a flat roof. This is an 'urban' house which will confirm his new life style.

Acknowledgements

This study would not have been possible without the support of people in Huancayo who shared with me their experience and knowledge of the growth of the city and of the process of formation of the *barriadas*.

My thanks go to Marcelo Juan Muñoz of the Office for Urban Planning of the Provincial Council of Huancayo who showed interest in my work and provided important information on new settlements. Thanks also to Manuel Soto and Ann Cosme of CICEP and Elsa Santillán of CEDEPAS who introduced me to *barriada* leaders with whom I enjoyed stimulating discussions about what is happening in 'popular' Huancayo. I would particularly like to thank Filomeno Ríos Varillas for his generous contribution and support.

Finally, I express my appreciation to the leaders of the three *barriadas*: Luis Aguilar of Justicia, Paz y Vida; Jeremías Arzapalo, leader of Santa Rosa de Lima and also President of the Federation of Human Settlements and *Pueblos Jovenes* ('young towns') of Huancayo and A. Villalba of Juan Parra del Riego. Through them, I would like to thank the residents who opened their doors and allowed me to share their opinions, needs and dreams about the building of their homes.

Technologies of survival in the slums of Santo Domingo

DAVID SCOTT LUTHER

Introduction

The Dominican Republic, like many other so-called 'Third World' countries, faces problems today of massive rural-urban migration. This process begins in the countryside where living conditions have reached crisis levels, with illiteracy running high, chronic food shortages, severe deforestation and exhaustion of arable land. An unjust property structure and land exploitation adds to a situation in which the rural population has few options except to migrate to the cities.

What migrants find in the cities, however, is unemployment, under-employment, urban overcrowding, housing unfit for human habitation, scarcity of drinking water, pollution, lack of medical facilities, falling standards of living among marginal residents, the concentration of incomes and privileges within few groups at the expense of underpaid workers. These are some of the factors which have led to a very low standard of living for the poor.

This massive migration towards the cities has had many and serious consequences and marginality for the masses has become a daily reality in our urban centres. This is shown in the fact that in Santo Domingo 64 per cent of the population, those living in overcrowded settlements, only occupy 19 per cent of the area. While annual population growth for the country as a whole is only 2.6 per cent, the capital city is growing at a rate of 6.3 per cent and the marginal settlements at about 10 per cent.

The situation prevailing in these settlements is truly alarming as they have no infrastructure for the supply of water, disposal of refuse, electricity supply, stormwater drainage or sanitation. No plans have been drawn up which would guarantee them the basic standards of comfort and security which are the right of every human being. This situation channels people into developing organizational, socio-economic, cultural and technological strategies simply in order to survive.

MR D.S. LUTHER (Dominican Republic) is a founding member and Executive Director of the Instituto Dominicano de Desarrollo Integral, Inc. (Dominican Institute for Integral Development). He is also a founding member and past Director of the Appropriate Technology centre for low-cost housing. He is an architect.

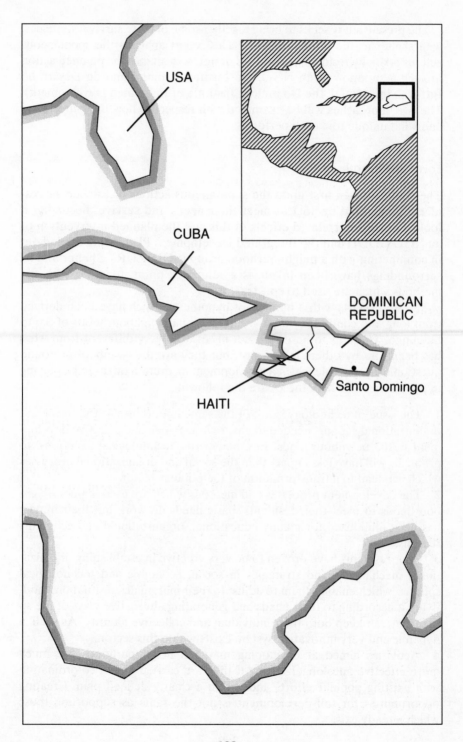

USA

CUBA

DOMINICAN
REPUBLIC

Santo Domingo

HAITI

The present study seeks to bring together some of these survival strategies, with shelter as the reference point. This report analyses the spontaneous actions taken by residents, organized or not. It examines the planned action in such a situation of an NGO, the Instituto Dominicano de Desarrollo Integral, Inc. (IDDI: the Dominican Institute of Integrated Development). The two approaches will be examined with respect to how they interrelate and what unique role each performs.

Focus and hypothesis

The study focused first upon the spontaneous actions of La Zurza's residents (organized or not) to meet their needs and survive. Secondly, it looked at the interrelated effects of this and the planned intervention of an NGO (IDDI) and the Integrated Development Plan, being carried out in conjunction with a neighbourhood group (SODIZUR). Shelter and its surroundings have been taken as a reference point, together with the methods which are used to construct it.

The study starts with a number of hypotheses which have been derived from long and continuous work in the marginal neighbourhoods of Santo Domingo. These hypotheses are not necessarily very different from what has been said by others in the past, but they are the results of profound questioning of the role which a development institution ought to be playing in poor areas. The hypotheses are the following:

1   The issue of technology is not of the same importance as the social and organizational support needed to ensure a sustained and effective development in the neighbourhoods. In other words, technological 'solutions' to problems will have less impact than the social and organizational processes which can lead to a transformation of the popular sector.

2   The development processes and methods which are used in poor neighbourhoods to meet their residents' basic needs do work but their impact has been minimized for mainly educational, organizational and economic reasons.

3   Poor residents have proven to be very creative in establishing organizational mechanisms and strategies in social, economic and technological spheres, which enables them to adjust to their marginalized situation, modifying it according to their needs and generating alternative ways of life so that they can keep both their individual and collective identity. As such, a dynamic and very innovative system exists within this sector.

4   Activities aimed at developing marginal neighbourhoods are much more effective and longer-lasting if they are carried out in co-ordination with existing popular efforts and within a clearly defined plan. Creating opportunities for self-development is not the same as supporting those which already exist.

200

5   The role of an NGO is that of a facilitator of grass roots control and not a substitute for it. This frequently exists, perhaps latently, as an indigenous form of self-development. When this is not recognized, more problems are likely to be created than solved.

Methodology

The methodology used to collect the data for this study was a combination of the traditional and non-conventional. It was traditional in the sense that it gathered information through interviews and questionnaires and non-conventional in so far as it involved participant observation and discussion with residents, members of some grass roots organizations in La Zurza and some IDDI officials. Both methods were used in order to compare spontaneous grass roots replies with the ideas put forward in the planned activities of the Integrated Development Plan. It should be pointed out that all the research methods were applied only in La Zurza and administered to those involved in the Plan. The methods can be summarized as follows.

A series of surveys have been carried out in La Zurza since 1985. These included some 256 household interviews for the 'Baseline survey for a housing improvement project' in October 1985. This was intended to measure the relative increase in the level of housing in the neighbourhood from then to the present and to place the data within a planned programme of action. There was also a survey of some 93 households under the title of 'Socio-economic study of La Zurza settlement' in August 1985. This made it possible to compare the change in landlords within the settlement from then to the present. A survey of 100 households called 'Survival Technology' in La Zurza in November 1988 was to record the spontaneous reactions of residents to existing housing, sanitary and service provision conditions. This survey was carried out totally independently of the Plan.

In February 1989 a 1,000 household survey, 'A study of the socio-economic and servicing situation', was carried out in La Zurza. The purpose was to compare the relationship of La Zurza Integrated Development Plan, IDDI and SODIZUR (the grass roots organization) with residents, taking into account the following:

1   the felt needs of residents;
2   the extent to which residents accepted these organizations;
3   how far residents accepted the Plan;
4   the degree to which the plan's organizational, building, economic, credit and educational activities were accepted.

The less conventional methodology used employed various techniques. These included conversations with some members of the community to form an idea of their view of IDDI, the Plan, grass roots organizations and how these different initiatives affected their lives. Conversations with representatives of grassroots organizations (mainly SODIZUR) helped to discover their point of view on the matter. Talks with IDDI officials gave an idea of what the Plan had in mind with regard to means of implementation and co-ordination. Personal experiences gleaned from extensive work in the neighbourhood added further information.

The spontaneous response

The ways in which the community responded spontaneously were examined. Existing conditions were looked at, including how people have been able to tackle problems through the mechanisms and strategies of survival which they have developed. One can sense tremendous effort in individual and group actions by residents, as well as collectively-organized initiatives which are outside the plan.

Housing conditions in La Zurza are a reflection of the marginal living circumstances of its population. Although average family size is six people, 59 per cent of houses have only one room and some 29 per cent have only two. The single-family house is typical (73.9 per cent of the total). This can be traced back to the individualistic way in which land was acquired. The majority of residents migrated from the countryside and are used to living in isolated houses. Only 6.8 per cent live in *cuarterias* (rooms or rented parts of a house). This shows the individualistic nature of the settlement's formation. It should be understood that the low-income resident is an urban peasant or, as they say in the Dominican Republic, a *campucho*.

Regarding house size, 61.7 per cent live in dwellings of less than 25m² which shows a high level of overcrowding. The land they occupy is also very small, having been acquired simply to erect a basic dwelling which could accommodate one family. The results of the survey show that 82.2 per cent of houses are occupied by a single family, with 10.7 per cent occupied by two families.

No family owns the land they occupy although 63 per cent have paid for improvements and another 33 per cent are renters. Over a third of those interviewed said that they had built their home there because there was nowhere else and 42 per cent because they would be close to their relatives. 73 per cent had to 'buy' the land on which they built, although the land did not belong to the so-called vendor.

The present houses of the heads of household interviewed are the result of a series of phases of development. A variety of building materials were used to reach the goal of a 'proper home of one's own'. The percentage of owner-occupied land in La Zurza is higher than that for the capital as a whole. In 1981 Santo Domingo had 52.8 per cent in this category while the settlement itself saw an increase in rented accommodation to a level of 44.9 per cent. This figure is influenced by the profitability of rented housing in

Santo Domingo compared with the type of housing which could be built in the marginal neighbourhoods, especially as the latter did not have any legal right to the land.

As for building materials, 88.7 per cent of houses have a cement floor which underlines the concern to improve one's dwelling, even perhaps at the cost of sacrificing other necessities. This figure is higher than the 1981 census data which shows only 63 per cent of houses with cement floors.

The material preferred for walls is wood (42.7 per cent of the total) and then a mixture of materials, including blocks (28.8 per cent) and finally some 19.3 per cent using throwaways such as cardboard and tin cans. What is used to build walls gives an immediate picture of the poverty of the sector and the limited resources available for house construction. This also shows up some instability in the sector. Families do not invest more in their houses because they may be living in dangerous areas such as steep hillsides which are always prone to landslides. Secondly, there is always the chance that the government might evict. Thirdly, families know the land does not belong to them. Fourthly, families do not invest more in their houses because they are located in areas of high crime rates.

Galvanized iron sheeting was the most preferred roofing material (54.8 per cent), followed by cardboard (16.7 per cent), a mixture (12.8 per cent), throwaway materials (11.6 per cent), asbestos (3.1 per cent) and reinforced concrete (0.4 per cent). It is clear that the roofing materials used have a short life-span. G.I. sheeting is cheaper than concrete but this is not the only reason it is more common in the settlement. An equally important fact is that the foundations of the houses have not been constructed to bear the weight of concrete. It is accepted that low-income housing is not built according to official standards. These are intended to ensure that buildings comply with certain minimum safety requirements.

Many innovations in construction techniques were developed when residents could not find a conventional low-cost method. Examples are those of foundations and the stabilization of hillside slopes. Here the innovations took the form of car tyres, sandbags and refuse of various kinds. This was often due to the fact that the settlement was in an accident-prone location. A conventional solution to this problem was beyond the means of the residents concerned.

As for service connections, the majority of sanitary facilities are latrines (93.8 per cent) while the rest are *inodoros* (a type of toilet). The average provision of toilets per family is 1.3. Only 31.1 per cent of respondents had domestic water connections while the rest had to find water where they could. The water-mains (*tomas de agua*) supply per family is 1.5. Given the scarcity of water, it is hardly surprising that there are few showers in the settlement. The proportion is in fact 1:18 which is very low. In La Zurza, water and the use of latrines and showers are sold as services. Some 33 per cent of respondents said they had to buy their water in this way. Exploitation exists at all levels. Moreover, it should be borne in mind that the settlement only receives water less than four hours a day and that sometimes there have been two weeks or more without water.

The result of the surveys was that half the houses are fit for human habitation while half are definitely not. Of the former, 34.7 per cent were in fair condition but only 15.6 per cent were found to be in good condition. That is, a large number of houses considered as 'fit for human habitation' are not really adequate.

Constructing a habitat

As far as the construction of the house is concerned, a settlement usually starts with people marking out a plot of land and then building their houses in stages. The materials they use for flooring, walls and roofs change according to family income. Poor neighbourhood housing has nothing to do with mass or serial construction involving fixed norms but is rather a response to circumstances which even the owners are unable to predict.

None of the houses were built using collective labour based upon mutual aid. When questioned, the builders said they were either bricklayers or carpenters receiving minimum payment from the householders, although the majority were relations, such as a brother, uncle or cousin. Some 81 per cent of houses were built at night in order to avoid police harassment. Police tended to stop building on land which was under litigation.

The initial stages of construction were undertaken at both the family and neighbourhood levels. Kinship networks provided input at the first level. Many families had not yet created relationships with other residents which would have provided a wider form of support. This only happened when houses already existed and the area was sufficiently settled. Another type of construction exists in La Zurza, although it was not to be found in the zone under discussion here. That is when new areas of the settlement are invaded by residents who want to encourage more people to settle there in order to give them greater security in collective terms. This could be called mutual aid through necessity.

It is commonly known that no sources for the financing of house construction can be found in the informal sector. Building is a slow process directly linked to family income at any specific moment. In sectors where housing is financed informally, as in La Zurza, house size is an indicator of the investment a family is prepared to make in order to get a roof. The larger the house, the greater the investment. Larger houses are found in the more secure areas such as the *llanuras* (flat lands) and in the areas near the streets.

On the other hand, one should not make a simple equation of size of house and amount invested because popular housing experiences a building process which is distinct from that in the formal sector. In the first stage, residents take possession of the land with a minimal investment until they are sure of both its security and convenience as a permanent site. Next, the house is built by stages depending upon the inhabitants' economic resources. This may take many years to complete from the initial ring of stones to the finished building.

Despite the fact that settlements have transient populations, there is a strong sense of community. Eighty-two per cent of those interviewed said they got on well with their neighbours. Communal work is undertaken at various levels of activity. Apart from the initial stage of building, neighbours also frequently co-operate in the execution of projects of common value. These include projects in times of emergencies such as heavy rains, landslides or a river overflowing its banks. People co-operate also on the installation of infrastructure systems such as drinking-water networks and pedestrian paths. Neighbours may also, to a certain degree, organize communal maintenance of these services.

The involvement of a popular organization in transforming a settlement is limited by its lack of resources and strong institutional structures. Other limitations are the absence of real democracy in the decision-making process and the fact that many of activities will be responses to immediate circumstances rather than being of a sustained and permanent nature. These groups have institutional weaknesses which impede their efficiency and effectiveness and as a result may disappear. There is no real co-operation between them and when co-operation does occur, it tends to be temporary and very specific.

The number of popular organizations in the settlement who are operating independently of the La Zurza Integrated Development Plan is increasing. Fifty-five per cent of all organizations active in La Zurza have been formed since 1982. Settlement residents are confident that they themselves can improve conditions (59 per cent believed this to be possible). However, their representative organizations have been unable to respond adequately to the needs of residents because of structural weaknesses and a lack of resources. Many of the organizations have limited interests and this affects their acceptance by and impact upon the general population. Many of the activities undertaken are important in terms of stimulating changes in the minds of residents but these organizations have a tendency to be more theoretical than practical in their attitudes. The consequence is that residents have reservations which the popular organizations must overcome in the future.

The planned response

The planned response is to be found within the parameters of the La Zurza Integrated Development Plan. This is based upon collaboration between a popular organization (SODIZUR) and IDDI. Inter-institutional co-operation extends from the grassroots of SODIZUR to its governing council and is multisectoral. It embraces four distinct areas of activity: social (organization and formation), health, generation of employment and physical infrastructure (housing improvement, community infrastructure and equipment).

Both the planning of collective and individual activities under the auspices of the plan and their implementation is undertaken in a collective manner. SODIZUR and its appropriate commission are the initiators of all that is done in the settlement in terms of the Plan's programme. As the present study is concerned with the habitat and its surroundings, we will describe only the activities in this sphere.

Housing improvement
The land where the settlement is located is under litigation between the Dominican Government and the Vicini family. Consequently, the first aim of the Housing Improvement Programme is to achieve legal recognition of the improvement, since it is not possible to legalize land ownership. This is done by the state, recognizing the permanent residence of families on land where they have lived for at least five years.

The Programme is carried out on the basis of a rotating fund which is managed by two committees. The first is the Committee for settlement credit/loans which is part of SODIZUR. The Committee is responsible for receiving applications, filling in the necessary forms, evaluating the social and moral condition of applicants and sending approved applications on to the IDDI's Technical committee. This carries out a technical and financial study on selections made by the Settlement committee. At the time of writing, 59 houses had been improved in the settlement. The same committee is also responsible for evaluating loan applications for economic activities, such as setting up small firms and shops. More than 400 loans have been granted.

Houses are improved in groups of five to ten and building is the responsibility of householders and their relatives. Technical supervision is provided by both SODIZUR and the IDDI. It is a pre-condition of the programme that householders must contribute their labour to improving the land around their houses — infrastructure such as pedestrian paths, stormwater drainage, domestic drains and collective latrines. This has been considered necessary in order to create a communal spirit, balancing individual and collective benefits. To date, this has worked reasonably well.

The householders were able to select building techniques most appropriate to their situation and take advantage of loans of up to seven years with favourable repayment arrangements. All chose block walls and cement floors, some 75 per cent G.I. sheeting roofs, and the rest, reinforced concrete. About 15 per cent decided to build two-storey houses which they share with another family living on the upper floor. This allows more space for latrines and recreation areas at ground level. The programme has achieved significant spontaneous co-operation among those residents in receipt of loans. Some 25 per cent have built latrines with the money.

Another interesting result has been that residents have been willing to continue improvements with their own savings. Similarly, other families who have not benefited themselves from loans have also improved their houses with their own funds, using higher quality, more permanent materials than before. When SODIZUR acquired sufficient experience in the efficient management of resources, IDDI transferred control of the revolving fund to it.

Building of physical infrastructure
This involves construction of pedestrian paths and steps, drinking water systems, the stabilization of slopes, the installation of latrines and storm-water and sanitary drainage. These activities are of collective benefit. Each project is supervised by a skilled craftsman and the labour is done voluntarily by residents.

Impact and consequences of the Settlement Development Plan
As a result of the support by the plan, residents have achieved access to a series of benefits which would not normally have been within their reach. These include loans for house building and legalization of tenancy. This gives residents a tremendous sense of security and inspires many of them to continue improving their houses without acquiring new loans. Other families not involved in the Programme are also improving their homes themselves. The technical and financial support for building physical infrastructure could only be achieved through this planned activity. The benefits from co-operation between an NGO and popular groups will be more profound and longer-lasting than spontaneous activity, no matter how well-intentioned. The question is to define when and how individual activities can be strengthened and pointed in the right direction for the well-being of the community.

With respect to SODIZUR's role in the settlement, our survey showed that only 40 per cent of respondents knew what the initials meant. This can be interpreted in different ways and only 20 per cent knew what IDDI meant. Of this 40 per cent, 76 per cent believed that SODIZUR was dedicated to solving the settlement's problems and another 7 per cent said that it implemented good works. Only 27 per cent had contact with a leader of the organization but about 56 per cent were aware of a project or activity which SODIZUR had undertaken in the settlement. This contradicts, to a certain degree, the fact that only 40 per cent of respondents knew what SODIZUR was. An explanation may be that some people did not know who was responsible for the projects or activities. Sixty-three per cent knew that there were projects in housing and latrines, and another 28 per cent knew of the activities with respect to pedestrian pathways and bridges. Only 11 per cent said that these projects had benefited them directly (40 per cent in the area of infrastructure, 25 per cent in housing, 20 per cent in health and 12 per cent in nutrition). A majority, 52 per cent, agreed that these projects had improved conditions in the settlement.

There was clear confidence on the part of respondents in SODIZUR's potential to improve life in the settlement. Eighty-eight per cent believed this to be possible although only 32 per cent participated in such activities of community development. Fifty-five per cent were willing to support the organization actively and only 7 per cent rejected any involvement. With respect to future activities, 50 per cent said that SODIZUR should concentrate upon building and 32 per cent that it should address the problem of basic services.

It is clear that SODIZUR has gained the confidence of those residents who know of its existence but it has not managed to achieve a sufficiently high profile within the settlement. This limits its capacity to transform life in La Zurza.

The role of IDDI in the settlement has not been to resolve problems but to be a facilitator of the organization and development of La Zurza. It has been the responsibility of IDDI to know when to support existing spontaneous activities and when to introduce innovative processes and activities. In this sense, IDDI has had to act with caution in La Zurza. IDDI has followed a method of responding to demands for support while at the same time being aware that sometimes it was essential to act as a catalyst of change. IDDI has not encouraged individual solutions which are isolated from a collective approach. As a result, impact at the family level has been less than at the neighbourhood and settlement levels. SODIZUR is responsible for activities at the individual family level. This defines an important aspect of the relationship between the two bodies.

Conclusion

By transferring the responsibility for the organization of settlement change to SODIZUR, the Plan will ensure sustained, planned activities with multiplying effects which will benefit the population. In this way, it is possible to preserve and direct spontaneous actions which emerge during daily life as a response to the thousand-and-one needs which exist in the settlement. The Plan has created a method for identifying the anxieties and needs of the population and providing a framework for their resolution through the planned activities of SODIZUR. Perhaps this is the most important contribution the Plan has to offer the settlement.

Survival is the daily objective of residents in the marginal settlements. People want the basic necessities of life such as access to water, employ-

208

ment, food, education for their children, adequate health conditions for their family, hygienic sanitary arrangements, provision of access roads and internal pedestrian pathways. Residents want to survive but they also want to improve their living conditions. There is a very definite merger of the need for survival and the desire for progress. This is shown at the family, neighbourhood and popular organizational levels, although the methods employed differ. We can make the following observations about these various activities:

1 The present image created by the existing informality of life in the settlements is one of chaos, disorder and illegality. However, this does not correspond with the real conditions pertaining there. On the contrary, one finds an order which is both defined and functional, with norms and rules which, although unwritten, are established and are accepted as law by residents. The settlement is a collective entity at all levels of organization and is recognized as such by residents.

2 The dilemma of neighbourhood settlement is located more in social and organizational processes than in technological ones.

3 It was a general conclusion that the innovations observed in the settlement were more of an organizational than technological type. Technological innovations were evident when conventional techniques did not provide the solutions to the problems residents encountered. If no low-cost solution was available then people had to innovate in order to be able to live in these places. Innovation was gradual, achieved in stages in order to meet the need for building on the hillsides at low cost. Others in the settlements copied these innovations.

4 It is clear that the impact of spontaneous activities is limited because residents do not have the resources to develop or sustain them themselves. If these activities are not supported by a more permanent process, they are likely to collapse. A positive aspect is that the activities based in the community, although often individualistic, and are a product of needs which are deeply-felt by residents. Planned activities which do not originate in the felt needs of residents could cause as many problems as they solve. This is where a popular organization can perform the function of taking the need and giving it a more coherent and permanent form.

5 Another important issue to be considered is when and under what conditions a spontaneous activity becomes a sustained, planned process. This requires an external agent or catalyst such as an emergency or the threat of eviction, strong settlement leadership or the support of an established body such as IDDI in La Zurza.

6 Mutual support is sometimes provided in the initial stages of house construction but never during the process of gradual improvement. This isdone by the individuals concerned without their neighbours' help. Spontaneous community support is most marked during emergencies and is

209

rarely planned or sustained. Planned activities are based more upon needs felt at neighbourhood than the individual level. These activities help the formation of popular organizations which achieve a greater or lesser degree of permanency within the settlement.

Recommendations

1 To be human is not simply to be the *object* of one's development but is also to be the *subject*, playing a central role in the search for solutions to problems. The human group which is affected by any plan, programme or project should be the first and final reference point in order to facilitate the group's control. All development initiatives should encourage the autonomy and independence of the group and individuals involved. The popular sector is not an exception to this rule.

2 In the final analysis, the responsibility for changing lives should be borne by the marginal population themselves. Consequently, their representative organizations should be strengthened in order to aid this process. This should not be done in a way which would destroy the independence of people. These groups can better represent marginal people because the groups understand living conditions, needs and desires better than any other body. An indispensable precondition is the promotion of solidarity and collective consciousness within the population.

3 The solutions which are produced by spontaneous popular activities should be valued, respected and supported. Where possible, these should be directed through planned programmes which can make them more permanent without detracting from their authenticity. This is mainly the responsibility of popular organizations themselves aided by the disinterested support of NGOs. It is essential that a balance is sought between the power of the NGOs in terms of institutional strength and disposable resources and the demands and needs of popular organizations. All should complement each other's activities.

4 NGOs are the tools and instruments best-suited to supporting the development of the marginal population in the short- and medium-term. However, NGOs must accept that their role is to *support* the marginal population and not *replace* it. This implies a search for and application of programmes and projects which respond to the real situation of the people. The role of the NGOs can be defined as one of channelling resources and information, of acting as mediators between the state and the popular sector and as promoters of alternative development policies. Formal institutions must seek to recover their credibility and the trust of the popular sectors if a greater fragmentation of Dominican society is to be avoided.

5 It should be an unconditional principle that all activities directed towards development must allow for the opportunity to be human and to

210

achieve self-fulfilment. We must commit our efforts to the qualitative development of both human beings and the physical world which surrounds and sustains us.

The emphasis must be upon balanced and integrated development of the individual, concentrating upon the growth of consciousness and self-fulfilment. The re-ordering of our society must begin with fundamental changes in the consciousness of each citizen, especially those who enjoy a high degree of decision-making power over questions of national development. These changes can occur either gradually through a sustained, directed process or in a dramatic manner in situations which are out of control. The ideal would be a slow period of adaptation and accommodation in order to be able to save what is positive in our present situation. The choice is ours.

Water, myth and technology in a Peruvian coastal valley

MARÍA TERESA ORÉ and GUILLERMO ROCHABRUN

During the time between 1930 and 1960, the peasants of the Ica Valley in Peru struggled to defend their land through control of the water supply. They were challenged by the expansion of the *haciendas* (large plantations) and growing state intervention, both features of the capitalist modernization of the country. The peasants relied upon traditional methods of building, the maintenance of canals and drains and the collective organization of irrigation.

Part of the collective memory of this period focuses upon victories gained and there is a strong sense of linkage with the past. However, another part of this memory recalls defeat and a lack of relevance of history to the present. It is the intention of this study to consider the reasons for this discrepancy.

The Ica Valley: history and legend

Our case study is the Tate community, which is located in the lower part of the valley. Lack of rainfall along the whole coastline means that agriculture is dependent upon irrigation. The indigenous people of the pre-hispanic period achieved an extraordinary level of agricultural development in these desert zones. They used different irrigation methods such as seasonal river beds, aqueducts and canals. The latter were most frequently employed and consisted in diverting surface water from a number of rivers to land which had no access to water. Many pre-Incaic canals were extended by the Incas, a policy which aided the consolidation of Imperial rule over subject peoples. This was not done without conflict.

The valley is crossed by the River Ica. However, the major part of the area is irrigated by a pre-hispanic canal known as La Achirana, which draws its water from the river. This canal facilitated historical growth of the Valley, particularly in this century. Unfortunately, the water level is variable and is particularly low between January and March. This results in a limited time being available for irrigation. The farmers have had to adapt themselves to these conditions.

MS M.T. ORE (Peru) is a sociologist. She is currently carrying out research on the problem of irrigation in Peru. This work is with campesinos in the rural coastal and mountain areas. Her special area of interest is the history and oral tradition of Peruvian campesinos. Before joining ITDG, she lectured in sociology at the Catholic University of Lima and was a Director of an NGO working with people's organizations.

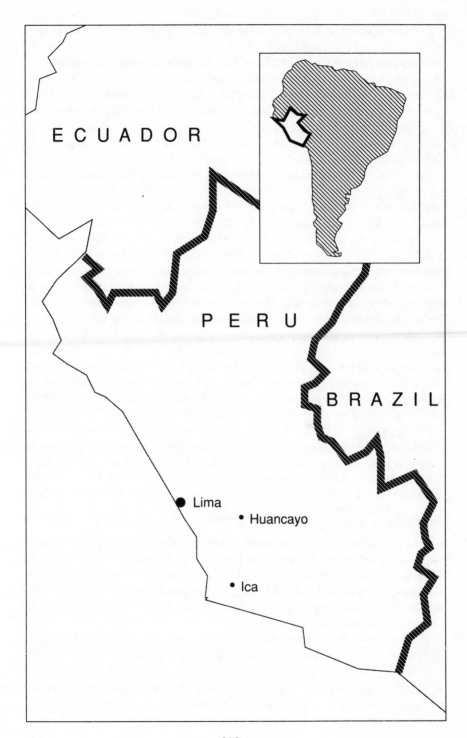

Popular legend has it that La Achirana was built by the Inca Pachacutec at the request of a local peasant girl, Mama Chiri, with whom he was deeply in love. The peasants say that Pachacutec's army built the canal's original 36km length in 40 days. Mama Chiri, who came from Tate, gave her name to the canal. As in other Andean myths, a woman obtains water for her village and the latter then assumes a priority over other villages in access to irrigation. Tate is located at the end of the original canal, a place where the most important Indian leaders lived. The Spanish accorded them a certain degree of respect.

In 1532 — when Spanish rule began — the valley's main products were wine and vines. The irrigated land was divided into an upper area which was dominated by *haciendas* and had greater access to the water and a lower part where the Indians lived. The Spanish Crown recognized Tate's ownership of the extensive Pampa de los Castillos. The peasants managed it collectively, obtaining firewood from the *huarango* trees and grazing livestock. They could not farm the plain owing to the absence of irrigation.

Cotton was introduced into the valley at the end of the nineteenth century. By the First World War, cotton had become the major crop, not only for the landowners but also for the Indians. At the same time, the state began establishing its control over the water supply. The cotton boom led to an expansion of the *haciendas*. Although there were, as yet, no land ownership conflicts, the *hacienda* owners had better access to water and irrigation. In response, between 1916–24, the Indians and *hacienda* workers formed a strong Federation. This was eventually repressed by the authorities. The village of Parcona, the Federation's headquarters, was razed to the ground.

The period referred to in our study begins a few years after these events. Before turning to it, we consider the historical, cultural and organizational structure relating to water and irrigation.

The culture and organization of irrigation

It is common for Andean communities to worship a lake or other important sources of water. Water is the original of life and is regarded as the symbol of ethnic unity. The peasants living alongside La Achirana lived in separate communities but all identified themselves as *achiraneros*. Their fathers and grandfathers had worked on the canal and it gave them a collective feeling.

The peasants had developed a complex system of obligations and rights with respect to the canal. Peasants paid water dues in terms of collective labour, but in return considered irrigation to be their right. The peasants' responsibilities consisted of the management of the irrigation process and the cleaning and upkeep of the canal. They regarded these activities as constantly renewing their relationship with the water.

214

These practical, voluntary activities attested to a large fund of technical knowledge and emphasized the symbolic value peasants attached to the canal.

The natural characteristics of the canal — the variability of the water supply and the limitations this placed upon the timing of irrigation — exerted a strong influence upon its use. Since colonial times, the head of the valley had been irrigated first — the *haciendas* by day and Indian land by night.

Management of the canal

As irrigation began at the top of the valley and finished in the lower part, it was vital to open and shut the water outlets at the right time so as not to waste water and to irrigate in sequence. A group of horsemen known as *corredores* (scouts) kept a constant watch over the canal and reported progress of the irrigation to succeeding sectors. Canal keepers were responsible for opening and shutting each outlet at the correct moment. The *corredores* also looked out for landslides which could obstruct the flow of water. If this happened, labourers selected for their strength and dexterity would rush to repair the damage. They were responsible for reinforcing the walls of the canal and for maintenance of the sluices.

Each village was responsible for its section of canal and a president was elected to direct the operation. He was elected by other residents and was considered by them to have great knowledge and authority.

Cleaning the canal

All the men, women and children of La Achirana were involved in cleaning the canal. Their main concern was to remove the sand left by the water on the bottom of the canal. They did this with very light wooden scoops made out of *huarango* wood. This activity, made necessary by the payment imposed on them by the State for the use of the canal, acquired the symbolic value of recognizing their rights to it.

Hacienda owners and peasants were involved in disputes over irrigation rights and the opening and shutting of the sluices. The Indians' organization assumed both demand making and union functions, and presidents of each sector represented their communities in conflicts with the landowners. Meetings and marches, sometimes of a violent nature, were organized to demand right of access to irrigation.

The growth of the valley

In the early 1930s, the state embarked upon a programme of development of the Choclococha Lakes whose wates flooded the River Ica each September. This project aimed to improve irrigation of land already under cultivation but was intended also to open up 10,000 hectares of the Pampa de los

Castillos to farming. Both the *hacienda* owners and Indians were interested in acquiring this new land.

During the same period, the *hacienda* owners began to dig wells in order to tap underground streams which were abundant at the bottom of the valley. The wells helped the introduction of a permanent method of irrigation which was not subject to variability of the surface waters. Irrigation was on a strictly individual basis. The cost of the installation and upkeep of the wells put them out of the reach of the Indians. This put the *hacienda* owners in an advantageous position with respect to the acquisition of the Pampa de los Castillos.

The Valley was expected to expand rapidly as a result of the use of the Choclococha waters and the drilling of the wells. The fundamental question was who would own the newly-irrigated land?

The Tate community had property titles to the Pampa which were granted by Charles V. The 1932 Constitution promised protection of communal land and prohibited their sale. Despite this, the *hacienda* owners began a campaign to take control of the land and eventually obtain legal title over it. They drilled wells and began cultivation, threatened the Indians and attempted to bribe leaders to sell land.

These methods provoked violent reactions: 'We decided to go out on the *pampas* and see how we could stop it. There were 14,000 of us and we were well organized. We went out in 10 lorries, both men and women, carrying axes and hammers with the aim of destroying the canals, section by section. Then the Prefect and the police arrived. He asked who was in charge. We said we all were and that we had come to take possession of the land . . . the Prefect told us that he was going to talk to Picasso and Rizo Patrón, and make them stop . . . Soon after that came the announcement that they would soon begin distributing the land.' (Interview with Nicanor Carhuallo, August 1987)

The State intended financing the Choclococha project through the sale of the Pampa de los Castillos lands. In an attempt to prevent this, the Indians decided in the 1940s to bring legal action against both the *hacienda* owners and the state. Defence was based principally on those colonial land titles held by Tate. However, in 1948, the dictatorship of General Odría ordered the case closed, divided the Pampa into plots and put them up for sale.

In an effort to appease the disgruntled Indians, the state proposed selling some plots at low prices provided the peasants relinquished their communal land and bought individually. A preferential offer was made to the residents of Tate and particularly their leaders, with the conscious aim of excluding other villages from the deal. Tate decided to accept, possibly influenced by the special rights given it by the legend.

The Indian movement was divided and the *hacienda* owners' expansion in the *pampa* was accelerated. In a final effort to keep their land, the presidents of the other villages ordered the occupation of strategic areas. They decided to extend the length of La Achirana to bring water to the new lands and so make this policy more effective. The project began in 1958, one year before the waters were expected to flow from Choclococha. Many of the wells had begun to dry up because the proposed canal from the River Ica to the *pampa* had not yet been built. Additionally, the canals built by the *hacienda* owners for the same purpose were not yet in operation. Neither project had thought of irrigating the *pampa* by extending the La Achirana canal. *This was the Indians' idea and was conceived because the canal was the symbol of their own identity.*

The project was regarded with scepticism by both the *hacienda* owners and those peasants who did not participate in it. In its execution, the Indians employed both their own technology and organizational forms. This was a collective activity begun and completed without any State support. The canal was extended by 18 kilometres on the basis of a design drawn up by the peasants. Decisions concerning design, the organization of labour, time, transport and the feeding of workers were taken by the peasants themselves. The canal was built in stages, each stage being the responsibility of the village through which it was passing. In the final stages, when success was evident, some *hacienda* owners also contributed in order to benefit from the irrigation.

By extending La Achirana, the Indians were completing the work of the Inca Pachacutec. The symbolic value had become a reality. One part of Tate, when it was elevated to the status of District, took the name of the Inca. Peasants remember that it was called 'the new Pachacutec'.

These events demonstrate several impressive features, including the organizational, technical and cultural autonomy of the peasants. Most notably, the events show the initiative and determination required to undertake a work of such great breadth and consequence. The peasants' efforts were successful from a technical and productive perspective in that 5,000 hectares were added to the Valley's cultivable land. However, the period is now remembered as one of defeat rather than victory. Why should this be so? One would have expected that the extension of La Achirana would have produced an independent peasantry in both economic, social and cultural terms. In fact, the reverse was true. We will now examine why this happened.

The pitfalls of modernization

The extension of La Achirana was the last recourse open to the peasants although they had already lost their organizational unity and with it the possibility of collective control over the Pampa de los Castillos. The extension gave them access to small plots which they had no possibility of enlarging and which they could not develop into prosperous, self-sufficient farming land. Large *haciendas* were established on the plains and these *haciendas* benefited more than the Indians from the new water source.

At the same time, the state was assuming control over a number of functions with respect to irrigation previously undertaken by the Indians. These included the cleaning and maintenance of the canal using modern machinery, supervision of the flow of water, repair of cracks and control of water distribution along the various sectors of the canal bank.

The peasant-landowner relationship had been replaced by a peasant-state relationship. This was characterized by impersonal, logical criteria based upon the application of standards of efficiency which were not suited to the economic conditions of the *minifundia* (small farms, individual plots). The peasants' relationship to the canal was now a contractual one based upon the payment of money.

In 1969, the military government of General Juan Velasco introduced an agrarian reform law which divided the *haciendas* into co-operatives which were handed over to their former workers. The *hacienda* owners became medium landowners allowed to keep up to 150 hectares for themselves. They managed these with very modern and efficient methods. Much social and political power in the Ica Valley stayed with the landowners. Another piece of legislation gave the state total ownership of water and created new irrigation organizations linked to new functions which the state had assumed. The peasants joined these organizations as small proprietors, while their old organizations disappeared. These are remembered today with nostalgia, despite their weakness in the face of individualism and apathy.

Today, the peasants see no future in smallholding. It seems increasingly inadequate in the face of the growing demands of modernization. The older people say the same of *huarango* wood. There is a gulf between generations and no possibility of transmitting traditional farming and irrigation techniques to the young. The latter leave agriculture and migrate to the cities.

The general consequences for peasant communities have been the loss of their land and water and a gradual loss of their autonomy and identity. The result is that only individual solutions can be sought to the problems of sustaining culture, organization and life itself. In these circumstances, the story of Pachacutec and Mama Chiri — despite its being made 'real' through the extension of La Achirana — has lost all relevance in the present. This is seen as evocation of a past which was just but is now unobtainable.

Technology, collective memory and the present

The collective memory possessed by Tate today has not always been the same. Such memories are neither constant nor necessarily accumulative. In contrast to what is happening today, different elements of their culture and

218

traditions (and, in particular, the story of Pachacutec) motivated the peasants when they were engaged in lengthening La Achirana. This had been the case also in the 1920s in the neighbouring district of Parcona. Both Parcona and Tate brought their past to life through their struggles. While Parcona remembers victory, Tate only recalls defeat. What is the reason for this?

At the beginning of this century, the small village of Parcona became headquarters of the valley's Federation of Peasants. This organization was violently repressed in 1924 and the village totally demolished. Over the next years, inhabitants returned and began the long struggle to recover their land and re-build their village. In contrast to Tate, they were successful but only because they preserved their organizational unity and independence vis-à-vis other social classes. This solidarity enabled the Parcona peasants to withstand the hostility of the authorities and other powerful groups, which was intensified by the violent death of the Prefect of Ica during the repression of the Federation. In this way, they were able to meet the challenge of modernization despite all the problems it brought with it.

While Tate has remained a rural settlement, Parcona has grown into one of the largest urban districts in the Province. This is as a result of the influx of migrants from neighbouring departments and from the city of Ica itself. Many of these new arrivals have adopted, in one form or another, the valley's tradition of struggle and adapted this to new situations. This is particularly true of the younger generation.

This tradition of struggle has preserved Parcona's vigour. It has been able to integrate changes arising from modernization. The identity of the residents of Parcona has been re-defined, incorporating new elements. As a result — and in sharp contrast to Tate — the present offers opportunities, and both memory and culture have a contemporary significance. The collective memory has been able to adapt itself to today's problems. It is not an evocation of an irrecoverable past but a mobilizing force.

If we want to understand the historical development of these different processes, we should bear in mind the following considerations. The decisive moment when the collective memory of Tate and Parcona separated was when Tate broke with the other villages and accepted the distribution of land on an individual basis. Thus legend portrays Tate as favouring division, whilst Parcona advocated unity.

It is true that the division did have positive results for the residents of Tate who became rich peasants. However, they lost their land, water, crops and their traditional role in the irrigation process. As a result, their culture and technology lost legitimacy. By repudiating collective forms of ownership and organization, they obliterated their means of defence against new challenges. They remained subordinate to the state and other social classes. Lacking organization, independence and identity, their present was divorced from

219

their past. As the myth could only produce feelings of nostalgia, their attempts to recover their land and lengthen the canal resulted in pain and anguish.

It should be mentioned, finally, that many of the symbols of modernity appear to be in crisis today. There is, for example, criticism of the way La Achirana is cleaned and maintained. The State is abandoning metal gates to return to ones made of *huaranga* wood. The division of the co-operatives following their organizational and productive collapse has resulted in the combination of cotton cultivation with that of traditional food crops. As a consequence of the over-exploitation of underground reservoirs, the Government has prohibited the boring of new wells.

It is clear that all this opens up new chances for the re-evaluation of 'traditional' technology, and this is the concern of many technicians and intellectuals. However, this re-assessment will only prove valuable to villages such as Tate if it results in the creation of a new, independent organization which will assume control over the community's relationship with water and the land. In this way, it may be possible to create a new link between the myth of La Achirana and the present in the Ica Valley.

Fire, water and innovation in Chilean farming communities

WALDO BUSTAMENTE GÓMEZ

Introduction

The agricultural communities of Coquimbo today find themselves in an unstable situation with respect to their levels of subsistence. Their socio-economic insecurity is compounded by environmental factors which are themselves deteriorating rapidly.

The residents' main economic activities are farming and livestock which are dependent upon natural resources such as soil type, access to water and the availability of wooded vegetation.

Water is a variable resource in the region. It is abundant in areas close to the river basins and scarce in unirrigated lands, where it is only obtainable from underground river beds and temporary outcrops.

The region possesses little wooded vegetation owing to a process of erosion which began during the colonial period. This erosion is linked to fuel consumption and livestock grazing. Fuel consumption for domestic use by the residents comes mainly from firewood collected in the neighbourhood of the villages.

The socio-economic problems faced by the communities would be reduced greatly if access to water could be extended, wooded vegetation increased and the use of wood as fuel rationalized. Water and fuel problems have not been solved either by various technologies proposed by outside agencies or by innovations introduced by the Communities themselves.

Efforts made by both external agencies and the Communities themselves were studied with the aim of discovering which factors explain the failure to resolve problems related to the scarcity of firewood and water.

With this aim in mind, the communities of Los Rulos and Huentelauquén were selected as case studies. The latter is located in the coastal sector on the northern side of the mouth of the River Choapa while Los Rulos is in the

MR W. BUSTAMENTE (Chile) is Director of TEKHNE, Centre of Experimentation and Training on Appropriate Technology, Santiago. TEKHNE is an NGO with scope to develop and promote technologies which use existing sources, material as well as human. Its purpose is to support popular organizations through diffusing such technologies. He has been a teacher at the Technology School, Professional Institute of Santiago and at the Civil Construction School, Catholic University of Chile.

interior of the Region. These communities were chosen because of contacts already made between TEKHNE and the residents.

The study looked at technological innovations introduced during the present century with respect to the problems of both firewood and water. It aimed to ascertain the residents' attitudes towards external proposals with respect to fuel and water needs. These centred upon measures for halting soil erosion and for increasing the water supply.

The technological proposals were made by CONAF, INGEDES and TEKHNE (Chilean NGOs) over the last fifteen years. The reason for this study is to identify the factors affecting technological change in the communities of Los Rulos and Huentelauquén over the last 15 years.

Communities in the region

The region is located in Chile's arid zone between 29°60′ and 32°36′ latitude south and 69°45′ and 70°45′ longitude west. Its surface area is 40,650sq. kilometres. There are 419,956 inhabitants of whom 74 per cent live in urban areas. In 1986, the Coquimbo Region contributed only 2.25 per cent of the gross domestic product of the country, one of the lowest-earning regions of Chile.

Economic development in the region is based primarily on mining, farming and manufacturing industry. In 1986, the first contributed 8.6 per cent to the regional gross domestic product, the second 15.2 per cent and the third 14.2 per cent. Coquimbo has the sad distinction of having the highest rate of poverty of any region in Chile, with 29.9 per cent of the population defined as 'poor'.

The Region suffers from desertification. The greater part of the soil has a low content of organic matter and this affects the surface structure and water retention. The magnitude and seriousness of the problem is reflected in the fact that some 40 per cent of the surface of the region shows severe levels of desertification, 16 per cent has a degraded herbaceous layer, 6.6 per cent can be considered desert and only 0.7 per cent does not show evidence of the problem.

Different forms of ownership co-exist in the region's communities. Amongst these are individual plots (*los goces singulares*) which are worked by a family living on them and are usually most productive. Another pattern of ownership is represented by *las lluvias*, these are lands handed over temporarily to *comuneros* (peasant groups) by the community. Lastly, there is what is termed the common ground (*campo comun*) to which *comuneros* have access for pasturage and collection of firewood. This common ground is regulated through payments per animal with a maximum quota of animals for each farmer.

The communities create administrative organizations in order to supervise use of the common ground and relations with public services. These

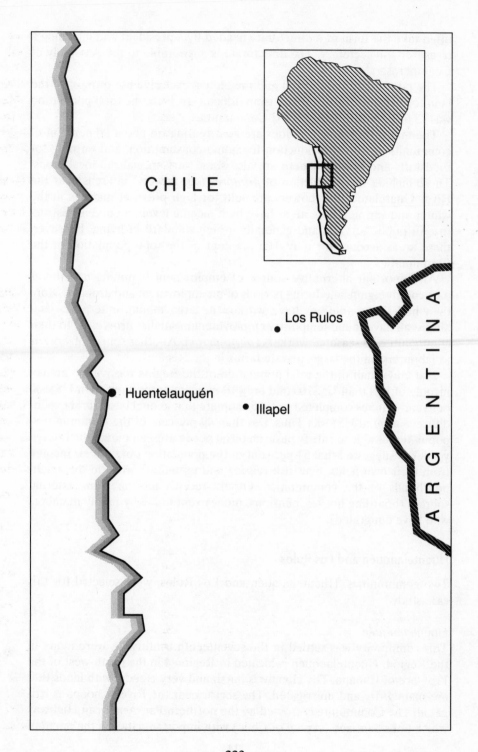

CHILE

Los Rulos

Huentelauquén

Illapel

ARGENTINA

223

often take the form of a directorate headed by a president and including a treasurer and secretary. The directorate is answerable to the Assembly of Comuneros.

The poor quality of the soil and the almost exclusive use of most of the land for livestock makes subdivision difficult. In 1976, the total population was 73,647 divided between 162 Communities.

The major economic activities are goat-rearing (in about 90 per cent of communities), cereal production for home consumption, and farming for foodstuffs and trading. There are also some very specialized local crops. These include the production of *primores* (cut flowers) in areas near the River Guatulame. The flowers are sold for high prices at markets in the winter and spring. These areas have high income levels, a good infrastructure of public services and generally a high standard of living. However, these areas account for only 0.05 per cent of the total population of the Communities.

An important alternative source of employment is mining and this is particularly significant during periods of unemployment and drought. More than half the *comuneros* have worked in large mining enterprises and almost all have found temporary employment in smaller firms close to their communities as seasonal workers (*pirquineros*). Another source of work is as labourers on the large, private farms in the Region.

Just under half of the total population of the Region receives an annual income of less than US$100 and only 10 per cent earns more than US$500 per year. Studies completed in 1985 estimate that annual basic rural expenditure is around US$100. Thus, less than 49 per cent of the Communities' population is able to satisfy basic material needs. Research over the last ten years has suggested that 51 per cent of the population obtain their income from their own fields, livestock rearing and temporary work in the neighbourhoods of the communities. Others receive income from external sources (boarding houses, pensions, money sent home by family members who have emigrated).

Huentelauquén and Los Rulos

Two communities, Huentelauquén and Los Rulos, were selected for this case study.

Huentelauquén
This community was settled in the seventeenth century, as were many in the Region. Huentelauquén is located in Region 4 in the north-west of the Province of Choapa. The climate is harsh and very cloudy, with lands that are mainly dry and unirrigated. The sector near the River Choapa is irrigated. The Community is crossed by the northern Pan-American Highway which links Santiago (capital of Chile) with important cities in the north of

224

the country. This has given Huentelauquén a privileged position with respect to communications as compared to other communities in the Region. Huentelauquén has drinking water and electricity in most houses.

The community's economic activities and patterns of land-holding are similar to others in the Region. Huentelauquén had 344 registered inhabitants at the time of the December 1971 census. About half of these people do not live in the village and so do not contribute in terms of labour or dues to the community. Huentelauquén possesses 7,426ha of land to which all *comuneros* have rights.

The Community has various organizations: the Agricultural Community itself, the Co-operative, two Mothers' Groups, a sports club and a Fathers' Group. It has also a goat herd, a forest nursery and a cheese dairy.

Los Rulos

This community's foundation had a character distinct from others in the Region. In 1943, land (6,600ha) belonging to the 'El Durazno' property was sold to a group of 37 tenants. The inhabitants are classed as *comuneros*, but Los Rulos is not an agricultural community. In theory it is a sector of the community of Canela Baja and the latter is responsible for its political organization and administration.

Los Rulos is located 30km to the north-east of Canela Alta and 35km to the south-west of Combarbalá. It is more dispersed than other communities. Its 'centre' includes an elementary school, medical post, social centre, a store with basic goods, a restaurant, a *media luna* and a sports centre which people do not use.

Los Rulos does not have either electricity or drinking water as a consequence of its isolated position. (This isolation is a result of harsh terrain and lack of adequate roads.) There is no collective transport to take inhabitants to the main road which links the closest villages.

Los Rulos has a population of 500 who are involved in the economic activities common to the Region. It has a Fathers' Group, a Neighbourhood Committee, a Sports Club and a Catholic Group.

Scarcity of firewood and water in the region

Over the last four centuries, economic activity in Coquimbo has been dedicated to farming, livestock and mining. Mining became important in the eighteenth century. By the nineteenth century, international and national bodies were drawing attention to the impact upon fuel supplies and the subsequent deterioration of the environment.

The need for mining fuel destroyed woody vegetation to a high degree. A number of mining sites had to be abandoned because of a shortage of firewood and water. At the same time, it was clear that livestock farming was depleting the pasture areas around the villages.

225

Desertification is also attributable to the impact of urbanization. Towns and cities were established in older mining settlement sites. Forests were cut down in order to satisfy demands for fuel and timber for building purposes. Finally, agriculture was under pressure to maintain high wheat production. Lands which were not really suitable for cultivation were farmed and this caused soil erosion.

Nearly all families (96 per cent) in the region use firewood as their domestic fuel source. Family consumption of firewood is about 10 tons per family per year. This amounts to a regional consumption of 146,000 tons if one considers only the inhabitants of the agricultural communities. If the firewood which is produced as charcoal is added, annual consumption reaches about 150,800 tons. The main domestic use for firewood is in cooking.

Impoverished social groups in both the villages and cities of the Coquimbo Region devote a great deal of time and energy to the collection of firewood. Only about 2 per cent of firewood needed for domestic consumption is purchased. The rest is collected from around the settlements. Each collection journey takes an average of four hours and is undertaken between one and four times per week. An average of 20km is travelled each day in order for each individual to collect about 15 kilos of firewood. The time spent per family per year is approximately 750 person-hours.

The region's water supply comes from rainfall which is absorbed by the soil and reappears in the form of springs (*aguadas*), channels (*vertientes*) and underground streams (*venas*). The supply also comes from precipitation in the Cordillera which, during periods of thaw, is transformed into water which feeds the rivers and streams in the valleys.

Water is taken up in homes for watering animals (goats), and in irrigation and farming. These are the major uses. Given that the Region's climate is of a mediterranean-type (semi-arid and with irregular precipitation), residents are never certain of obtaining sufficient water supplies.

Residents of Los Rulos and Huentelauquén maintain that vegetation has disappeared and firewood has become more scarce over the years. They remember times when less effort had to be made to collect firewood and when vegetation was more abundant.

There are considerable differences between the two communities in their use of water. These differences are based upon the availability of the resources in each place. Huentelauquén is located near to the River Choapa. The *comuneros*' plots are close to the river and are irrigated by a system of channels supplied by it. Only those fields which are unirrigated have problems. Although Los Rulos has the Maitén brook in its territory, this lacks sufficient water. (Most of it is underground.) *Comuneros* living close by can use this as a water source but it is a serious undertaking because they have to build channels on the surface in order to direct the water to fields. Some water is inevitably lost through leakage and evaporation. In some cases, it would be easier to get the water from watering stations. This is the only way to obtain it for those *comuneros* living far away from the brook.

The domestic use of water is also markedly different in the two communities. Huentelauquén has sufficient drinking water; only those *comuneros* living away from the village have problems in obtaining it. In contrast, in Los Rulos water for family consumption has to be drawn from wells. Thus the scarcity of water is a more important problem for Los Rulos than it is for Huentelauquén.

Technical change and the communities

The CONAF proposal

A programme of reforestation began in the Coquimbo Region between 1974 and 1978 under Decree 701 which established government control over forest resources. A total of 40,000 hectares were re-sown, 90 per cent with fodder shrubs such as *Atriplex repanda* and *Atriplex nummularia* and the remainder with *Eucalyptus globulus* and, to a lesser extent, *Prosopis chilensis* and *Shinus molle*.

The state through CONAF (National Forestry Corporation) contributed 75 per cent of the total costs of reforestation using workers from schemes for unemployed labour. This programme represented the first attempt at reforestation in the Region. It aimed to enrich and increase the productivity of the soil and produce fodder for goat herds, one main economic resource for the communities.

The land around Huentelauquén was reforested between 1976–78 with *Atriplex nummularia* and *Atriplex repanda*. At first, the community resisted the scheme because residents feared they would be forced to leave their land. However, once CONAF had ended its involvement, the *comuneros* continued the programme themselves. This about-face was not explained by ecological concerns but because the peasants saw that reforestation could be profitable. Given that the state subsidized 75 per cent of the costs calculated by CONAF, the community's contribution was reduced and a profit could be produced.

Overall, 2,700ha of land were planted with trees. Of these, 1,800 were planted by CONAF. The Community of Los Rulos rejected CONAF's reforestation programme mainly because it would increase the value of the land. As Los Rulos is under the legal jurisdiction of the Community of Canela Baja, it is forced to pay contributions for the use of the land to the latter. The cost depends upon the value of the land:

The INGEDES proposal

This NGO is concerned with economic programmes. In 1987 it proposed the following development plan for the area:

227

1 the creation of agro-industrial enterprises in the agricultural communities;
2 an increase in the application of fuel technologies of an intermediate character;
3 technical assistance to community organizations for development projects and
4 technological training, particularly for young peasants.

It was hoped these would generate employment and raise residents' incomes. INGEDES has concentrated its activities in Los Rulos, where it is building a cheese dairy. Improved management of the goat herds has been linked to the production of cheese. With the aim of satisfying basic food needs, technologies for water conservation (hand pumps and wind generators) are being introduced. INGEDES is being aided in this by TEKHNE. The water will be used mainly for irrigating the alfalfa crop.

Professionals from both INGEDES and *comuneros* have been involved in the design, planning and implementation of these activities. A legally-registered company was formed to manage the cheese dairy. At present, ownership is shared between the *comuneros* and INGEDES but eventually the former will take control.

The TEKHNE proposal

TEKHNE's programme in Huentelauquén is based upon the productive and domestic activities of the *comuneros*. Included amongst the economic activities are a cheese dairy (using a wind generator and solar water heaters) and a co-operative nursery for the production of shrimps/prawns to which TEKHNE has contributed cultivation techniques. Unfortunately, this project has not achieved the results expected of it.

Inhabitants have been instructed in the building of domestic ovens and stoves. There is now a more efficient use of firewood. These activities, developed since 1986, have centred upon the importance of involving intended beneficiaries in the design, planning, implementation and evaluation. An Ovens Committee, involving women, has been set up.

Innovations from the communities

The Huentelauquén residents have developed new cooking techniques in response to the firewood problem. At the beginning of the century, a system of open fires placed at ground level either inside or outside the houses was the norm. Bread was baked by using stones heated by burning either animal excrement or firewood as fuel.

By the 1930s, clay ovens were being used for baking. At the same time, elevated stoves appeared. These were built on a base of stones and clay and incorporated a toaster at the top. Charcoal braziers also became common. Charcoal is produced in the communities. In some cases, wood is burnt in holes dug in the ground.

In the 1940s, peasants began to use glazed earthern ovens (*hornos de medio tarro*) for both baking and cooking. Kerosene stoves were introduced in the 1960s and gas stoves in the 1970s. These were purchased in villages such as Los Vilos (40km to the south of Huentelauquén) and Illapel (50km away).

New technologies based on firewood have been introduced into the Community since 1986 by the Programme of Fuel Research (PRIEN) of the University of Chile.

Traditional skills with respect to the detection, extraction and storage of water are practised by Los Rulos' residents. Thus, underground water is detected by the presence of certain shrubs on the surface. Amongst these can be mentioned the *palqui* (*Cestrum palqui*, a medicinal plant). Detection is also by mineral deposits. *Piques* (holes) are built on hillsides and wells dug. Water is stored in *pircas de contención* (dry stone walls) and protected cultivation shrubs and trees close to the watering stations. There are irrigation channels from natural sources and dams, and also water wheels obtained from a resident of a neighbouring community.

In Huentelauquén, there are wells in the area around the River Choapa and its tributaries, and also wells in the arid regions. There is a system of irrigation channels supplied with river water. As the Community has had a drinking water supply since 1980, technologies of water-catchment for domestic use have disappeared. Tributaries in this sector are used only to water livestock.

Conclusions

There is an uncertain technological response to the firewood problem. This is probably because wood is not yet a totally exhausted resource. It is used mainly by women and is not regarded as linked directly to the generation of family income. Firewood can still be collected although it is more scarce than fifty years ago. As a result, inefficient use is not a significant problem for families although all members, including children, have to find time to collect wood.

This activity could be viewed as part of cultural tradition and the socialization process for adults and children. Those residents whom we interviewed had strong memories of accompanying parents in the search for firewood. The activity clearly constitutes part of the collective experience of *comuneros*.

The predominance of women in the domestic activities of cooking and baking bread may account for the lack of technological innovation in the use of firewood. Women do not have access to the skills necessary to construct equipment. Furthermore, domestic duties occupy a large part of a woman's day. Even if she had the skills, she probably would not have time to spend on innovating. No observable interest has been shown by men in the building of cooking equipment. It is a subject which is seen as solely a female concern.

Additionally, firewood is used in activities which do not make profits and the *comuneros* are most interested in activities that enable them to become involved in the commercial market. Thus, the savings that could accrue from a technological innovation linked to cooking are not of paramount interest.

In Los Rulos, the supply of water for domestic and agricultural use is more restricted than in Huentelauquén. As a result, the technological innovations introduced by residents of the former have been more varied. However, even before the advent of drinking water supply in Huentelauquén, technological experiments were less diverse than those of Los Rulos. This is because of Huentelauquén's privileged position near the River Choapa and its proximity to the river's tributaries. Underground streams have aided the irrigation of fields and provided domestic supplies.

The greater variation in technological innovations with respect to water as compared to firewood may be explained by the former's scarcity, its association with productive activities (which are dominated by men) and its importance in the generation of family income. As noted earlier, it is the men of the family who devote themselves to farming for their own consumption and for the generation of profits. Their dedication to agriculture coincides with their concern with finding solutions to the water problem.

In general terms, the technological innovations introduced by residents of the two communities display a greater diversity in the case of those linked to income–generation activities. The *comuneros* regard the receipt of profits as a necessity of the highest priority.

Diversity of technological innovation is linked directly to the *comuneros'* hierarchy of needs. The greater the scarcity of an identified necessary resource, the greater the diversity of technological response to its satisfaction.

Finally, there may be a relationship between the sexual variable and diversity in technological innovation.

Dialogue between social organizations and external agents gives the latter a better understanding of the behaviour, attitudes and values of the former. If the objective of a technological proposal can be clearly identified, then its acceptance will be made all the easier.

PRIEN built communal stoves and bread ovens in the offices of the Huentelauquén social organizations but residents did not use them. This was because food preparation is seen as a family activity and some of the stoves were made by youth groups who had no part in this activity. PRIEN's project aimed to show the potential of a technology for more efficient use of firewood rather than to demonstrate the technology itself.

On the basis of this idea of participation, and bearing in mind PRIEN's earlier experiences, TEKHNE directed its efforts towards women householders organized in the Mothers' Group. It was decided that ovens and stoves for domestic use should be built in each house. This Committee has now taken over the construction of stoves and ovens with a small degree of technical support from TEKHNE. The women demonstrate an aptitude for building and are also running a materials' bank.

Involvement with the women's group enabled TEKHNE to understand that the concept of 'community' is linked more to the common ownership of the land than to collective activities. The cooking of food and baking of bread is a *family* activity. TEKHNE realized that the need to improve cooking equipment originated with the *women*, as they were the users of the technology.

TEKHNE aimed to introduce cooking equipment which will help save firewood. The women's stated needs at the onset of the project were mainly concerned with energy-saving and with environmental issues related to smoke fumes. Women only mentioned the need to save firewood as a secondary consideration. Only after a number of conversations with the TEKHNE staff did the women begin to mention aspects related to firewood.

Some defects in the behaviour of local social organizations appeared. For example, the Huentelauquén community was one of the most advanced in developing CONAF's forestry programme. The nurseries planted by the *comuneros* made a profit. However, leaders of the community organization turned this to their own advantage by claiming the profit as an example of their good management. CONAF only became aware of this manipulation at a later date.

Another example of manipulation is that undertaken by the Huentelauquén Co-operative (whose leader is also the president of the agricultural community) with respect to the Committee for stoves and ovens. It was decided that the Committee, formed by the women, should become part of the Co-operative and as such would offer its services to Co-operative members and the community as a whole.

What the Co-operative's leaders wanted was to use this to legitimize their organization in the eyes of the community. This has sometimes complicated the relationship between the Committee for stoves and ovens and TEKHNE.

These experiences lead to the conclusion that contact between external agents and the leaders of social organizations is in itself insufficient for the acceptance of new technologies by a community. In some cases, exclusive contact with leaders makes communication between agents and users more problematic.

In the *comuneros'* hierarchy of needs, those linked to the generation of profits come first. Technological proposals linked directly to this type of activity will be accepted most easily. Thus the INGEDES project, which concentrated upon economic activities, has been very successful to date.

231

Beneficiaries have shown a strong desire to participate by, for example, forming work committees to build the dairy. This generates income for those working and also has a productive impact upon other activities. The *comuneros* involved in the construction of the dairy are also interested in the project concerned with the manual water pumps. The water collected by these methods is used to irrigate the alfalfa plantations which provide fodder for goats. The reforestation project captures the imagination of the *comuneros*, as it too will provide livestock fodder.

The above experience suggests that in implementing income-generating activities for *comuneros*, it may be possible for agencies to bring in environmental objectives of which the residents are not yet conscious. This will be possible, however, only if a suitable community organization exists — one that seeks ends which are likely to satisfy the *comuneros'* needs, rather than consciously mis-representing external proposals.

Finally, external pressures brought to bear upon communities will make the acceptance of new technologies slower. CONAF's reforestation programme only came about because of pressure exerted by its central management committee in Santiago. CONAF Region had to prepare the proposal in three months or risk dissolution. It decided to plant *Atriplex* without sufficient preliminary study. CONAF fieldworkers did not have the necessary information regarding growing patterns or its use as pasturage or fuel material. As a consequence, CONAF professionals were able to train residents in correct care.

Short-term projects do not help planning processes for integrated participation methods involving social organizations in the communities. As a result, short-term projects do not produce the solutions which the unstable living conditions of the inhabitants demand. Short-term financing, arbitrary decisions imposed upon NGOs and administrative pressures coming from within state agencies make the development and dissemination of new technologies for communities all the more difficult.

Organizations which have a high level of participation by members can stimulate closer participation between agents and beneficiaries. This allows for a more effective assimilation of new technologies. Innovations are accepted more easily if they are directed towards income-generating activities.

232

From three-stone fires to smokeless stoves in Venezuela

LUIS MIGUEL ABAD

Introduction

Our study focuses upon the experiences of a popular organization (health committee) in its attempt to introduce clay stoves (*fogones*) and ovens (*hornos*) to the Villanueva area of the State of Lara in Venezuela. We hope to suggest what general conclusions can be drawn from a specific project with respect to the diffusion and transmission of technology amongst popular groups.

Villanueva is a town in the Andes of western Venezuela. It is located in the State of Lara which has the fifth largest population in the country and is 100km (two hours travelling time) from the state capital, Barquisimeto. In this study we shall use Villanueva as a generic title for a mainly coffee growing area of about 70 small peasant settlements.

At the end of the 1970s, an Australian priest named, Father Vicente arrived in Villanueva and was responsible for the creation of an evangelical movement known as the Legion of Mary. During the following years, Legion groups (mainly consisting of men) were founded in 45 Villanueva villages. In the late 1970s, the Jesuit Fathers of the Centro Gumilla in Barquisimeto set up a co-operative of coffee producers on the basis of these Legion groups. This co-operative aimed to give religious, social and economic impetus to the peasants to help them unite as a group and so strengthen their role in the production and sale of coffee. Twenty-two co-operative unions now exist in the area.

In the early 1980s a Carmelite priest, Father Manolo, was invited to Villanueva by Father Vicente to give a course on natural medicine and nutrition to Legion members. He had been involved in similar projects in other places in Lara.

Using the religious and organizational base provided by the Legion, Father Manolo established health committees whose aim was to improve health and nutritional standards and treat illnesses through the use of natural medicines. Twenty committees are now operating in the parish.

Father Manolo instructed health committee members in the application of natural remedies and people rapidly began to treat themselves. Natural

MR L.M. ABAD (Venezuela) is a member of the Centre for Development of Popular Technology. He is a psychologist and community organizer with experience in politics and the administration of technology.

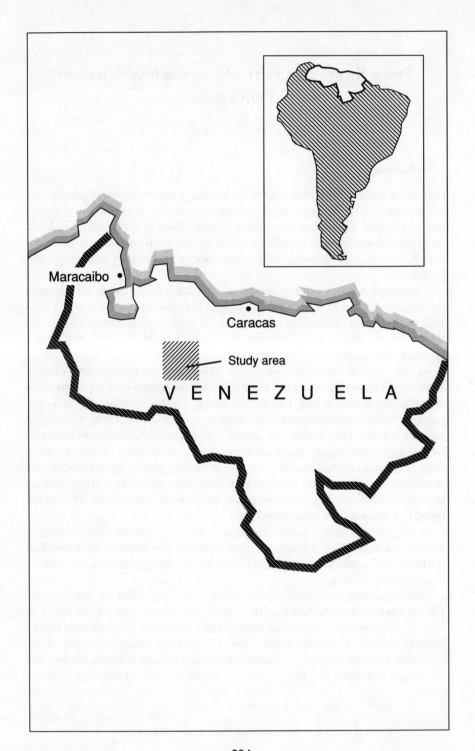

Maracaibo •

Caracas •

Study area

V E N E Z U E L A

234

medicine spread throughout the villages of Villanueva. Following this, the health committees began nutritional work through the setting up of family allotments for the cultivation of vegetables which were previously absent from peasant diets. The committees based their work upon the principle that in order to be healthy and prevent illness, one must eat properly. This project soon spread throughout the area.

Beginning the project

In the course of developing these activities, Father Manolo decided that many health and hygiene problems were caused by smoke and fumes produced by the *topia* stoves. These problems included respiratory and eye disorders, unpleasant-tasting drinking water, bad odours in clothes and cooking stains on house roofs and walls.

The *topia* consists of a platform or table made of soil and stones, on top of which are placed larger stones, small logs or blocks of cement (or all three) which provide the base for cooking pots or frying pans used for cooking and for the firewood which is arranged between them.

On a visit to a colleague, Father Manolo discovered a book on appropriate technology which mentioned a smokeless clay stove and oven. Father Manolo invited his colleague to hold a workshop on the building of these stoves and ovens for the members of the Health Committees. Such a workshop was held and an L-shaped clay stove and oven was built. The design was based upon a model suggested in a *Manual of appropriate technologies* produced by the Canadian Hunger Foundation and the Brace Research Institute. Unfortunately, the stove and oven did not work properly and cracked and fell apart after a short time.

Following this initial failure, a series of activities were developed with the aim of introducing the *fogones* (smokeless clay stoves) in Villanueva. This was done very much on a trial-and-error basis on the part of Father Manolo and the health committees.

These activities of dissemination and adoption were not done in the same way or with the same intensity in all the villages. Some dissemination activities were aided by health committee members and/or the families for whom the stoves were intended. Some people built their own stoves after having observed the construction of prototypes either in their own village or at the parish house in Villanueva.

These attempts at the diffusion off the new stove were characterized by a constant process of trial-and-error given the lack of knowledge and mastery of the techniques. Experiments were made with different types of building materials such as clay and stones, different designs (right-angled or L-shaped), modifications to different parts of the stove (for the firewood entrance, the grate, the chimney, doors for keeping in heat).

The original oven (*horno*) was built in the mid-1980s. This was the

235

result of a handbook produced by a Brazilian agricultural extension institute which outlined the method of building an oven with metal barrels (*horno de pipa*). Father Manolo initiated the project by building the first *fogones* and *hornos*. The health committees only really became involved in the second stage of diffusion in their villages.

To date, about 250 *fogones* and 80 *hornos* have been built in 20 villages. The great majority of health committee members have *fogones* in their homes. However, those villages in which more than half the houses have them remain in a minority. Most *fogones* and *hornos* are used constantly for cooking, some only intermittently. Others have broken down.

The *fogones* are of two basic designs, the 'right-angled' and the 'L-shaped'. *Hornos* are made of metal barrels. Although both units are treated as one in this study, there are important differences between them.

1 *Fogones* were adopted mainly for health reasons caused by cooking fumes while the *hornos* were seen as offering the possibility of preparing new food dishes. (*Hornos* had not been available in the area before.)
2 While *fogones* are built with local materials, the barrels for the *hornos* are purchased outside and brought into the parish for installation in the houses.
3 The *fogones* have undergone a process of alteration and improvement since their introduction, as users have identified problems. The *hornos* have not been modified and no significant problems have been reported.

The most important result of the introduction of the *fogones* has been in resolving health problems caused by fumes from the *topias*. Use of *fogones* has had other repercussions in the community, the most significant of which are:

1 reducing the time spent in cooking, allowing the peasant woman to spend more time caring for her children and cleaning the house;
2 allowing more time for agricultural production (harvesting coffee, family allotments);
3 community organizations such as the Legion of Mary and the Health Committees playing a more active role.

The *hornos* have facilitated the introduction of new food dishes (different types of bread, cake, biscuits) and also different methods of preparing traditional foods such as *auyama*, yucca and bananas (*cambures*).

The project's structural framework

We have decided to view the project on three different levels — cultural, political and technical — in order to deepen our understanding of the process. In this way, we hope to analyse the context in which the innovation has been adopted, the relations established during the process and the elements necessary for an effective transfer of technology.

The cultural dimension

By 'the cultural' is understood the totality of practices, meanings and beliefs by which a population defines its relationship to its surroundings. In this sense, the 'technological' is always cultural and the success of introducing technological innovations will be determined by cultural implications.

In many cases, 'need' is defined by external agents (institutions, groups, individuals) whose geographical and socio-economic backgrounds are different from that of the subject community. These agents identify 'problems' and suggest 'benefits'. This is often based upon a simplistic conception of what a community needs, with problems and/or benefits being reduced to purely technical or methodological categories and their wider context being ignored. External agents do not take the cultural aspect sufficiently into consideration. People give meanings to and have expectations about the elements involved in a 'problem' which are closely linked to their history, environment and daily life.

Father Manolo identified the health problem caused by the *topias*. However, when peasants were questioned about the benefits produced by the *fogones* and *hornos* they mentioned other factors besides the prevention of illness. These included:

1 less time spent on cooking and more free time for other jobs;
2 absence of fumes within the home;
3 less firewood used and unseasoned wood burns well in the new stoves;
4 greater variety of food dishes and new ways of preparing old ones;
5 greater safety: women and children are not burnt by overturned cooking pots.

Thus the *fogones* were evaluated in terms of the element of time as well as that of health and the former was given an equal if not superior importance. Members of the health committees tended to stress the health element more. Peasants preferred a *fogone* which cooked quickly but gave off fumes to a slow-cooking stove which was smokefree.

One must remember that, when cooking with a *topia*, the woman had to spend the whole day in the kitchen because of the slowness of cooking caused by constant loss of heat and the need to tend the fire. This was a particular problem during harvest-time when she had to feed all the workers and temporary labourers. Fumes were a real problem and their disappearance was important as well. It should be noted again that a majority of committee people had *fogones* but this was true for less than half of all households.

The health/fumes element acquired a significance for health committee members because it was a condition of their organization and history.

237

However, the fumes did not have the same relevance to non-members. If this distinction had been apparent, it could have led to the development of strategies appropriate to both sectors.

Most peasants deal with the problem of smoke and fumes by knocking a hole through the roof of their houses, although this is not always successful. Smoke is a real problem in the daily life of peasants and they have attempted to resolve it via the exit in the roof. At the same time, the 'time' problem was also an important factor in the peasants' adoption of the *fogones* and *hornos*.

The *cultural* dimension of 'need' involves understanding the reasons, perceptions and meanings that ordinary people give to problems. Their values are determined by their history, environment and daily life and these may be very different from those of external agents.

The technological model

Another important factor with respect to experiments in the dissemination and transfer of technologies is how the technology is conceived and how it relates to the daily life and customs of the people.

The prototype *fogone* in Villanueva was based upon the smokeless stove from Ghana because information about this was available in the book on appropriate technologies owned by Father Manolo's colleague. He also had some experience in building it. Thus, the stimulus for the introduction of the new types of cooking stoves came from the availability of information and not only from the suitability of the model.

Data collected in the villages on the problems and difficulties in the use of the *fogones* and *hornos* offers interesting clues concerning the relationship between the technological model and innovations. These include:

1 *preparation of* arepas (maize pancakes): They come out hard and split from the *horno*. If you cook them with cold hands, you get spasms. You need two people to cook *arepas*, one to knead the dough and the other to tend the *arepas* because the *horno* gets hot very quickly.

2 *maintenance of the chimney*: Cleaning the chimney is a chore. The chimney fills up with tar and because of this people hate the *fogones*. The chimneys get blocked up very quickly and are corroded.

3 *the* fogones *collapse*: People have to repair them with clay plaster. The interiors have to be reinforced to prevent them collapsing and the tiles crack.

4 *getting used to the* fogones: is difficult initially.

As one can see, the introduction of the *fogones* produced a series of new practices and customs which were absent in the technological model of the *topias*. Some problems have been rectified already as a result of the technical assistance which accompanied the process. Other problems have been solved by the users themselves with great imagination and creativity. What is of interest here is the absence of analysis and understanding of the *topias'* technological model when the new type of technology was being considered. The health problem was emphasized but not those related to cooking with *topias*. Neither the specific context nor meaning for the peasants was considered — a case of not seeing the forest for the trees.

On the other hand, it is significant that many of the problems linked to the use of *fogones* did not exist with the *topias*. Thus, *arepas* cooked normally. *Topias* did not collapse nor did they have to be plastered. They did not have chimneys and did not require maintenance. They were easy to use. The innovative technology differed from and in some cases conflicted with the existing technological model.

In order to illustrate this point, we can mention the problems associated with the preparation of *arepas*. The majority of *fogones* observed had openings for firewood larger than those recommended in order to conserve heat and regulate the entry of air. This resulted in a loss of efficiency. People prefer the larger opening because it allows them to arrange several *arepas* at a time in the cavity in order to keep them warm. This reproduces the method of cooking *arepas* with the *topia*. Some families prefer the 'right-angled' *fogone* because it enables the firewood to be put into the bottom without impeding placing *arepas* in the bottom to keep them hot.

Thus, the introduction of the innovation (*fogones* and *hornos*) did not consider the technological model of the *topias* in the preparation of *arepas*, a vitally important part of the peasants' diet.

Another aspect is the actual construction of the *fogones*. Although men are needed to build them, the campaign with respect to their acceptance was directed mainly at the women. A number of respondents referred to the importance of the men's participation in the adoption of the innovation: 'The men have . . . to build them because it requires physical strength. The women hope the men will help but if the men do not recognize the importance of the innovation, they will not.' 'If the men will not help, you cannot maintain the *fogones* or rebuild them'. It was felt that men should become a target group for the dissemination of the technology. 'You should call a meeting of the husbands in order to involve them because building the *fogones* is a man's job . . .'.

There is no agreement on whether less, the same or more firewood is used by the *fogones* as compared to the *topias*. Although some say the *fogones* use less, it is difficult to know if this quantity is perceived in absolute terms (fewer kilos or bundles) or in relative ones (the same quantity of firewood producing more dishes). There is certainly a tendency to use more firewood than recommended. In this sense, the *topias'* technological model still influences practices and so affects the use of the innovation.

The political dimension

This dimension has two aspects: the role of the promoting agent and the participation of the community. These should be considered together because of their interdependence. The 'political' is present in every stage of any process — from the identification of needs to the evaluation of a project.

Father Manolo was decisive in initiating the project to introduce *fogones* and *hornos* in Villanueva. His influence was based not only upon his authority as a priest but also because the communities held him in great esteem. One resident said: 'At the beginning . . . when we arrived in the parish . . . (people) were apprehensive because no one knew what he was going to be like. The people did not understand what the *fogones* were. The majority built them because Manolo told them to. One peasant said that he built a *fogone* out of respect for the Father; it was the Father's command.'

The positive effects of natural medicine and allotments campaigns also generated confidence in him. The health problems connected to the *topias* had existed for many years but Father Manolo gave them an urgency and incorporated their resolution into the work of the health committees. He motivated the work of the health committees but later they took over the organizational impulse.

Therefore the process was shaped initially by the opinions and decisions of Father Manolo in his role as promoter and not through the participation of the health committees. Indeed, the latter had little opportunity of commenting upon the need or problem in question or of evaluating or redesigning the process while it was evolving.

During the second stage, introduction of the *fogones* and *hornos* into the villages, the committees played a far more dynamic role, explaining and organizing the project to the peasants.

Four conclusions can be drawn from observation of the project. Father Manolo, a man trusted and held in esteem by the peasants, facilitated the introduction of the *fogones* by the health committees. His role as priest, his authority and ability to exercise power shaped the dynamics of the project during the initial stage. However, this was done at the expense of involving the community in discussions and decisions with respect to the execution of the project.

Secondly, the pre-existing organizational structure in Villanueva presented fertile ground for adoption of the new technology by a majority of members of the health committees and by some other families. These organizations espoused values such as respect for the individual, religious faith and belief in the unity of the community.

Thirdly, this organizational framework is the reason why the *fogones* and *hornos* were accepted more in some villages than in others. Those villages where more than half the families have adopted *fogones* are those where

240

the health committees count upon the participation of a majority of the inhabitants and hold regular meetings, and so play an active role in the community.

Finally, there is an observable correspondence between acceptance and continuing use of *fogones* and *hornos* and stable marriages based upon equal relations between husband and wife. As we have noted earlier, the involvement of the man in the building of the *fogone* is indispensable. If a husband is concerned about his wife's situation and actively shares in the activities which represent a large part of her labour, he is more likely to be open to the introduction of a new technology.

There are two elements related to the participation of the users in the modification and improvement of the technology of *fogones* and *hornos* and the community's evaluation of its own participation in the project. One encounters residents who are not health committee members building their own *fogones* and introducing various changes in the building and function- ing of the stoves. Amongst these improvements can be included:

1 use of *adobe* bricks made of clay and cement and cow dung to plaster the *fogones* and prevent them cracking
2 use of pieces of recycled metal, rubber rings, brake disks etc. to rein- force the *fogone's* structure, give a longer life to the ranges (*hornillas*) and provide better support for the cooking pots
3 construction of wider chimneys with cement tubes and a higher cover in order to facilitate the exit of smoke and so reduce the frequency of cleaning
4 introduction of a special cooking range for making *arepas*, consisting of a hot plate and grill which could be interchangeable during the different stages of cooking
5 design of a special *fogone* for cooking *arepas*
6 design of a *fogone* with two openings, one for firewood and the other for collecting the ashes
7 design of a *horno* fitted into the wall with its body outside the house in order to save space
8 design of a *horno* with divided sections for keeping cooking utensils
9 use of corn husks as fuel

One can see from the above that the users have adapted the innovation in line with aspects of their previous technological model for cooking. In the process they have made better use of the *fogones* and *hornos*. This demonstrates the importance of communal participation in the processes of diffusion and transfer of technology. The people understand their living conditions best and can make the best use of innovations.

The technical dimension

As mentioned, the process of imparting information about and promoting the acceptance of a specific technology by popular sectors is affected by cultural and political factors. Diffusion is also influenced by specifically technical factors related to the skills required to use the technology properly. The following would seem to be the most important of these:

1 mastery of and adaptation of the technology
2 transfer of the technology
3 technical assistance and follow-up support

The first factor, mastery and adaptation of the technology, refers to the capability to operate, maintain, adapt and improve the technology. If the users do not enjoy this mastery there may be serious implications. It is also necessary, and this is related to the category of technological model, to adapt the technologies to the host environment.

The second factor, transfer of technology, involves more than just the simple transmission of 'know-how' with respect to using the technology. This includes all the accumulated information necessary to give the user a real mastery over the technology in the terms indicated earlier.

Finally, the whole process of diffusion and transfer of the technology demands technical support and follow-up activities. These would guarantee adequate management, adaptation and improvement of the whole process.

If we apply these three factors to the Villanueva project, we note that there was a lack of mastery of an information about the technology. There was no process of selection between technologies, no discussion of which would be most suitable. Rather the decision was made on what was 'nearest at hand'.

The first *fogone* built in the parish house did not work and soon fell apart. The same happened with those made in the villages: 'Those that Manolo made collapsed. It took a while for him to make them properly'. The majority of people who have *fogones* have had to build them more than once either because they did not work properly or because the stoves had begun to fall apart.

As a consequence of this lack of mastery of the technology, the process of diffusion was haphazard and based upon constant trial-and-error. Thus, in the beginning, the dissemination and transfer of the *fogones* was influenced more by spontaneous conditions than by technical features of the *fogones* themselves. When people told Manolo that the *fogones* were not working, he replied that people should 'make the effort until the stoves do work'. Despite the commitment of the health committees, the religious element which was pervasive in the whole process and the confidence invested in Father Manolo to say 'persist' and 'make the effort' was not enough. The villages *had* to master the technology and be creative in their management of it.

It must not be forgotten, however, that there never can be real dissemination of a technology without a process of trial-and-error. Thus the peasants built the *fogones*, the stoves broke down, people then built them differently, attempting to correct the faults.

The emphasis appeared to have been more on the 'building' of the *fogones* rather than in the transfer of technology. The peasants' statements are clear on this point: 'Manolo installed it quickly in Pedro's house.' 'Manolo made them so quickly that they broke.' 'Manolo made them in haste.' 'We couldn't copy the way Manolo worked.' The quantity and variety of activities undertaken in order to spread the technology confirm this view.

Finally, there was no provision of technical assistance and follow-up for the project. Some people felt they had been left without help. Additionally, the health committee members were offered no opportunity to evaluate the development of the project or to share their experiences of it in order to rectify mistakes and consolidate their efforts.

These technical aspects had a direct influence upon the extension of the *fogones* and *hornos* project in the Villanueva area. Indeed, the reasons some people gave for not using the *fogones* are directly related to faults in the process of mastery, transfer of and support for the technological innovation. These include:

1 excessive use of firewood.
2 lack of technical assistance and support: A person could not embark upon the project alone. He or she needed help. A number of people had bad experiences because they did not know how to use the stoves. People who had no experience of them did not want to install them. There were no support visits and no information allowing people to be independent. Many people felt insecure because of the lack of support. There was no one to provide back-up in the villages.
3 breakdowns: The *fogones* broke down a lot and people stopped using them because of this. One must bear in mind that if the *fogones* are well-constructed, they use less firewood than the *topias*. This is one of the main advantages of *fogones*. The first *fogones* collapsed because they were built badly.

When questioned, the promoters stressed their support for the process but it is quite clear to us that lack of technical assistance and follow-up activities significantly affected the spread of the *fogones* and their maintenance once installed. The early failures had an adverse effect upon their adoption by other peasants. The majority did not build *fogones* because the first ones had not worked. These experiences must lead promoters to make sure that there is in every future project someone who understands the technology and that people are taught how to make and maintain the innovation.

Lessons of the project

The many aspects of the Villanueva project discussed in this document can be drawn together to arrive at a general understanding of the experience.

The initial impression is that the project to introduce *fogones* and *hornos* to Villanueva was modified, supported or presented with difficulties depending upon how the cultural, political and technical dimensions of the process were handled.

The *cultural* dimension offers an explanation of how and why changes were made to the technology. The need to 'control the fumes' was transformed into the benefit of 'saving time'. The technological model of the *topias* altered and influenced the way in which the innovation (the *fogones* and *hornos*) was implemented in terms of building, use and cooking methods. This helps us to understand that the 'technological' also acquires meaning through its appreciation of the perceptions of local people.

The *political* dimension covers many of the aspects which contributed to the development of the project: the organizational history of the Villanueva region, the religious factor, the role of the health committees, earlier experiments in the management of technologies and the participation of the community in improving and changing the technology of the *fogone*.

We believe that it is the *technical* dimension that contains the largest number of elements which explain the problems involved in the adoption of the technology. These include that there was no mastery of the technology by promoter or community, there was a constant process of trial-and-error in application and there was no technical assistance.

Our involvement as external agents is not purely technical. It is dependent upon values, attitudes and ways of facing reality. It behoves us to consider our form of involvement and role as promoters as well as the community's participation in decision-making and the implementation of projects. We would like to make some recommendations on the basis of the Villanueva experience:

1   It is necessary to obtain a better knowledge of and mastery over the technology in order to facilitate modifications and improvements to be made to the *fogones* and *hornos*. This will prevent frustrating experiences which delay acceptance.

2   The main improvements and changes to the *fogones* should be gathered together in order to produce a more effective design.

3   The technology should be 'sold' to people not only on the basis of the 'absence of fumes' but also in terms of 'time-saving' because this is a major problem in a peasant's daily life.

4   Men are an essential resource in the process of adoption of the *fogones* and *hornos*. Campaigns should explicitly encourage their participation.

5   Particular attention should be drawn to the creative improvements introduced for the cooking of *arepas* in the *fogones*.

6   Follow-up and technical assistance facilities should be available to people using *fogones* and *hornos*. Information should be available and accessible to communities with regard to their construction and efficient use.

244

The adoption and adaptation of solar energy technologies in the Bolivian Altiplano

ROXANA MERCADO RODAS

Introduction

This work presents the findings and conclusions of a study of a population involved in the adaptation of technology for the development of protected crops in Pacajes Province. It should be pointed out that this is not complete or exhaustive but a pilot study to be continued later.

In the Bolivian 'altiplano', solar energy technologies have been introduced for use in organic agriculture. These include greenhouses, cloches and cold frames. This is one of the most widespread types of activity in the field of rapid social change in which non-governmental, and some official departmental development corporations have become involved.

Geographical and climatic conditions in the altiplano are particularly harsh on open-air agricultural production because of the high incidence of frost, hail and the scarcity of water for irrigation. Rates of crop success under such conditions are generally poor.

The search for viable alternatives which would safeguard levels of production while allowing crop diversification into more nutritious varieties led to the new solar energy technologies being considered for use in protected crop cultivation. It was hoped they would provide viable solutions to the problems of low production which were directly affecting the nutritional standards and living conditions of the inhabitants of the region. The efforts of organizations to have these initiatives taken up on a larger scale seem to be facing difficulties in transmission of knowledge of technologies and with people's adaptation and use of them.

Of special interest here is why projects aiming at introducing innovative agricultural production techniques have met with so little success. Equally interesting is the investigation of how some innovations are modified by the people. This allows us to understand something of popular perceptions of appropriate technology and its environment.

Geographical context

Pacajes Province has a typical *altiplano* landscape, mainly flat in the centre and

MS R. MERCADO (Bolivia) is a teacher at Universidad Mayor de San Andres, La Paz. She has researched appropriate technology amongst the rural population of Almara. Her area of special interest is educational administration and planning.

245

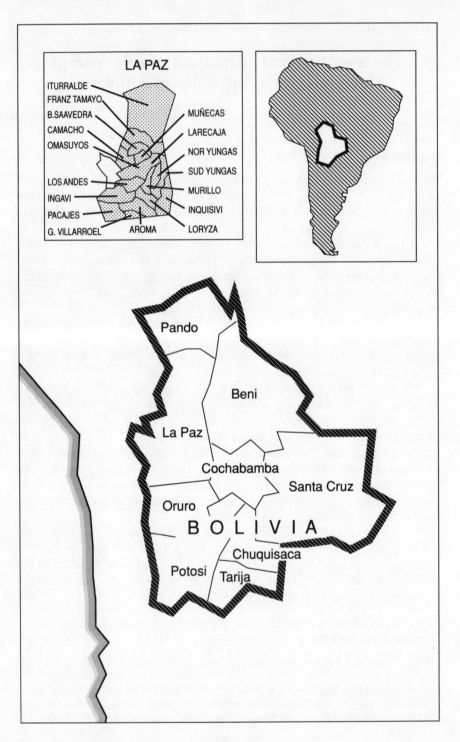

LA PAZ

ITURRALDE
FRANZ TAMAYO
B.SAAVEDRA
CAMACHO
OMASUYOS

MUÑECAS
LARECAJA
NOR YUNGAS
SUD YUNGAS

LOS ANDES
INGAVI
PACAJES
G. VILLARROEL

MURILLO
INQUISIVI

AROMA
LORYZA

Pando

Beni

La Paz

Cochabamba

Santa Cruz

Oruro

BOLIVIA

Chuquisaca

Potosi   Tarija

bordered by gently sloping hills. It is lined from north to south by ranges of hills varying in height from between 4,320 and 5,784m above sea level. Most rain falls between December and March, with an annual total of 400mm.

Frost occurs throughout the year and is caused mainly by extreme diurnal changes in temperature. Hail is common in September and October. The main river is the Desagüadero into which various tributaries flow. Pacajes is bordered by Peru and Chile in the east, Ingavi Province to the north and the Department of Oruro in the south.

Pacajes includes 532 communities, each with its own agricultural union. These are affiliated to their respective cantons which form agricultural sub-centres. Fifty-two cantons, divided into four sections, are recognized by the state. The sub-centres are affiliated in turn to the Pacajes Provincial Peasants' Federation, itself represented in the La Paz Departmental Federation of Peasants with the national body being the United Confederation of Bolivian Peasant Workers (Unica).

The agricultural unions play an important role in community organization and in defining issues to be decided upon in the area of communal civic works. Above all they constitute the sole legal link between the community and the state. The position of Secretary-General of the agrarian unions is held on a rotating basis for one year by each head of household. While this establishes a type of obligatory service to the community, the limitation upon the period of leadership makes continuity difficult in communal projects and weakens the organization.

According to estimates by the National Statistical Institute, based upon the 1976 census, the Province of Pacajes had 102,124 inhabitants in 1987. The reliability of these figures, however, is open to some doubt as they do not distinguish between natural growth and a rapid rise in migration.

Protected productive infrastructure in Pacajes

The 1982–83 period was dominated by a great drought. Initial efforts to assist victims were geared mainly towards meeting food needs after the total crop had failed. Another concern was how to revive production when the drought was over. Non-governmental and official organizations helped in this through their respective assistance projects.

In the *altiplano*, technological assistance began to be directed towards exploring technological alternatives to safeguard agricultural production against the region's severe climate. Moreover, in much of the region, protected crops were being tried out which would in the first instance seek to guarantee self-sufficiency.

Six institutions can be identified as developing protected crop projects in Pacajes Province. Here we shall present a general overview of these projects followed by extracts of the most relevant points which emerged from interviews with each of the following organizations:

247

1 Fundacion Contra el Hambre [Anti-Hunger Foundation] (International Non-Governmental Organization)

This organization started its cold frame project in February 1986 and it is still operational. The project involves the setting up of 'development modules' with infrastructural facilities aimed at the demonstration of, and training in, agricultural methods. The modules comprise twelve cold frames, forestry, rabbit breeding and poultry units, an 'animal bank', administrative offices, classroom for training, a tanning workshop, a ceramics kiln and housing for technical staff. Four development modules have been set up in Pacajes, namely in Calacoto, Ulloma, Callapa and Agua Rica.

The dissemination and implementation of family-operated cold frames started in February 1988 with the training of trade union leaders at subcentre level. By December that year 150 cold frames had been installed and an equal number of leaders trained. The materials needed for construction were divided into 'local' (to be provided by the beneficiaries) and 'non-local' (such as polyethylene, wood, doors, windows and seed) which were donated by the Foundation. The dissemination of cold frames through leaders was intended to have a multiplier effect amongst other community members.

The training courses lasted two days per community and involved basic education in nutrition, horticulture, animal husbandry and peasant organization. The community provided manual labour for the construction of the modules and the installation of the family cold frames. The Foundation reciprocated by providing food rations.

Training in cold frame operation for beneficiary families was given only at community level along the lines mentioned above. There were no regular visits for technical assistance back-up and no follow-up of the replicability of the technology within the communities. The present project extension only envisages the provision of polyethylene to families interested in constructing cloches.

2 Alianza Noruega [The Norwegian Alliance] (International Non-Governmental Organization)

In this project cloche installation started in 1983 as a complement to livestock support work. In the three years to 1986 — the publicity phase — 50 family cloches were donated. Training courses and individual technical assistance were provided.

Since 1987 the organization has sold only 'Agrofilm', seeds, insecticides and technical assistance to those expressing interest when this has been channelled through the Achiri office where consultations are held. No monitoring records on the cloches constructed during the promotion phase are available. However, sales figures for Agrofilm show that 56 families purchased it in the period 1987–88, implying that a similar number of cloches were built.

3 Programa de Microproyectos Rurales 2-CEE-CORDEPAZ [Second Rural Microproject Programme-CEE-CORDEPAZ] (Decentralized State Body)

In this programme the demonstration phase of the cloche project started in August 1986 and continued into the first quarter of 1987, during which time twelve communal cloches of 30m² in size were constructed. Non-local materials were donated by the programme and complementary technical assistance was given during weekly visits to each community. In addition, occasional community-level training courses in horticulture were given. Today the continuation of the project is being considered along the lines of offering credits to families in the form of polyethylene priced at 7 bolivianos per square metre, up to a total of 210 bolivianos (approximately US$84). Technical assistance in the construction and operation of the cloche would be given also.

Between 1987 and 1988 three requests for such credits had been officially received.

4 Corporacion Regional de Desarrollo de La Paz — CORDEPAZ [La Paz Regional Development Corporation — CORDEPAZ] (Decentralized State Body)

The CORDEPAZ cloche project was implemented throughout the *altiplano* between 1985 and 1987. Although it has now finished it deserves mention for the impact it has had on the province.

The project approach defined two levels of beneficiary — families and communities. In communities, the organizational units they opted to work with were mothers' clubs and, to a lesser extent, community labour unions. Special attention was paid to mining centres. In the case of Pacajes this meant Coro Coro. Twenty-five cloches were built in the province.

The agreement CORDEPAZ reached with beneficiaries stipulated that the community or family would contribute locally available materials and labour. CORDEPAZ would extend loans in the form of non-local materials when these cost more than 85 bolivianos (US$34), i.e. nylon, wood, seeds. It also gave technical assistance. Credit was repaid either in *kind*, to the area school (that is, the beneficiary would give part of his production for the school to use for its own purposes), or in *cash*, through the community organization or association so that the credit 'revolved' and became available to other families.

There was no systematic monitoring of credit repayments nor of the continuation of the project. Technological transfer took place through 'training courses' in the following subjects: one general course on cloche construction, six courses on different horticultural crops, one course on plant husbandry and one course on nutrition. Each training course lasted approximately three hours. Today a large number of the cloches built at family and community levels have totally run down.

5 Federacion Departmental de Clubes de Madres [Departmental Federation of Mothers' Clubs] (Non-Governmental Organization)

The cloche project in this case was undertaken as a training exercise for mothers' clubs. It was hoped that a model would be provided for individual families to replicate spontaneously.

The project started in 1987 and lasted until December 1988 and around 35 cloches were constructed in Pacajes. Because of its nature, the organization's approach to implementing the project was somewhat special. The Federation of Mothers' Clubs distributed the gifts of food to depressed urban and rural areas of the country. Would-be supporters had to be women who were required to form themselves into clubs. The main goal of the clubs was to raise domestic and community living conditions through actions to improve health, education, nutrition and the promotion of profitable artisanal activities. Beneficiaries could obtain food at half the local market price. Proceeds from sales were divided as follows: 30 per cent to the mothers' club to be deposited in a bank current account, 15 per cent to the Departmental Federation of Mothers' Clubs, 5 per cent to the National Confederation and the remaining 50 per cent to the National Food Aid Office (Oficina Nacional de Asistencia Alimentaria — OFINAL). This last organization is a decentralized body dependent on the Office of the President and responsible for the acquisition of foreign food aid.

With respect to the construction of the cloches, the community's mothers' club would provide locally-available materials and non-local materials would be purchased with the bank funds referred to above. An official of the Federation would calculate the amounts needed in the latter case.

Training courses were very infrequent although these were complemented with pamphlets on horticulture. There was no monitoring of the replication achieved within participating communities and technical assistance was provided irregularly.

6 Semta — Servicios Multiples de Tecnologias Apropiadas [Comprehensive Appropriate Technology Services] (Non-Governmental Organization) The provision of greenhouses and mulches in Pacajes Province was part of SEMTA's rural programme. The main goals in this were to increase production through the introduction of alternative agricultural technologies and to stimulate community organization for local economic growth as a move in the direction of independent peasant economic development.

The rural programme defined two areas of work — traditional and intensive cultivation. In the first, assistance was given through a revolving fund operated by trade union organizations and consisting of the provision of silos for seed storage, veterinary products, equipment and permanent technical assistance. The SEMTA plan for intensive cultivation was to implement a 'technological package' which would introduce protected cultivation (greenhouses and mulches) and a microsystem of water storage and irrigation to suit the target communities (wells, hand-pumps, windmills, elevated water storage tanks, reservoir or ponds).

Since 1984 'technological packages' have been introduced in 24 communities on commonly-held land and these serve as training and agricultural production centres. Each such centre has its own greenhouses, mulches and water collection system.

250

Technological transfer is made through a continuous training plan consisting of two teaching modules. The first, called 'intensive training', is aimed at community leaders and is carried out on the organization's training and experimentation farm. The second is 'community training' which involves individual families once a month throughout the year and is carried out in the training and agricultural production centres. The topics dealt with in each are construction, horticulture, animal husbandry, forestry, trade unionism and organization, administration, traditional medicine and nutrition. Each is covered over a period of four days within the intensive programme for leaders and one day under the community training programme.

Each training and production centre has its own monitoring and evaluation system for training and management development aspects. The centres were constructed jointly by SEMTA and the community. Management is the community's responsibility while SEMTA provides technical assistance by means of regular weekly visits.

In the 1988–89 year a family credit plan was started for the building of greenhouses, mulches or irrigation systems. This is one way in which training work for families is put into action. There is also a community credit scheme for the organization of production co-operatives. In this case training takes the form of credit management and co-operative formation.

Technologies supplied and the people involved

Here we examine how individual families have been affected by technology adoption and adaptation.

Twenty families were interviewed. Altogether these included 128 people, of whom 90 were children. New technologies were adopted by seven families, 35 per cent of the total.

Pacajes is considered one of the least agriculturally productive areas of the country. According to estimates made by the National Agrarian Reform Council, only 15.41 per cent of the land is suitable for cultivation. Taking this into account, the following data only refers to land occupation in cultivable areas.

Of the 20 cases under consideration, 16 families (80 per cent) held cultivable land of medium or small size, with only four families (20 per cent) occupying large holdings. There is a greater degree of new technology take-up amongst families with medium-size (10–20 hectares) cultivable landholdings.

Pacajes is more of a cattle raising province than it is agricultural. Traditional crops are intended mainly for personal consumption. Potatoes are far and away the main crop. More potatoes are eaten than any other food, they have unlimited storage and preservation potential when they are dried and there is such a wide variety that the peasant can overcome the harsh

251

climate by selecting suitably resistant seed. Traditional cereals also contribute to the region's agricultural output as well as the fodder which compensates for the poor natural pastures. All families grow potatoes, 95 per cent grow barley, 90 per cent *quinca*, 45 per cent millet, 30 per cent wheat, 25 per cent *oca*, 10 per cent oats and 15 per cent *papaliza*. The average area cultivated annually, by crop rotation, is between one-and-a-quarter and one-and-a-half hectares per family. This is due to the relative scarcity of manual family labour.

Livestock provides a secure source of cash income for families in the region. To peasants, livestock ownership is not a measure of profitability in any real sense of the term but rather a means of saving which also gives them liquidity. The number of animals a family owns is determined by their finances and not by how much grazing land they have.

The main kind of livestock is sheep. These are used mainly to supply the family with meat and for petty sales. The latter determined the family's cash income and depends on the size of the flock.

Cattle are used for animal traction in agriculture while they are growing and being fattened. When they reach maturity they are sold and this represents an important source of income which is then re-invested in the purchase of calves to repeat the cycle.

Small animals, such as chickens and pigs, are reared for domestic consumption. The native llama has been replaced almost totally as a means of transport and source of food.

Families taking up new technology own less livestock than those who do not. The ratio is two-to-one in favour of the latter. For example, non-adopting families own 66 head of cattle between them while those adopting own only 32. For sheep the figures are 560 and 295 respectively.

Making estimates of peasant household income is very difficult. This is particularly so when we remember that information on families themselves is only calculated in money terms. No consideration is given to income in kind which is derived from agricultural work and which generally ends up as domestic consumption.

Comparing estimates of the incomes of families adopting new technologies and those who do not, it seems that the former receive less. The average income of adopting families is 66 pesos (US$27) while that for non-adopters is 83 pesos (US$33). Adopting families are less likely to be involved in any additional or parallel economic activity compared with families not adopting. This is a point which will be returned to when we look at technical barriers to technological acceptance.

Garden vegetables are of particular interest as they are the crops which protected productive infrastructure aims to stimulate. The main horticultural products sold in the markets are onions, carrots, tomatoes, lettuce, peas and broad beans — the first three being the most popular.

Much has been assumed about the lack of any tradition of garden vegetable consumption in the *altiplano* and various projects for protected crop promotion have had as one of their main goals the introduction of garden vegetables in daily diets. But in the cases examined, those products already make up part of the families' food intake. In the case of families adopting new technology, garden vegetables are limited to those which they grow themselves. Non-adopting families consume a wider variety which are obtained from local markets.

Although garden vegetables can be bought at the markets, they are more expensive and supply is variable. So, families relying on them are unable to maintain a stable diet throughout the year.

The province of Pacajes is considered to be one of the main sources of population outflow towards the departmental capital, La Paz and other migrant-recipient areas. To talk about the frequency of itinerant migration implies discussion of a category of migrants which is distinct from those who leave their place of origin to establish themselves firmly in another. Itinerant migration is a phenomenon of temporary mobility, with the family itself remaining fixed to its community of origin. We are talking about a community member who goes back and forth to the city on a frequent and regular basis for a variety of reasons: to sell agricultural produce, to buy goods, to attend to official matters, to seek short-term employment, and so forth. There is a tendency for non-adopting families to visit the city more frequently than families who have adopted new technologies.

The standard by which we measure levels of education is given by the national education system which has three levels:

1   basic, lasting 5 years
2   intermediate, 3 years, and
3   middle, 4 years, at the end of which the title of *'bachiller'* is awarded which enables the student to go on to higher studies.

The majority of women in the study had not progressed beyond the basic level of education. With regard to technical training courses held in the community, both husband and wife attended in five out of seven adopting families, but in only four out of the 13 non-adopting families.

Routes to adoption and technical barriers

Defining technical barriers to technology adoption purely in technical terms would be shortsighted and would ignore much of the problem. By analysing the reasons given by families for adopting or not adopting a particular type of protected cropping method we shall try to determine what these technical barriers are.

Remember that all the families interviewed received technical information on protected cropping. In most cases, in the community in which they lived there were greenhouses, cold frames or mulches.

Adopting families: reasons for doing so

Family 1 — to produce strains which are not found in the area
— to save on the cost of food

Family 3 — to see whether it is possible to grow garden vegetables in the altiplano
— to be able to eat green vetegables without spending money
— to see if it is possible to sell green vegetables to neighbours

Family 4 — to save on the cost of food
— to improve diet

Family 6 — to save on the cost of food

Family 7 — because the communal greenhouse was seen to be successful
— to save on the cost of food

Family 16 — because the communal greenhouse was seen to be successful
— to save on the cost of food

Family 20 — out of interest in experimenting
— to save on the cost of food

Non-adopting families: reasons for not adopting

Family 2 — no water available close to the house
— the high cost of the crops
— not having a fixed source of income

Family 5 — lack of time

Family 8 — lack of time
— lack of money

Family 9 — not having enough water

Family 10 — lack of time
— not enough money to spare

Family 11 — lack of time
— not enough money to spare

Family 12 — not seeming profitable

Family 13 — not enough water nearby

Family 14 — not enough water nearby

Family 15 — lack of time

Family 17 — lack of time
— not enough money to spare

Family 18 — lack ot time
— not enough money to spare

Family 19 — no water nearby

We can see that in the case of families adopting protected cropping methods the reason which all gave was that of saving on the cost of food. This meant the cost of buying garden vegetables at the district market. We can relate this reason to the fact that the average monthly cash income of adopting families was less than the non-adopters. If we also take into

254

account that every one of those families who constructed their greenhouses or cloches/cold frames did so using their own funds, we can state that lack of money is not an important technical obstacle.

The most common reason given by non-adopting families was lack of time. This is understandable if we refer back to the figures on parallel economic activities. More non-adopting families than adopting families were carrying out some other work apart from agriculture. Therefore, availability of time is indeed a technical obstacle.

Irrigation of horticultural crops requires large quantities of water. How far access to sufficient water is a technical barrier is illustrated by the fact that the mean distance of landholding to water supply for adopting families is 43 metres while for non-adopters it is 338 metres. It should be noted that access to sufficient water is not just a matter of distance but also of quantity which, in many cases, is only enough to meet household needs.

Technology adoption

Let us first discuss the infrastructural prototypes for protected cropping which were disseminated in the area. In most respects these did not differ significantly from each other despite some variations in shape and size. The most important difference was the use of plastic film in some cases while more durable plastic sheeting was used in others.

Two main directions were taken in technical development. The first was the construction of greenhouses of approximately 60m² in size and mainly carried out at communal level. Individual family greenhouses average 15m². The second line of development was that involving cloches/cold frames or mulches. The main features of these were smaller dimensions, the use of plastic film and, following logically from this, a lower cost of installation.

The main materials used for prototypes were stone, cement, sand and grass for foundations and floor (*sobrecimientos*) in the case of greenhouses, or just mud and stone in the case of small cold frames; adobe for the walls, plastic sheeting in some greenhouses, plastic film in smaller ones and in cloches/coldframes or mulches; fillets (*listones*), beams, nails and rope binding for the roof or covering; wood for doors and windows. In addition, roofs were sloped towards the north in all cases to take maximum advantage of the sun's rays.

While the original designs made use of the most durable materials, the change families made showed a greater concern for saving on investment costs at the expense of strength and durability. Such priorities are decided by what materials families own and their resources. Most families stated that although their construction would not last long, they had permanent access to the local materials used to make repairs or to rebuild. This was especially important as the garden vegetables produced by protected cropping were not going to bring in any profits but were only for personal consumption. This shows the creativity displayed in most cases in adapting materials for the purposes desired. Everybody was willing to experiment to find the solution most suitable to their own needs.

Regarding problems of crop management, the majority agreed that garden vegetables were very sensitive to pests. The main difficulty families faced was not having specialist information available on how to deal with them.

Families also pointed out that the difficulties they faced with some varieties would be minimized if constant technical assistance were available in the form of courses. These could build up both practical and theoretical knowledge of crops, their dietary importance and the ways in which they can be prepared for eating.

Conclusions

Many argue that rural dwellers are fiercely resistant to change and use in evidence the failure of projects seeking to stimulate technological innovation. What we see, however, is that ordinary people have a critical attitude towards technical proposals which fail to take into account important aspects of their daily lives. This attitude has no other way of showing itself except in the rejection of such proposals.

The replicability of a technology which is drawn from outside traditional methods of production will depend on the amount of free time available to try it out in practice. In this way the new technology is subject to the dictates of daily family life.

Replicating smaller-scale projects aimed at domestic consumption holds greater interest for families who own medium-size holdings of cultivatable land, small livestock herds and lower cash incomes. This is the case despite the fact that environmental conditions affect those with relatively high incomes equally as far as their food needs are concerned.

To interpret family incomes only in money terms is to exclude the value of labour power which is invested in agricultural work and the products which are derived from it. The latter are intervening variables in the way in which life-enhancing technological innovations are rated by prospective beneficiaries.

There is a greater predisposition to adopt technological innovation amongst those families where the women participate in technical training. The need to save on expenditure is shown to be a prime condition in whether new productive technology is taken up or not.

The identification of technical problems with new technologies must involve beneficiaries as well as technicians in order that the viability of the project in question can be established at an early stage. In adapting a new technology to its environment local people prefer to make maximum use of local resources even when the durability of the technology is reduced.

256

Table 1 Modifications and adaptations

family	model adopted	modification and adaptation made
1	greenhouse	– doors and windows of used tins; frames from waste wood
		– strips of used tyre rubber in place of binding rope
	cold frame	– no covering; only side walls
3	cold frame	– no fixed covering; in bad weather cover temporarily with jute sacking
4	greenhouse	– half underground (one metre deep) to save on *adobe* for walls
		– no windows; two-part roof, can be lifted
6	cold frame	– *tapial* (mud) walls
		– no covering; only hardy crops grown
7	greenhouse	– foundations of mud and stone
		– mud walls (*tapial*)
		– doors and windows – canvas stretched on poles
		– ropes replaced with twisted sheep's wool cord
		– *caito* for holding down the cover
	cold frame	– mud (*tapial*) walls
16	greenhouse	– bottle glass windows
		– mud (*tapial*) walls
	cold frame	– covering made of noodle packets sewn together and reinforced with plastic flour packets
17	cloche/cold frame	– no modifications to original design

Source: Own Compilation, Communications and Training Unit, SEMTA, 1989

Technological transfer has to be considered in the context of rural daily life or there will be a divide between technical 'expertise' and popular knowledge.

In most of the projects for technological innovation in protected cropping in Pacajes, there has been a lack of technical assistance, monitoring and evaluation. Above all, there has been a lack of a clear policy on training approaches to be used in technological transfer.

257

Killing artisanal fishing with kindness in Nicaragua

OCTAVIA TAPIA

Introduction

Aserradores is located in a calm bay which is protected from winds and tides and bounded on the east by hills and offshore by an island. The highest point of Aserradores is approximately ten metres. Potential fishing grounds stretch along the tranquil coast from the port of Sandino to the gulf of Fonseca. The bay, which is encircled by mangrove swamps, is an ideal place for the cultivation of oysters and crayfish. However, this resource has been underexploited and indeed has been severely affected by the indiscriminate use of agro-chemicals in the cotton industry which is the main monoculture in the zone. There are abundant shoals of shark, braize and other species. Sea routes to El Salvador and Honduras are swift and communication by land with Chinandega, the departmental capital, takes less than one hour. Temporary work in cotton, sugar cane and banana cultivation provides alternative sources of employment. Small-scale farming co-operatives are being set up although land is limited. Family farming activities attain only subsistence levels of income.

A model of development based upon small-scale, artisanal fishing has been applied to the area. Like most models, it has been unable to reproduce reality and indeed has misrepresented it. The model has found itself at the centre of discussion.

Schematically, societies develop on two levels. One is the formal level, that which can be seen. Power and political economy in a society is imposed through ideological and political means. The other level is informal, the struggle for survival, the necessity to meet present problems without projects or planning. The latter is the new civil society, in which 60 per cent of the present population of the Third World live. It is a world suspended between hope and need, resolving the practical circumstances of everyday life in an uncertain and unforeseen way.

Nicaraguan context

Nicaragua has approximately three million inhabitants and a surface area

MR O. TAPIA (Nicaragua) is an architect. He worked in Chile, France, Algeria, Spain and Nicaragua. He is currently Co-ordinator of ECOTEXTURA, Centre of Innovation and Development of Appropriate Technologies.

of 140,000 sq. kilometres. There has been a struggle for popular revolution since 1979 and the country has experienced since 1987 one of the most acute and sustained hyper-inflations in Latin America.

The background to the project can be understood more easily if some economic factors are considered:

1 The impact of the war of liberation (1977–79). Estimates of direct damage include a reduction in the gross domestic product (GDP) to 1971 levels and a massive flight of capital (approximately $500 million) which was equivalent to 78.5 per cent of the total exports of 1977.

2 In early 1979, the new government began transforming the productive structure and the internal and external dynamics of the Nicaraguan economy on the basis of a mixed economic model. The new role which was assigned to the state significantly increased the importance of public expenditure and the role of public enterprises. This had a strong impact upon prices in the economy as a whole.

3 Armed opposition against the revolution was supported by the United States. A number of economic consequences included the need to finance the destructive capacity, the mobilization of resources which it provoked and the political alliances which it demanded. People working in the defence sector constituted one-fifth of the economically-active population and consumed quantities of food and goods which were already in short supply.

The Aserradores project is located in the Second Region of the country. In 1988, it had a population of 632,021 which was 18 per cent of the national total. The inhabitants are mainly urban, with 355,330 living in towns and cities. The Region is principally agricultural and agro-industrial. Agriculture is devoted to export-orientated goods but weak in production of goods for internal consumption. The area produces 90 per cent of the national output of cotton, 50 per cent of sugar cane, 100 per cent of bananas and 60 per cent of garlic — but only 11 per cent of rice, 4 per cent of maize, 3 per cent of beans and 23 per cent of sorghum.

The Aserradores project is located in the north-east of the Department of Chinandega in the municipal region of El Viejo. The project impinges upon the entire area known as the Aserradores Peninsular. The land is part of the Aposentillo Hacienda. It has soil of high agricultural potential and is protected by coastal mangrove swamps. There are two distinctive types of landscape: the fertile valleys and slopes reaching 30m in height on the northern side and the mangrove swamps of the coast. The annual total precipitation satisfies the requirements of the tropical farming practised in the region but is irregular in its distribution. Torrential proportions are often reached in some areas. The zone has a hot, humid climate and is situated in a sub-tropical, wooded biological area.

The inhabitants are either landless peasants or those with very small plots of land located on the boundaries of large estates and common land on the coast and inlet. People supplement their incomes and diet through fishing, growing sorghum, maize and sisal and working as temporary labourers on the cotton and sugar plantations. The fishermen also work as shell and firewood collectors and popcorn sellers. This is a transient population, one which is constantly moving from place to place within the zone and to other zones.

The project is located in a small area which forms part of the ancient dry, tropical Pacific forest which is now used mainly for pasture land and cotton fields and, to a lesser extent, for a few subsistence crops. Both the wind system and surface waters which drain into Aserradores Bay carry along with them what is estimated as dozens of tons of highly toxic synthetic agro-chemicals a year. It has proved impossible to remedy this situation on a local level. Biological agents originating many kilometres away constitute a problem which affects the entire western Pacific zone. The indiscriminate use of agricultural toxins and their lasting residual effects upon the coastal and mangrove areas is intensified by the marine traffic in the bay.

The toxins which contaminate coastal waters blend with the sediments and the living fabric of aquatic organisms and cause the latter's metabolisms to change in many ways. These effects include a reduction in the reproductive potential of species and the poisoning of fish and crustaceans. The viability of eggs and larvae are endangered, so reducing the biomass of species which can be used for commercial purposes. The coastal area is an important site for the reproduction and incubation of larvae and young fish.

The zone is one of the most over-exploited areas of the municipal region. Cotton is the main crop, followed by sorghum, maize and banana to a lesser degree. A wooded strip approximately 15–20m wide separates the cotton plantations from the coast and there are also small stretches of trees on the hillsides. The mangrove tree is found in all the inlets of the bay and provides subsistence for the families. The proximity of the cotton plantations poses a severe threat to the ecosystem of the area because of the use of agrochemicals and pesticides which have damaged the fauna of the mangrove swamp and the bay in general. The other problem is deforestation as a result of the exploitation of timber as fuelwood and as a building material.

Artisanal fishing

The artisanal fishing industry in Nicaragua is located along both seaboards and on the rivers, lake and lagoon basins of the country's interior. Fishing is done from small boats driven by oars, sails or outboard motors and the methods employed vary from region to region. With a few exceptions, fishermen have managed to rise above subsistence fishing production. The main problem is that the dispersed, often remote fishing communities lack infrastructure and basic services and many do not have land routes to the rest of the area. There is also a lack of fishing equipment, a lack of capital to finance its replacement and a resulting dependency upon middlemen who buy the catches, supply equipment and determine the prices of both. Many fishermen depend upon one buyer for the sale of their product.

Fishermen often work as agricultural labourers when fishing is impossible. They may combine both activities as a result of the absence of state support in the provision of certain indispensable goods such as fuel, lubricating oil, ice and food. These factors and others, such as the lack of an infrastructure for the collection, processing, conservation and distribution of the fish, have created a sense of insecurity at the workplace and in the men's incomes. This forces them to work at other jobs which are often badly paid.

After the triumph of the Popular Sandinista Revolution and the creation of the Nicaraguan Fishing Institute (INPESCA), a survey of the various fishing communities in the different zones and regions was undertaken. This survey aimed to discover which communities might be suitable for the installation of storage centres for the fishermen's catches, and for subsequent processing, conservation and distribution. These centres could be the basis for later development of the communities. Several sites, on both the Atlantic and Pacific coasts and the river basin of the Lake of Nicaragua, were selected and a support plan proposed. These sites have been designated 'poles of development'.

Each of these levels moves forward by similar methods although with different aims. Each has its own support structure which intervene, aid and create possibilities. Each has created social organizations which are entrusted with designing a believable vision of utopia. These enable a social group to endure its existence and explain its causes. Similarly, these organizations propose tactics to enable a social group to confront different sets of circumstances.

The Aserradores project

The Nicaraguan Institute of Fishing (INPESCA) proposed the projection in 1982. This aimed to offer support to small-scale, artisanal fishing with the objective of 'giving the population access to low-cost protein'. Fishermen were offered training, technical assistance and infrastructure, under the 'poles of development for artisanal fishing'. Aserradores was listed as one of these poles. In 1983, financing for the project by different international organizations was sought. Norwegian People's Aid (NPA) offered to finance the project in 1984, after a team of experts visited the area.

The object group, the fishermen, organized the 'Mario Carrillo' cooperative in 1980 with the institutional support of the Institute of Natural

Resources (IRENA) and AID. Originally the group included 13 fishermen who did not fish in Aserradores and who were not native to the village. They were individuals trying to survive on the basis of fishing and also, occasionally, as peasants, drivers and smugglers. Fishing was only another way of surviving during a period of economic crisis. The fishermen travelled between Jiquilillo, Potosí and Padre Ramos. They had no permanent home, sleeping in their boats. The fishermen were not members of a guild or a village or even a nomadic community, but simply men trying to survive. They arrived in Aserradores in 1984, slept under a temporary structure of branches and visited their families in distant communities at weekends. The men now numbered 25, some using a small fishing line with 30 hooks (*anzuelos*) while others used trammel nets (*trasmaloos*). The site had no access by main road. INPESCA and Norwegian People's Aid learnt of their presence in Aserradores and selected them as the project's object group.

These improvised fishermen now witnessed a stream of visiting experts and officials, saw bulldozers constructing roads and building installations and understood that the site of their settlement was being transformed into the co-operative's port. The fishermen were the protagonists of the project despite the fact that no one had consulted them. Their fishing tackle was improved and they received different types of outboard motors for their hollowed-out tree trunks (*cayucos*). The men were promised boats of an unfamiliar size and also houses, schools, training centres and a processing plant producing 10 tons of frozen fish per day.

The co-operative has both grown and declined as an organization, with many of its leaders and members leaving because of a lack of understanding of what was happening. Of the original 25 fishermen who arrived in Aserradores, only three now remain. However, the organization now has 52 members. While the size has grown, there are problems related to cash supply, book-keeping, grants, loan repayments and housing loans. The men say that they do not have the ability to manage what they have and have had to hand over the ice factory and the warehouse to INPESCA as part of the price of remaining within the project. Sixteen families are living in the new houses in the new village and another 16 will arrive soon.

The families have frustrated the financial agency (NPA) because they remain unaware of their own worth. They have learnt to negotiate and are moving timidly into the new situation created for them. Some have benefited while others have suffered from the experience. They have learnt to navigate on the high sea and have trained new members of the co-operative. They always prefer to recruit individuals from outside the fishing industry because they believe professional fishermen to be too individualistic and unlikely to work for the good of the co-operative.

ECOTEXTURA, a local NGO, became involved in the project in 1987 in order to design the fishing village. ECOTEXTURA's function was to survey the physical location, liaise with the fishermen and reach some common understanding on the context of the project. One of ECOTEXTURA's immediate discoveries was the level of existing contamination caused by the encirclement of the site by cotton plantations. Pesticides were found everywhere, including the wells and in mothers' milk. The fish had moved out more than 15 miles from the coast and the shellfish had disappeared. Another important point was that no fishing culture existed. The fishermen had learnt how to catch fish but knew nothing of the traditions linked to fishing and their families were ignorant of conditions in this part of the country.

Fishing techniques in Aserradores

There are 18 *cayucos* made of hewn-out tree trunks, but three are not operational because their motors need new crank shafts. Twelve boats are used for trammel nets and are four to five metres in length. Boats fishing with hooked lines are six to seven metres long. Trawlers were provided as training boats to instruct the fishermen in the handling of intermediate-sized vessels which were to be donated later. However, the intermediate vessels never arrived. The trawlers provided are made of reinforced fibreglass. They arrived in Nicaragua from La Paz in 1983. After a few hours in operation, their transmission boxes broke. New boxes were received in 1984 but the same thing happened again. It was found that the boxes could not support the revolutions per minute produced by the motor. New boxes with different specifications were sent and were accompanied by a Norwegian naval technician. He made various changes to the new boxes such as taking away the hydraulic system of the propeller's axle shaft and fixing the propeller with a new, adapted part. This reduced the vessel's speed. The barges remained at anchor until the arrival of a Mexican technical expert and instructor but as they did not have the equipment necessary for fishing, the barges were used to carry the co-operative's *cayucos* to Puerto Sandino and to take part in the recruitment of fishermen. When fishing with nets and hooked lines was attempted, their transmission boxes were disconnected. It was finally decided to renovate the holds in dry dock while awaiting parts sent by INPESCA.

The barges began working in January 1989 and have experienced many problems of a mechanical, fishing and social nature. The latter involved the fishermen. It was necessary to redefine the relationship the latter would have with the vessels. For example, who fishes from the barges, who equips them and who finances their maintenance? To date, NPA has been responsible for the costs of the numerous renovations of these difficult vessels.

The Co-operative's output is based upon two techniques: hook-and-line and gill netting. The selection of the type of fishing method to be used depends upon the fishermen themselves. They are organized in crews of three and, with a few exceptions, are chosen by the co-operative's management. Crew members are responsible for the tackle, the vessel and the motor. Crew decide upon the distribution of fuel, minor repairs to the motors and the provision of supplies for the journey.

Storage and marketing

The Aserradores storage centre is managed by INPESCA and was initially a container intended for temporary storage, a Thermoking which stopped working. A small office which was irregularly supplied with ice from Chinandega was added. The fishermen were frequently prevented from going out fishing because of the lack of storage facilities and the insecure nature of the sale of their produce. This happened often in the early summer. The fish are frozen and the day's catch is stored in a thermal trailer to await transportation to Chinandega and other INPESCA depots. We can give an example of the marketing of the catch from August 1988. Fishermen were paid 70 córdobas for one pound of Class A fish but INPESCA sold it to the public for between 150–170 córdobas. That is a mark-up of 210 per cent. A pound of shark fillet was bought for 40 córdobas but sold to the consumer at between 90 and 110 córdobas, an increase of 250 per cent.

Fish processing

NPA's contribution has been instrumental in giving Aserradores the profile and significance it enjoys today. The agency has effectively assumed total investment in the project. Since 1982 the state's involvement has been limited to supervising and training the fishermen and even this has been done in a superficial and irregular manner. Indeed, it could be said that both INPESCA and the fishermen have played fairly passive roles.

Table 1 overleaf, details the total investment in the 'pole of development for the artisanal fishing project' in Aserradores.

Despite the amount already invested, the plant has not yet begun to function on a regular basis because drinking water has not yet been connected. The Nicaraguan Electricity Institute (INE) has not made the connection for the pump motor. The plant now has electricity but the village is still waiting. The road is in good condition and a bus route now offers services for the village. The technicians' house is finished and ECOTEXTURA members are living there while conducting the training programme. The fishing village has 30 houses, one primary road, one training centre, a primary school and a children's playground.

The financial agency has various investments still pending, such as six 40-foot trawlers (whose beneficiary is unknown), a shipwright's yard, a docking jetty, a system for handling fishing refuse and a workshop for building small vessels to replace the *cayucos* (which, according to the NPA, have a

Table 1 Investment in artisanal fishing project, Aserradores

item	cost in US dollars
the plant	478 990.06
– building	89 704.59
– cooling equipment (freezing, ice-making, maintaining frozen goods)	334 043.47
– processing equipment	55 242.00
drinking water system	209 024.00
electrical system	116 166.03
main road	108 204.04
technicians' house	19 000.00
co-operative's logistics and fittings	40 000.00
fishing village (30 houses, residential development and equipment)	475 000.00
total investment US$	1 446 384.97

useful working life of only three years). The NPA has also contributed new funds for running the co-operative.

Problems with the project

The Aserradores project formed part of a national programme for developing artisanal fishing. There are two main obstacles in the way of this development. One is the lack of a stable market (in terms of quantity and prices) for the sector's product. The other is the lack of a regular source of consumer goods.

The project has opened up a number of perspectives. For example, the availability of ice could make fishing more independent and improve the quality of the product. However, the vessels, the *cayucos*, are small and need to be replaced. The external market is now accessible because of the freezing facilities but to enter it with advantage the fishermen would need to rely upon the administrative support of the government. Up to now, this support has not been forthcoming. The internal market has remained stable as a result of the state's role but we have already discussed the pricing problem. The population could live in better conditions and fishermen's families could participate in fish-processing activities such as repairing nets, drying and adding brine to the fish. This would help increase their incomes.

The project was unable to create the necessary dynamism because of the following contradictions:

1 The contradiction between the plant's capacity and the artisan catch: The imbalance between these points to the problem of the profitability of the project as a whole. The plant's semi-industrial character allows it to produce 10 tons of ice cubes, process 2,000 pounds of cleaned fish

266

(fishermen gut the scaled species and remove skin and fins from the shark) and conserve 25,000 pounds of fresh and frozen product per day. The plant needs a volume of fresh catch of between 6,500 and 10,000 pounds per day in order to function properly, but is faced with a very limited supply. There are normally 16 *cayucos* available for fishing in Aserradores and field research has shown that the whole zone has only 27 *cayucos* for 118 fishermen.

The total fishing catch in Aserradores between September 1987 and August 1988 amounted to 150,000 pounds of processed fish. The plant works on a daily basis and needs 6,000 to 10,000 pounds of fish per day. To resolve this problem, you would have to expand the *cayuco* fleet so that the number of vessels exceeded the number of fishermen in the zone. Both INPESCA and NPA saw the 40-foot boats as a solution. However, we are already aware of the history of the boats and we still await six new vessels.

Another way of making the plant profitable could be INPESCA's shrimping barges. The storage capacity is now known but only 20 per cent of the catch is shrimp while the rest is braize, mackerel, eel, *curbina*, haddock, cod, *wicho* and other fish with no commercial appeal. These catches could be processed by the plant and make it profitable. However, the consequence would be that the artisanal fishermen would then become marginalized suppliers and the project's objective — to develop the artisanal sector — would also be marginalized. The artisanal fishermen would merely share in the multiplying effects of a semi-industrial plant which was, by chance, sited in Aserradores.

2 The contradiction between the public entity (INPESCA) and the population: INPESCA is the actual owner and manager of the plant and aims to build up highly profitable enterprises. Following its reorganization, its corporations are now managed on the basis of INCAE (Harvard Business School) criteria. The Aserradores project, which is not yet highly profitable, was donated to the state entity in order to ensure its continued functioning. The donor organization agreed to finance the director of the plant and his technical personnel. This was because INPESCA had little confidence in the undertaking and was suspicious of the conditions imposed by the donor (co-ownership by the co-operative, INPESCA and a fishermen's union, which still does not exist).

This arrangement enabled INPESCA to enjoy control over purchase of fish from local artisanal producers and control with respect to the sale of consumer goods and also the fish product itself. This does not constitute an advantageous position for the fishermen because the internal market, even if restricted, is often flooded by donations of tinned fish from the Soviet Union.

INPESCA's pricing policy is determined by sectoral strategies and is not linked to local costs. The fishermen, who are concerned to increase

267

their income, see that the market of middlemen and external trade (smuggling to El Salvador) offer higher income possibilities in the short-term than do INPESCA's operations. Thus, different people have different conceptions of profitability. The object of desire, the plant, becomes a theatre of confrontation rather than a lever of development.

An alternative model

The fishermen have begun bringing their families to the new village and there are now 16 families living there. Electricity is already installed. There are roads and drinking water will arrive soon. The ice-making factory and the processing and freezing plant are all under construction, under the management of INPESCA. Basic infrastructure has been built including a training centre, primary school and playground. A small shipwright's yard for reparing motors and vessels is being built. NPA has given money for the financing of the co-operative for the next months. The installations are being completed and relations with the state's administration appear clear. The project should now begin to function and the fishermen ought to be able to finance themselves and the remainder of the project.

However, with the introduction of a different model, people have been forced to change their roles. The institutional structure no longer appears as a mother-father figure. Instead, it seems cold and even a little hostile. The financial organism shows signs of fatigue and is happy neither with itself nor with the project which has not produced expected results. The fishermen, confronting their own loneliness, appear a little stupefied and want to find new godparents/protectors.

In Aserradores, there was no fishing culture. Some people had no knowledge of the sea, the majority being of peasant origin. They arrived in a suspicious frame of mind, generally liking the new houses but finding the yards were not big enough to keep animals (hogs, hens, cows, etc). People did not like the idea of a communal laundry for 16 families. Twelve of these families had not had electricity in their previous homes, 14 had used well-water (mostly contaminated) and 11 did not have latrines. In general, their houses had been single room hovels made of straw and lacking furniture (10 beds for 49 people).

ECOTEXTURA is trying to create a fishing culture which could act as a support for the project and which would affect both the co-operative and the community. ECOTEXTURA aims to do this through a locally produced development plan and through training. The situation of the emigrants and their fight to survive should be regarded as a trampoline rather than as a handicap and has suggested new ground rules based on this perspective.

ECOTEXTURA made a suggestion to NPA which the latter accepted.

This was that the fishermen should have a total vision of the project and a strategy for implementing it. The fundamental aim of the plan is to revitalize the co-operative and the community as an independent entity. This would enable an improvement in the productivity of the fishing activity and potential economic sectors (artisans, collectives, family firms) as well as raising the quality of life for the inhabitants in the short-term.

The objectives can be summarized as:

1 stimulating artisanal production, preserving traditional forms and improving quality;
2 replacing and improving vessels and methods of fishing;
3 promoting alternative ways of processing and storage in the form of small, family firms;
4 ensuring the survival and productivity of such firms;
5 using appropriate technologies and re-using waste materials;
6 organizing an autonomous marketing system;
7 creating a centre to promote development alternatives for artisanal fishing.

The lessons of Aserradores

The efforts of the international financial aid agencies should support the poorest groups in society. This should be done without conditions, without expecting results in unrealistic time periods, without demanding that such activities be part of a more general plan and without regarding these groups as 'objects' to be activated by foreign representatives who are constantly changing.

The goal of appropriate technology is to help create better lives for people. Appropriate technologies are tools of liberation which give their users a greater sense of self-value and fulfilment. There must be a way of determining needs and the capacity for work with the aim of establishing a creative social process based upon permanent training and participation.

Appropriate technologies have to be endogenous, or to reinforce what is endogenous, so that new tools can become part of the daily life of the community. These technologies can be introduced with lower investments and can promote new forms of self-government and management within the designated social group.

At the same time, appropriate technologies should be instrumental in beginning the process of re-organizing production habits. Machinery could become profitable, plant and buildings could be modified and innovations introduced. When workers improve, look after and maintain their machines and equipment they have knowledge about and control over these implements.

269

The productive sector of Third World countries must be re-structured and the emphasis placed upon small producers and those working in the so-called 'informal' sector of the economy. This is where the poorest and the most vulnerable people live. This is where the most substantial improvements could be made quickly and without vast financial investments.

We must guarantee these sectors each access to credit, technological innovation and the domestic market. These people are the groups who produce the major part of what most people consume. We must give more attention to women, to encourage rather than hinder their liberation, and thus stimulate their economic activity. In Africa, female labour is responsible for around 80 per cent of food production.

Finally, in an attempt to summarize the problems facing Latin America, we will quote the words of Gabriel García Marquez:

'Poets and beggars, musicians and prophets, soldiers and scoundrels, all creatures of that turbulent reality, we have not had to ask much of our imaginations because we have been preoccupied with trying to make sense of our lives with the tools given us.'

Bibliography

Nkonoki

Bomani, P., *Kongamano la Chama Juu ya Utekelezaji wa Azimio la Arusha*, (Party Symposium on the Implementation of the Arusha Declaration), mimeo, p. 3, Dar es Salaam, 1987.

Brewin, D.R., 'Kilimanjaro agriculture' in *Tanzania notes and records*, No. 64, Tanzania Society, p. 115, Dar es Salaam, 1965.

Government of Tanganyika, *Annual report of the Department of Agriculture 1934*, Government Printer, p. 25–26, Dar es Salaam, 1935.

Government of Tanganyika, *National paper on science and technology*, UNCSTD, New York and Addis Ababa, 1978.

National census, Central Statistical Bureau, Dar es Salaam, 1988.

Mwamadzingo

Agarwal, Bina, 'Diffusion of rural innovations: some analytical issues and the case of wood-burning stoves' in *World Development*, Vol. 11, No. 4, pp. 359–376, 1983.

Baldwin, Samuel F., *Biomass stoves: design, development and dissemination*. Princeton University, 1986.

Barnett, Andrew, Martin Bell and Kurt Hoffman, *Rural energy and the Third World: a review of social science research and technology policy problems*. Oxford: Pergamon Press, 1982.

Board of Science and Technology for International Development, *Diffusion of biomass energy technologies in developing countries*. Second Edition. Washington, D.C.: National Academy Press, 1984.

Gamser, Matthew, S., *Innovation, user participation and forest energy development*. Unpublished PhD Thesis, Science Policy Research Unit, University of Sussex, 1986.

Gill, Jasvinder Singh, *Traditional fuels and cooking stoves in developing countries — a technical, social and environmental assessment*. Unpublished PhD Thesis, Energy Group, The Open University, 1985.

Hyman, Eric L., *The economics of fuel-efficient household charcoal stoves in Kenya*. Appropriate Technology International, 1985.

Juma, Calestous, 'Intellectual Property Rights for Jua Kali Innovations' in Juma, Calestous and Jackton B. Ojwang, eds, *Innovation and* sovereignty: the patent debate in African develoment. Nairobi: African Centre for Technology Studies. pp. 123–144, 1989.

Kamweti, D.M., *Review of cookstoves and charcoal production in Kenya.* Nairobi: African Development and Economic Consultants Ltd., 1983.

Kinyanjui, Maxwell and Laurie Childers, *How to make the Kenya ceramic jiko.* Nairobi: Energy/Development International, 1983.

Krugmann, Hartmut, *Review of issues and research relating to improved cookstoves.* IDRC Manuscript Report No. 152e, 1987.

Mwamadzingo, Mohammed, Calestous Juma and C. Bhadwaj, 'Biomass From Waste: The Case of Apro Energy Enterprises', Nairobi: African Centre for Technology Studies, Mimeo, 1988.

Mwamadzingo, Mohammed and Dominic Walubengo (forthcoming), *Rural electrification in Kenya.* London: The Panos Institute.

Obel, Elizabeth, 'Utilizing agricultural waste' in *Kengo News.* Vol. 1. No. 1, 1984.

O'Keefe, Phil, Paul Raskin and Steve Bernow, *Energy and development in Kenya: opportunities and constraints.* Stockholm: The Beijer Institute, 1984.

Pathak, B.S., *et al.*, 'Characteristics of crop residues' in *Energy Digest*, 1984.

Republic of Kenya, *The Development Plan 1989–1993.* Nairobi: The Government Printers, 1988.

—— *Improved cook stoves in Kenya: experiences of the renewable energy development project.* Nairobi: Ministry of Energy and Regional Development, 1986.

United Nations, *Yearbook of energy statistics.* New York, 1982.

—— *1982 Statistical Yearbook.* New York.

Walubengo, Dominic 'Personal Communication', Friday, 9 June 1989.

Ncube

Hancock, D. & Hancock, G., *Cooking patterns and domestic fuel use in Masvingo Province*, Zimbabwe.

Mandala, G.S., *Limited — dependent and qualitative variables in econometrics*, Cambridge University Press, Cambridge, 1983.

Ncube, M., *Rural industrialisation in Zimbabwe*, Economics Department, U.Z., 1986.

Ncube, M., *Rural non-farm industries in Zimbabwe*, ILO Paper, 1989.

Stewart, F., *Technology and underdevelopment*, Macmillan, London, 1977.

Sutcliffe, R.B., *Industry and underdevelopment*, Addison Wesley, London, 1971.

Massaquoi

Aberra Yonas, *Feasibility of large-scale salt manufacture from salt-laden-silts*, M. Eng., University of Sierra Leone, 1989.

Industrial Development Unit (IDU), Commonwealth Fund for Technical Co-operation. *Sierra Leone: development of the salt industry.* Mission Report IDU/SLE/2, Commonwealth Secretariat, London, October 1986.

Gbakima, A., *Solar — Evaporation of Brine from Silts* B.Eng, USL, 1989.

Kamara, M.Y., *Construction and testing of an improved wood burning stove for use in a small-scale salt processing project*, B.Eng. (Hons) project, University of Sierra Leone, June 1985.

Manner, M.G.V., *Guidelines for the establishment of solar salt facilities from seawater, underground bines, and salted lakes.* Chapters 3, page 30, UNIDO/IS 330, July 1982.

Massaquoi, J.G.M., *Technology choice in the informal sector. The care of salt production in Sierra Leone.* Report for IDRC Contract No. 3-P-84-0164-014 (IDRC Canada), 1987.

Massaquoi, J.G.M., *Introduction of improved technology in the small-scale salt processing operation.* Report prepared for Plan International Freetown, 1985.

Sierra Leone Government, Programme Evaluation, Monitoring Services Unit (PEMSU) Agriculural Statistical Bulletin No. 2, February, 1983.

Adjebeng-Asem

Adjebeng-Asem, S., 'Social factors influencing the translation of innovation into entrepreneurship', IDRC Module 186e, IDRC, Ottawa, 1988.

Agarwal, A.N., *The university and the international dissemination of managerial techniques*, R.A. Solo and E.M. Rogers, 1972.

Almazan, A.M. (1988) 'Selection of cassava varieties for processing and utilization', paper presented at IITA–UNICEF Interregional Experts Groups Meetings — Exchange of Technologies for Cassava Processing Equipment and Food Products, IITA, Ibadan, 13–19 April, 1988.

Bass, L.W., *In technology transfers: successes and failures.* San Francisco Press, 1974.

Carr, M. and Ruby Sandhu, 'Women, technology and rural productivity', UNIFEM Occasional Paper No. 6, UNIFEM, New York, 1987.

Cock, J.H., Cassava, new potential for a neglected crop, Boulder and London, pp. 23–53, Westview Press, 1985.

Freeman, C., *The economics of industrial innovations.* Penguin Modern Economics Texts, 1974.

Gamser, Matthew, 'Innovation, technical assistance and develpment: The importance of technology users', World Development, Vol. 16, pp. 711–721, 1988.

Grace, M.R., *Cassava processing*, pp. 81–102. Food and Agriculture Organization, Rome, 1977.

Hahn, S.K., *et al., Breeding low cyanide cassava varieties and effect of traditional processing methods on the residual cyanide content in the final pro-*

ducts, paper presented at the First African Conference of Food Science and Technology at Cairo, Egypt, 14–17 November, 1983.

Kwatia, J.T., *Cassava processing in Ghana: technology, experiences and problems*, paper presented at IITA–UNICEF Interregional Experts Group Meeting — Exchange of Technologies for Cassava Processing Equipment and Food Products, IITA, Ibadan, 13–19 April, 1988.

Ladipo, P., 'Introducing Appropriate Technology for rural development: The case of a maize sheller', Research Report, University of Ife, Nigeria, 1978.

Cassava products and recipes. Food Investigation Project. Enugu, Nigeria.

Onabolu, A.O., 'Development of new cassava for products', paper presented at IITA–UNICEF Interregional Experts Group Meeting — Exchange of Technologies for Cassava Processing Equipment and Food Products. 13–19 April, 1988.

Onwueme, I.C., *The tropical tuber crops*, John Wiley and Sons, Toronto, Canada, 1978.

Opaleye, O.A. and C.P. Adams, 'Development of food processing equipment problems and constraints', paper presented at IITA–UNICEF Interregional Experts Group Meeting — Exchange of Technologies for Cassava Processing Equipment and Food Products, 13–19 April, Ibadan, Nigeria, 1988.

Platt, Adam, *The introduction and verification of household level technologies*, paper presented at IITA–UNICEF Interregional Experts Group Meeting — Exchange of Technologies for Cassava Processing Equipment and Food Products, IITA, Ibadan, 13–19 April, 1988.

Platt, B.S. 'Tables of representative values of food commonly used in tropical countries'. Medical Research Council Special Report, Series 302, London, 1962.

Rogers, M.E., *Diffusion of innovations*, (3rd Edition), Free Press, London, 1983.

Rothwell, Roy, 'Tough customers, good design', 1985.

Schmookler, J., *Invention and economic growth*, Harvard University Press, 1966.

Smith, S.S., 'Roots and tuber processing and utilization: a case study of Sierra Leone', paper presented at IITA–UNICEF Interregional Experts Group Meeting — Exchange of Technologies for Cassava Processing Equipment and Food Products, IITA, Ibadan, 13–19 April, 1988.

Basant

Basant, Rakesh, 'The development of animal-drawn implements by artisans in Gujarat', *Appropriate Technology*, Vol. 14, No. 4, December, 1987.

Basant, Rakesh, *Agro-mechanical technology in a developed area: a study of its diffusion*, Ahmedabad, The Gujarat Institute of Area Planning, 1988.

Basant, Rakesh, *Technology diffusion in an agrarian economy: a study of agro-mechanical technology in Gujarat*, Ph.D. Thesis submitted to the Gujarat University, Ahmedabad, India, 1989.

Basant, Rakesh and K.K. Subrahmanian, *Diffusion of agro-mechanical technology in a backward region*, Ahmedabad, Sardar Patel Institute of Economic and Social Research, 1987.

Biggs, S.D. and E.J. Clay, 'Generation and diffusion of agricultural technology: a review of theories and experiences', *World Employment Programme Working Paper No. 122*, Geneva, International Labor Organization, 1983.

Fransman, Martin, 'Conceptualising technical change in the Third World, in the 1980s: an interpretive survey', *Journal of Development Studies* XII, 4, 572–652, 1985.

Hemmi, Kenzo, 'Mechanization as a strategy for agricultural and rural development', paper presented at the seminar on *Mechanisation of Small Scale Farming* held at Hangzhou, The Peoples Republic of China, 22–26 June, 1982.

Rogers, E.M., *Diffusion of innovations* (Third Edition), The Free Press, New York, 1983.

Rosenberg, Nathan, *Perspectives on technology*, Cambridge University Press, 1976.

Schon, D.A., *Beyond the stable state*, Random House, New York, 1971.

Starkey, Paul, *Animal-drawn wheeled tool carriers: perfected yet rejected*, German Appropriate Technology Exchange (GATE), GTZ, Eschborn, Germany, 1989.

Haque, Islam, Islam

Ahmed, Q.K., *Promotion of employment and income through rural non-crop activities in Bangladesh*, BIDS Research Report No. 45, BIDS Dhaka, Bangladesh, 1986.

Ahmed, Q.K. and Chawdhury, F.A., *Rural industrialization in Bangladesh; a synthesis based on studies on rural industrial development in selected upazilas*, BIDS, Dhaka, Bangladesh, 1987.

ASM: *Metals Handbook*, American Society for Metals Handbook, Metals Park, Ohio, 1948, 1961.

BARC, *Indigenous agricultural tools and equipments of Bangladesh*, Agricultural Engineering Division, Bangladesh Agricultural Research Council, Dhaka, 1982.

Basant, R., *Indigenous knowledge and technology diffusion: a case of agro-mechanical technology in Gujarat*, Working paper No. 16, The Gujarat Institute of Area Planning, Gota, Ahmedabad, India, 1988.

BBS, *Bangladesh Statistical Yearbook 1986–87*, Bangladesh Bureau of Statistics, Govt. of Bangladesh, Dhaka, 1987.

BSCIC, *Bangladesh Small and Cottage Industries Corporation: A survey*; Bangladesh Small and Cottage Industries Corporation, Dhaka, 1983.

Gamser, M.S., *Power from the people*, IT Publications, London, 1988.

Gamser, M.S., *Mobilizing Appropriate Technology*, IT Publications, London, 1988.

Haque, M.M., 'A method for promoting indigenous innovations', *Science and Public Policy*; Volume 16, No. 1, 1989.

Hossain, M., *Credit for the rural poor – the Grameen Bank in Bangladesh*; Research Monograph: 4, BIDS, Dhaka, Bangladesh, 1984.

IACB, *Engineering industries in Bangladesh – a review*, Investment Advisory Centre of Bangladesh, TIP, Govt. of Bangladesh. Dhaka, 1985.

Muller, J., *Liequidation or consolidation or indigenous technology*; Development Research Series No. 1, Aalborg University Press, 1980.

Planning Commission, *Third Five-Year Plan 1985–90*; Govt. of Bangladesh, Sher-e-Bangla Nagar, Dhaka, 1985.

Rosegger, G., *The economics of production and innovation*; (An Industrial Perspective), Pergamon Press, 1980.

Van Ufford, P.Q. et. al., *The hidden crisis in development*: Development Bureaucracies, UN University, Tokyo and Free University Press, Amsterdam, 1988.

World Bank, Bangladesh, *Promoting higher growth and human development*; A World Bank country study, Washington D.C., USA, 1987.

Shrestha, Singh

ADB/Nepal; Appropriate Technology Unit, 1955.

AIM Consulting Group (Pvt.) Ltd., Evaluation Study of ADB/N/UNICEF Supported MPPU, July, 1987.

Bachmann, A. and Nakarmi, A.M.; *New Himalayan water wheels*, November 1985.

Bajracharya, Deepak, *Decentralized energy planning and management for Hindu Kush — Himalaya*, ICIMOD, September, 1986.

GATE, *Activating traditional indigenous techniques*, 1983.

Hulshcer, W.S., *Dissemination of rural energy technologies — the private sector*, Twente University, The Netherlands, September, 1988.

Gimpel, Jean, *The horizontal water wheels — how to light the Himalayas*, The Rising Nepal, Kathmandu, 15 April, 1985.

Joshi, C.B.; *Traditional water wheels and small water turbine in Nepal*, RECAST, Tribhuvan University, Kathmandu, 1981/82.

Kattel, Jiwan and Bach, Manfred, *Improved ghatta construction manual*, September, 1985.

NRECA, Nepal, *Private sector approach to implementing micro-hydro-power schemes*, October, 1982.

Rudolph, Klaus, 'Ghatta — the Himalayan water mill'. GATE, March, 1988.

Shrestha, Ganesh Ram, *State of the art of micro and MPPU hydro-power in Nepal*, Five Energy Workshop Report, WECS, September, 1985.

Shrestha, R.B. and Pradhan P.M.S., *State of the art of small hydro-power development in Nepal*, Five Energy Workshop Report, WECS, September, 1985.

Singh, Kiran Man, *Financing small hydro-power schemes through the Agricultural Development Bank of Nepal*, June, 1985.

WECS, HMGN, *Energy sector synopsis Report*, 1985/86.

Kadappuram

Achari Thankappan, T.R., *Fish aggregating devices and artificial reefs*, Kerala, India. FRC, PCO, Trivandrum — 695 039, 1987.

Bay of Bengal Programme, *Marine Small-scale Fisheries of Tamil Nadu: A General Description*, 1983.

Brock Richard E., et al., Sea Grant Quarterly, Vol. 6, University of Hawaii, 1984.

Dept. Of Fisheries, *Kerala Fisheries — An Overview*, 1987.

Fernandez, John T., *Dissemination of Information: The PCO Experience*, Moving Technology, Vol. 3, No. 1, Feb 1988.

Gross, Grant M., *Oceanography, A View of the Earth*, Third Edition, 1982.

Grove, Robert and Sonu, Choule, Report number 8, 3-RD-137 by the Southern California Edison Company, Rose Mead, California — 91770.

Kurien, John, *Knowledge Systems and Fishery Resource Decline*, A Historical Perspective Paper presented at the Fourth International Congress on the History of Oceanography, Hamburg, West Germany, 1987.

Raj Sanjeeva Dr, *Artificial Fish Habitat Technology for Small-scale Fishworkers*, paper presented at the National Workshop on Technology for Small-scale fishworkers, 1989.

Rao, S.N., *Present Status of Small-Scale Fisheries in India and a few neighbouring countries*. CMFRI Bulletin, 30 B, 1981.

Sheeby, Daniel J., *New Approaches in Artificial Reef Design and Applications*, Aquabia Inc., Annapolis, Maryland 21403–6130, 1982.

Monzon

Alberti, Giorgio Y Sanchez, Rodrigo, 'Poder y conflicto social en el valle del Mantaro', Colección Peru Problema No. 10. Instituto de Estudios Peruanos, Lima, 1974.

Arguedas, Jose Maria, 'Evolución de las comunidades indigenas en el Valle del Mantaro.' Revista del Museo Nacional. Tomo XXVI, pags, 78–151. Lima, 1957.

Arquimiba, Prudencio, 'Wasi priqay/Construcción de una casa' tomado de 'Tecnologia Andina' Rogger Ravines (compilador) Instituto de Estudios Peruanos, Lima, 1978.

Henriquez, Narda, 'Migraciones y estructura productiva regional', Pontificia Universidad Católica del Perú. Departmento de Ciencias Sociales. Lima, 1980.

Instituto Nacional De Estadistica, Censos Nacionales: VIII de Población y III de Vivienda, Lima, 1981.

Vildoso, Abelardo; Monzon, Flor De Maria, 'Seguir construyendo con tierra: Realidad socio-económica de la construcción con tierra en zona andina. Valle del Río Mantaro — Perú', CRATERRE, Lima, 1984.

Oré, Rochabrun

Banco Central de Chile. Boletīn Mensual No. 727. Santiago, Septiembre, 1988.

Bustamante, J., Flores, L., Guzman, G., Moncayo, L., Vivanco, J., 'Huentelauquèn: una Comunidad humana de zona en Desertificaciòn', Universidad del Norte-Chile. Centro de Investigaciones para el Desarrollo Rural. Coquimbo, Diciembre, 1979.

Castro, Milka y Bahamondes M., 'Surgimiento y transformaciòn del sistema Comunitario: Las Comunidades Agrīcolas, IV Regiòn, Chile', Ambiente y Desarrollo, Volmen II. No. 1, pp. 111–126, Santiago, Mayo, 1986.

Del Valle, Alfredo, Investigador PRIEN. Universidad de Chile. Contacto personal. Santiago, Abril de 1989.

Galilea, S., 'La Planificaciòn Local: Nuevas Orientaciones Metodològicas', EURE No. 41. Instituto de Estudios Urbanos. Pontificia Universidad Catòlica de Chile, Santiago, Diciembre 1987.

Hernández, Hilda, 'Diagnòstico Socio-Econòmico, Cultural y Educacional de 6 Comunidades de la IV Regiòn', CPEIP. Santiago, Noviembre de 1987.

Hernández, Rodrigo, Ingeniero Forestal, Entrevista personal. Ovalle, Abril de 1989.

INE (Instituto Nacional de Estadisticas). Compendio Estadistico 1988, Santiago, Julio de 1988.

INGEDES, 'Documento Institucional', Santiago, 1988.

INGEDES, 'Una Propuesta de Desarrollo para las Comunidades Agrīcolas', Santiago, Noviembre, 1987.

IREN–CORFO. Estudio de las Comunidades Agrīcolas IV Regiòn, Informe Final, Tomos I, II, IX y X. Santiago, 1977.

Peña, Alberto. Ingeniero Forestal. Entrevista personal. Santiago, 5 Abril, 1989.

Sàez, Juan Carlos, 'Energia para el Desarrollo Rural: El Caso de las Comunidades de Coquimbo', PRIEN, Universidad de Chile, Santiago, 1986.

Urquiza, Alberto. Investigador PRIEN, Universidad de Chile. Contacto personal. Santiago, Abril, 1989.